RAISING THEM RIGHT

RAISING THEM RIGHT

THE UNTOLD STORY OF AMERICA'S
ULTRACONSERVATIVE YOUTH MOVEMENT
AND ITS PLOT FOR POWER

KYLE SPENCER

An Imprint of HarperCollins*Publishers*

HarperCollins books may be purchased for educational, business, or sales promotional use. For information, please email the Special Markets Department at SPsales@harpercollins.com.

Ecco® and HarperCollins® are trademarks of HarperCollins Publishers.

FIRST EDITION

Designed by Paula Russell Szafranski

Library of Congress Cataloging-in-Publication Data has been applied for.

ISBN 978-0-06-304136-3

22 23 24 25 26   LSC   10 9 8 7 6 5 4 3 2 1

To Seth, of course.

CONTENTS

INTRODUCTION

T he roots of this book first took hold on a November evening, two days after the 2018 midterm elections, in a glass-paneled auditorium at Cleveland State University. There, a couple hundred hippies, hipsters, gym rats, and nerds networked near an oversized sign that read "BIG GOVERNMENT SUCKS," as Aaron Tippin's defiantly patriotic country anthem, "Where the Stars and Stripes and the Eagle Fly," blasted from the sound system. From tables in the lobby, attendees snapped up posters, buttons, and laptop stickers with slogans like: "Political correctness has ruined football, academia, comedy, the media, Hollywood, and patriotism" and "I support helping the needy; I oppose funding the lazy."

The event was part of a national speaking series touring the country, titled Campus Clash, a barn-storming mix of comedy, Christian values, and right-wing politics. Anyone who'd ever watched a Trump rally or a few minutes of Tucker Carlson railing against his many enemies on Fox News would recognize the targets that would be mercilessly lampooned on the auditorium stage over the next few hours: the PC Police, Alexandria Ocasio-Cortez (AOC), and transgender bathrooms, to name a few. The mood was simmering fear and outrage, not yet at the embittered stage, but spoiling for a fight.

"If we don't speak up for ourselves against the libtards," said a sandy-haired attendee with a dab of a mustache that wouldn't look out of place in the trendier parts of Brooklyn, "who's going to? Our professors? I don't think so."

As the music came to a stop, the evening's headliner, Charlie Kirk, a then-twenty-five-year-old true believer who skipped college to get a head start on becoming the future of the Republican Party, catapulted onto the stage, wearing trendy dress pants, white Adidas, and a slick-looking navy blue blazer. The young man President Donald Trump once referred to as a "great warrior" settled his six-foot-four frame into a cushioned chair, slid a well-manicured hand through his crown of short, chestnut-brown hair, and flashed a cocky frat-boy grin. His look: pop-star preacher.

Charlie, who toured the country so frequently he had yet to move out of his childhood bedroom, was the founder of Turning Point USA, the organization that was sponsoring the event. Turning Point USA was the fastest-growing youth activist group in GOP history. And its sister organization Turning Point Action was planning on raising $15 million for a Get-Out-the-GOP-Vote campaign, with its eye on 2020. Though I was a frequent *New York Times* contributor and a registered Democrat (I voted for Bernie Sanders in the 2016 Democratic primary and Hillary Clinton in the November general), Charlie had parted the curtain for me on a world that had largely shut out journalists, allowing me rare access for my research into young conservative activists. At that point in his career, Charlie was not yet a household name in the Fox News–watching world, and he apparently welcomed any opportunity to expand his profile, even via coverage from the so-called liberal media. We'd spoken several times at various student events and I was struck by his outsized drive and energy, though I still hadn't grasped how he and his group fit into the bigger conservative picture.

A white kid from suburban Chicago, Charlie was the son of a successful architect who was the project architect for Trump Tower in midtown Manhattan. He had confidence in spades and seemed to have no problem sharing the stage with an equally charismatic co-host, his "thermodynamic" Turning Point USA colleague Candace Owens, a twenty-nine-year-old Black conservative and Fox News regular whom he introduced to booming applause. Candace, too, had been attracting my attention in recent months, with her ability to fire up college-aged audiences. The month before, I'd witnessed her electrify a room at the Turning Point USA–sponsored Young Black Leadership Summit, where she'd implored a new generation of African American voters to abandon the "emotionally-abusive" Democratic Party and vote Republican.

"Hey guys," cooed Owens, slinking onstage in a charcoal gray pantsuit and high-heeled boots. Settling next to Charlie, she crossed her legs smartly and let her almond-shaped eyes rest lightly on the man she would later describe to me as her "political twin."

"Thank you so much for having us."

Candace grew up poor, in Stamford, Connecticut. Until recently she'd considered herself a liberal. Now, she had close to a million Twitter followers (the count will balloon to over 3 million by the time this book heads to press) and Kanye West had recently told his 20 million Twitter followers that he loved "the way Candace Owens thinks."

And what did Candace think? She told the room that she was sick of the left's obsession with "victimization" and its delight in sorting Americans "into collectives," pitting men against women, Blacks against "illegals," and Bible-fearing Christians against nearly everyone else. She called LGBTQ activists "The Trans Army." Referring to Florida's first African American gubernatorial nominee, Andrew Gillum, who earlier that week had lost to the hard-right Republican Ron DeSantis, Candace raised her voice and scoffed that he had just had his "Black card declined on a national level!"

"You are allowed to say that," Charlie said, inferring that as a white male, he could not in fact say that. Then he grinned mischievously, as if to say: *Can you believe I found her?*

The mostly white audience roared with glee.

That night onstage, Charlie's trademark confidence never flagged. Even though Democrats had made big gains in that week's elections, taking the House back from the GOP, handing two seats to Muslim women, and electing the first openly gay governor in nearby Colorado, you'd never know it from Charlie's upbeat manner.

". . . It was a good week in Ohio, right?" said the self-proclaimed optimist. ". . . The governor's race, a lot of statewide offices, a supermajority in the state legislature."

Candace's eyes glistened. "It was a red wave!"

The lights piercing down on him, Charlie furrowed his brow and called the new Democratic-led House "the clown parade" and AOC "the Communist from the Bronx." The crowd howled. "The teachers' unions," he continued, "we call them the cartel."

This act went on for hours, the hard-edged ribbing at times giving way to starkly moralistic pronouncements, as when Owens attacked Democrats' unsuccessful efforts to thwart the confirmation of Supreme Court Justice Brett Kavanaugh. Of the citizens and politicians who sought to hold the nominee accountable for a credible, decades-old accusation of sexual assault, Owens intoned: "These people are evil," resting a hand on her chest. "In my estimation, they are absolutely evil. And if we don't band together and fight them, we're going to lose this country."

The two claimed Turning Point USA was giving voice to a new "silent majority" of young people who were fed up with the left-leaning agenda pushed by Hollywood, the mainstream media, and the Democratic Party. Watching them together, I noted that, like Trump, they shared a gift for harnessing cultural signifiers and celebritydom, and clearly understood that it was not so much issues that grabbed voters and connected them to candidates, it was emotions. They also had youth on their side, exuding a kinetic, camera-ready energy rare for two people who hadn't taken a slew of college acting classes, and even rarer in young politicos who purported to care more about budget deficits than Beyoncé. Perhaps most advantageously, they were storming college campuses at an opportune cultural moment, when left-wing college activists who had done so much good work—mainstreaming feminism, empowering the LGBTQ community, and emboldening minority voices—were becoming just as well known for fostering a "cancel culture" that banned controversial speakers, censored students, ousted outspoken professors, and incessantly demanded apologies from those with differing opinions. Having long reported on student politics, I'd seen firsthand that students of all political stripes were starting to get fed up with all the "wokeness."

I was still inclined to believe that, in spite of cancel-culture backlash, Democrats still had the youth vote in the bag. Trump may have had his grip on certain Boomers and members of the Silent Generation (born between 1928 and 1945), but Generation Z (born in 1997 onward) was, at least according to recent Pew research polls, remarkably inclusive: pro-government, supportive of same-sex marriage, and committed to racial and economic equality. Only about a quarter of voters between eighteen and twenty-three approved of President Trump. Seventy percent of Gen Zers believed that "government *should* do more to solve problems," and 62 percent of them said that "increasing racial/ethnic diversity is good for society." This young generation had grown up with and overwhelmingly approved of President Barack Obama's progressive policies on transgender rights, universal healthcare, and climate change.

But as I filed from the Cleveland State auditorium along with hundreds of attendees barely older than my high school–aged son, I had an unsettling sense that while young right-wingers were certainly outnumbered by their left-leaning counterparts, they were also showing up at campus political events in surprisingly high numbers, with a distinct desire to be heard. And it seemed naïve to overlook how incredibly inspirited so many of them appeared. That's when I overheard a group of young people chatting in the CSU lobby, using acronyms that were foreign to me.

"We did a GOA thing last semester," a doughy-faced young man in rumpled khakis and a gray Campus Clash T-shirt relayed casually. He stood next to a table piled high with Turning Point "swag."

A girl with long brown hair mentioned some talk about "organizing an NRA U." And that, she intoned, was a good thing.

Back in my hotel room, I opened my laptop and googled GOA. The event the young man was talking about had been hosted by the Gun Owners of America, a firearm advocacy group with a "no compromise" attitude about gun ownership. NRA U, I soon learned, was short for NRA University, a heavily advertised initiative that brought speakers to colleges around the country to teach students how to debate "anti-gun spin doctors." The NRA even had a "collegiate coalition," with the aim of opening campus chapters. I pulled up my files on some of the other ultraconservative activist groups I'd been researching. I noted that they, too, were aggressively peddling their free "training" and "educating" to young people, often by appearing decidedly mainstream. The Intercollegiate Studies Institute (ISI) didn't look fringe or obscure. In fact, its flashy website, which invited students to "fill the void" in their education, seemed like the kind of place a lot of intellectual twenty-somethings would find appealing. The home page made it clear that ISI was conservative. But missing was the fact that a sizable chunk of ISI funding came from a foundation run by the powerful DeVos family. And one of its primary goals was to promote the superiority of Judeo-Christian traditions. The website for the Foundation for Economic Education (FEE), backed by some of the richest right-wingers in the country, looked inviting, too. Missing from its homepage was its deep ties to the Koch network.

Also on the list of organizations I'd been exploring was The Gloucester Institute, which sought to sell young African Americans on the free market; and The Leadership Institute, a massive, forty-year-old umbrella organization, with forty-seven different political training classes—all teaching a unique political skill—devoted to producing "a new generation of public policy leaders unwavering in their commitment to free enterprise and limited government."

It finally crystallized for me: Charlie Kirk and Candace Owens weren't just some swashbuckling anti-establishment renegades; they were now key players in a heavily endowed, incredibly well-organized and interconnected initiative to lure as many young people into the ultra-conservative cause as possible. Charlie talked about building the most powerful youth movement the American right had ever seen. That evening, I realized: he wasn't doing it alone.

Could this endeavor succeed?

This book is the result of my quest to find out.

OVER THE NEXT FOUR YEARS, I WOULD FOLLOW THE METEORIC rise of the far-right youth movement largely by following Candace and Charlie, staying as close on their heels as they would let me as they zigzagged across the country to spread their gospel at colleges, churches, and conferences from Washington, D.C., to Newport Beach. I also became fascinated, early on, by another rising star in their world, the rough-and-tumble libertarian Cliff Maloney, who at the time was building the Koch network–affiliated organization Young Americans for Liberty into a political force to be reckoned with and solidifying his own power and pull inside conservative circles. While Candace and Charlie were media stars, Cliff worked largely behind the scenes. If they were the shiny evangelists, he was the master strategist—cut from the same cloth, I came to think, as Karl Rove.

Throughout this time, I spoke with as many young conservative activists as I could to learn what made right-wing politics so alluring to them. My sole job was to get these young activists to open up to me. I was always honest and candid about my own political leanings. Still, even when I vehemently disagreed with their views, I most often held my tongue. "Tell me more about that" was one of my most common responses. As the fifty-something mother of two teenagers, my interest in understanding what made a young person susceptible to right-wing rhetoric was deeply personal. And I suppose I presented as more maternal than menacing. As a result, young people did talk to me. They talked to me a lot.

Many of the ultra-conservative young people I met had been raised by homeschooling parents and in fundamentalist churches in the South, the Midwest, or Central California. They seemed to have missed any teachings on systemic racism and American imperialism. No surprise, then, they tended to blame poverty on the poor and downplay racism as a way to excuse people who were "too lazy" to work, telling me things like: "My parents taught me how to budget, we don't spend money we don't have," and "Anything is possible in America. There's no reason not to be successful."

Their views, I would learn, were further cemented at swanky, heavily subsidized conservative conferences, where they were often wined and dined and always entertained by a charismatic cast of speakers, many of whom had become glittering celebrities in their own right. These same speakers repeated the same tropes about the ills of socialism and the destructive liberal agenda. The same pamphlets, paid for by the same right-wing activists who often donated to these causes through secret funding vehicles like

DonorsTrust and Donors Capital Fund, were prominently stacked on tables for the taking. (The messaging was strikingly direct: *The Minimum Wage Can't Solve the Poverty Problem, Competitiveness Means Limited Government and Greater Economic Freedom, Defeating the Regulatory State Is Key to America's Survival as a Free Country.*) And when donors did want the credit, it was the same foundation names that kept popping up as bankrollers of the groups sponsoring these gatherings. There was the Lynde and Harry Bradley Foundation; the foundations started by the infamous oil magnate Koch Brothers; ones overseen by Liz and Dick Uihlein, whom the *New York Times* once dubbed "the most powerful conservative couple you've never heard of"; and foundations that blossomed under the tutelage of the now-deceased Richard Mellon Scaife, known in giving circles as "the Funding Father of the Right." All the events were aimed at spreading the hard-right word and teaching young people how to effectively proselytize that gospel to their peers.

By January 2019, data I had culled from open source investigative sites and tax returns of "dark money" nonprofits confirmed that I was onto something even bigger than I'd thought: a deep-pocketed, hyper-organized network of institutions, agencies, and online education outlets that sought total domination of society. And they were working together. To that end, far-right donors were spending tens of millions of dollars a year to target young people, close to three times what their progressive counterparts were dolling out. And their commitment to that cause was only growing. In 2019 alone, DonorsTrust, the largest arch-conservative funding consortium in the country, donated more than $3 million to groups targeting young people and women. Close to a million of that went to Turning Point USA. That same year, Koch family foundations spent $112 million on campus-related programming, more than ten times what they had spent a decade earlier, according to data gathered by the Center for Media and Democracy and the watchdog group UnKoch My Campus.

The deeper I dug into this network, the more apparent its aim: to normalize the far-right's divisive ideology with the help of charismatic figureheads like Charlie and Candace. The goal was to give it an attractive, relatable face—or as Donald Trump Jr., with whom Charlie would headline rallies in the 2020 campaign, liked to put it: to "show the world we are not terrible people."

It also became apparent to me that the right's efforts at harnessing young conservative energy to door knock, phone bank, and take to the web to push arch-conservative ideas was successfully changing the political complexion of the nation, from state legislatures all the way to the White House. What was their next move, and what could be learned from their hyper-organized tactics?

Their playbook, as I think of it now, is not being written from scratch. It's rooted in an infrastructure that the far right has been building since the 1960s, when conservative activists—many holdovers from Barry Goldwater's failed presidential bid—united with extraordinarily wealthy private citizens and began organizing to counter America's progressive tendencies. From the beginning, leaders in the movement understood the power of delivering their message to young people. As Charles Koch opined at a conservative conference in New York City in 1976, there is no other time in people's lives when they are more "open to a radically different social philosophy."

An unlikely mix of free-market libertarians, social conservatives, and anti-communists, they peddled the golden image of a bygone era, before the birth of the American welfare state, when government was small and Judeo-Christian values reigned supreme. Over the past five decades, these ultra-privileged donors have worked tirelessly to will the nation their way. During the Obama years, they stealthily underwrote the Tea Party movement. And every step of the way, it should be noted, their foot soldiers imitated the successful strategies of lefty grassroots organizers before them, even co-opting a 1971 guide written for progressive activists: Saul D. Alinsky's *Rules for Radicals: A Pragmatic Primer for Realistic Radicals.* While Alinsky's thirteen rules for empowering radical change, including "Power is not only what you have but what the enemy thinks you have" and "Pick the target, freeze it, personalize it, and polarize it," can seem all but forgotten by today's Democrats, they've been effectively harnessed by the right—including the Tea Party and the white supremacist Andrew Anglin. It's little wonder that the far-right is proving so successful at undoing much of the progress that the grassroots left helped to make—from rolling back abortion rights; to reversing regulatory measures on the fossil fuel industry; to legislating local tax cuts; to thwarting laws that would restrict guns in churches and college campuses; to curbing the teaching of historical realities about our nation's strengths and weaknesses inside our schools.

Historically, these ideologues and mega-donors had aimed to disrupt the political system as stealthily as possible. Knowing their ideas were objectionable to much of the public, they remained in the shadows, working through PACs, lobbyists, front groups, and politicians. Even much of their work on college campuses was seen as best done behind the scenes. In 1979, the John M. Olin Foundation, a far-right funding source named after the arms manufacturer John Olin, initiated the "beachhead" strategy, a way to discreetly spread conservative ideas by funding professorships, grants, publications, and entire campus centers at top universities. What happened at these universities, the theory went, had a trickle-up effect. The mode of thinking swirling through the campus would eventually find its way into the mainstream, reshaping institutions, courts, and government. In a 2005 essay, James Piereson, then the head of the foundation, offered tips for his philanthropic comrades seeking to spread their influence through the beachhead strategy, including: don't attract unwanted attention by using political-sounding names for the professorships and campus centers.

Today, however, many on the right openly hawk an arch-conservative agenda that's purposefully designed to dazzle disaffected young students into joining their ranks, and they are willing to do just about anything to be heard. It's in this climate that firebrands like Candace and Charlie have redefined and reenergized the culture wars that had seemingly been fought to a standstill under President Barack Obama. Turning Point USA—along with groups like the Koch network–connected libertarian outfit Young Americans for Liberty, the NRA's collegiate arm, Students for Life, and the online education site PragerU, a breeding ground for ultra-right influencers—is giving voice to what they call a "silent majority" of young people who are receptive to their seductively clean-cut narratives: student debt is the fault of an overly paid academic elite; illegal immigrants and lazy welfare recipients drain our treasury; identity politics undermine our culture and impinge on our freedoms; and government is not to be trusted.

There is a hopeful supposition among many on the left that the rise of the far right is a temporary glitch in society's fabric that will, despite the indelible horrors of January 6, 2021, eventually dissipate in the post-Trump era. Having gained unprecedented access to today's most influential far-right youth groups and their captains, I will argue otherwise.

Right up to the deadly attack on the U.S. Capitol, none of these leaders seemed all that surprised by the right-wing rage engulfing the nation—in large part, it seemed to me, because they had spent years fomenting that rage. In Charlie's case, his group Students for Trump heavily promoted the #Stopthesteal march online. Then Turning Point Action, one of his sister organizations, sent busloads of protesters to Washington, D.C. One of the apparent riders stormed the Capitol and has been charged with assaulting several police officers. (As of this writing, he has reached a plea agreement with the government, the terms of which have not yet been made public.) For Charlie and many others in the ultra-conservative movement, this was just the beginning of a new era, where rage against the left has morphed into a full-fledged battle against tyranny. "We have warned against this," Charlie remarked on January 6, as he and his podcast team monitored the riots—adding a few minutes later that as far as he was concerned, what was transpiring was "predictable." As of that point, no one had died.

While it's true that young people still vote overwhelmingly blue, and that a wide swath of them support dynamic progressive leaders like Stacey Abrams, Elizabeth Warren, and Alexandria Ocasio-Cortez, what deserves close attention is the growing fervor and radicalization of those young people who already consider themselves conservative. A review of three national studies of 10 million respondents between 1970 and 2015, conducted by researchers at San Diego State University and Florida Atlantic University, tells us that when Baby Boomers were polled as they were finishing up twelfth grade, about 17 percent identified as far right. When asked more recently, about 22 percent of twelfth graders identified as such. Some polling also shows that young voters, while more liberal than their parents on issues like same-sex marriage, legalizing marijuana, and the death penalty, are more likely than their parents to take libertarian positions on issues like gun control and national healthcare.

These young voters are also more likely than their parents to find themselves disenchanted with political parties and less likely to say one party represents them better than another. This indicates that young voters may in fact be more up for grabs than the left has acknowledged. And conservative youth groups seem to understand this, as they seek new and increasingly innovative ways to lure students to the right, like first attracting them through issues with bipartisan appeal. For libertarian groups, that means emphasizing criminal justice and drug legalization laws. For Turning

Point USA, that means standing against campus wokeness. These issues can be and often are used as gateways to more radical ideas.

AS THIS BOOK HEADS TO PUBLICATION, WE'RE APPROACHING THE 2022 midterms and the 2024 presidential election. If there was ever a moment for the Democrats to draw inspiration from their grassroots-driven victories of the past—from women's suffrage to civil rights to sending the first Black president to the White House—this would be it.

The reality is that firebrands like Candace and Charlie are already ten steps ahead. They don't need to win over many young people to the GOP to make a big impact if they can simply continue to activate their growing base of radicalized young Republicans.

Cliff, too, with his tactical game plan, one that I watched him unfurl over the course of this reporting, has helped author a powerful political schema designed to snag disgruntled undecideds, particularly young men, to a screw-you government libertarianism that promises a kind of every-man-for-himself, independent dignity that the Democrats aren't selling. Even as Cliff faces a slew of allegations—and, as this book goes to print, a criminal court battle—his confidence in his ability to serve the liberty movement has been largely unwavering.

If these activists and their followers are successful, their impact will no doubt play forward for years to come. The outcome: a generation of free-market natives who will enter their twenties and thirties with individualistic principles so socially conservative and economically punishing that they risk further threatening our very understanding of American democracy.

In other words, the far right's success at selling their counternarrative to the next generation will likely determine the kind of America our children will inherit—and the stakes could not be higher.

Many of us have long conceived of the United States as distinct from certain nations in Southeast Asia, parts of Eastern Europe, and the Middle East, where oligarchical governments and religious persecution have stamped out democracy. But if the far-right youth movement continues to spread unrivaled, the United States of America risks joining our reactionary neighbors in an international repudiation of pluralism, in favor of theocracy and oligarchy—systems that can now feel so normalized at home that, frighteningly, they seem to elicit no more than a collective shrug from some young people.

In the coming pages, I'll take you back to the Obama era, Charlie Kirk's high school days, Cliff Maloney's college years, and the early days of Candace Owens's rise to prominence, showing you exactly where some of the most impassioned conservative influencers came from and how they became emboldened activists.

Ambitious, power-hungry, and willing to stop at nothing to do what many of them say is God's work, today's far-right political influencers have co-written the playbook for winning young hearts and minds in the social media era. That playbook is here, in their stories. What will we take from it?

PART I

CHAPTER ONE

The Rise of a White, Male Obama-Hater

In early winter 2009, as Barack Obama was adjusting to the demands of the Oval Office and life inside the White House, excitement about America's first Black president reverberated through the cacophonous halls of Wheeling High School, a large, increasingly diverse school on the outskirts of Chicago—the very town that birthed the forty-fourth president's political career. But if there was one Wheeling student who was firmly inoculated against Obama fever, it was Charlie Kirk, a lanky freshman, already north of six feet, who would one day call America's first Black president a "National Disgrace."

"If you were not wholeheartedly worshipping the guy you were considered like the worst human being ever," Charlie would later explain, adding: "Well, that was me, and I found a lot of satisfaction in it."

In 2009, many of the high schools that made up Chicago's suburban collar were still quietly segregated learning communities that boasted mostly-white parent associations and heavily endowed education funds that bankrolled luxurious upgrades to theater departments and school gyms.

Not Wheeling. Sometimes referred to as "the ugly duckling,"

it drew from a spattering of middle-class subdivisions, like the one Charlie's father, Robert, a local architect, had designed and that Charlie's family lived in. But it also pulled from modest blocks of low-hanging ranches and postage stamp–sized yards as well as a series of squat apartment complexes built in the 1970s that surrounded the school. These blocks—tucked behind thick ribbons of highway that led commuters out to the interstate—housed the area's growing Latino population, men and women who had arrived with families in tow but without papers, fleeing vicious drug wars in northern Mexico and Peru. They worked as gardeners, housekeepers, and mechanics, as they pursued futures for their children that were no longer possible back home.

Wheeling was a trailblazer, but not an outlier. Neighborhood schools in nearby Rolling Meadows and Elk Grove Village were experiencing similar influxes. Indeed, as Charlie wound his way through high school, suburban America was changing. Wealthy white professionals were moving en masse to newly gentrified urban neighborhoods, while poor Black, Hispanic, and East Asian families were being priced out of cities and heading to the 'burbs. Indian grocery stores and Spanish-language daycare centers were popping up in and around Wheeling, but also on the edges of middle-class subdivisions all over the country in what was once lily-white terrain—changing the face of suburban Detroit, New York, and Chicago and injecting a more international flair into these once purposefully anodyne locales.

The change—by 2010, minorities made up more than a third of all suburban residents in the United States—spurred studies about school integration and white papers on how to serve the varied needs of this new suburbia. It also shifted the political landscape. Once reliably Republican suburbs were increasingly voting blue, at least for a while. Obama took all the ones in Illinois in 2008 and most all of them in 2012. And local school boards were increasingly preoccupied with the needs of students of color. By the early 2000s, Wheeling's elementary schools needed so many Spanish-speaking teachers they were hiring them from Spain.

That September, as Charlie, a Reagan-obsessed fourteen-year-old, was learning how to navigate Wheeling's bustling hallways, Wheeling was doing its own adjusting. After years of demographic change, it had flipped—just a year earlier—from a mostly white school to a mostly Black, brown, and Asian one. Charlie was a minority in his high school, outnumbered in classrooms, hallways, and athletic fields by young people of color.

Wheeling's principal Lazaro Lopez didn't just welcome students from diverse backgrounds, he made a successful career out of accommodating them, earning himself an Illinois Principal of the Year award. Wheeling held regularly scheduled Spanish-language family nights, produced a bilingual parent newsletter, and affectionately referred to the school's soccer team, made up of the sons of die-hard "futbol" fans, as Los Gatos, a nod to the school's efforts to be inclusive and open. The other teams maintained their original name: the Wild Cats.

This was the fast-changing universe young Charlie faced as he glinted toward adulthood and puzzled about what kind of man he would become. He was growing up in the backyard of a president he despised, during a time when the power structures and demographic makeup of his childhood home were forever changing, in a school where the status of a young white man was diminishing, and in a nation where the power and pull of people of color was on the rise. Charlie's father had built many of the homes and at least one of the glass and steel office buildings that jutted into the sky in and around Wheeling High School, helping to form the physical makeup of the suburban region where he grew up. But it was the hundreds of aspiring immigrants and their sons and daughters who sat next to him in classes, fought with him on athletic fields, and rustled through the halls with him who were now setting the tone. America was changing. And the American suburbs were where a lot of that change was happening, as it increasingly welcomed a diverse crowd of young people seeking opportunity and advancement. Charlie Kirk would soon lead a movement that sought to stop at least some of them from reaching their goals.

In later years, during conference speeches and chats with me, Charlie would profess a cheerful admiration for his school's ethnic makeup and for the school as a whole. "Wheeling has been great to the Kirks," he wrote in a post around the time of his younger sister's graduation in 2014. But that benevolent telling contradicted a harsher view Charlie would later hold about some immigrants in America. One high school friend described those views like this: There were good ones; they were documented and paid taxes. And there were bad ones. Charlie would later refer to the latter as "trespassing foreign nationals."

The high school Charlie attended had a stated mission of integrating recent immigrants—almost all of them non-white—into American economic and cultural life. He understood the challenges poor people, immigrants, and the disenfranchised faced. In fact, he watched their struggles up close, for years.

"I knew people that were in this country illegally," he said years later. "I went to high school with them. So, for me, it was really a personal connection."

CHARLIE'S CHILDHOOD HOME—A FIVE-BEDROOM BRICK MCMANsion with a three-car garage and a spacious backyard—lacked the refinement and historic charm of the Tudors and late-stage Victorians that graced tonier suburbs like Winnetka, Glencoe, and Wilmette that surrounded him. But for Prospect Heights the Kirks appeared to have made it. Many classmates at Wheeling, and before at Douglas MacArthur Middle School, considered Charlie rich.

Charlie's father, Robert, a square-shouldered descendant of

German immigrants, spent his teen years in an upscale Long Island bedroom community, thirty miles from midtown Manhattan, where the mostly white residents lived in large homes, paid high taxes, and sent their children to top-rated Jericho High School. Robert graduated from the University of Oregon with a degree in architecture, then cut his teeth at a series of architecture firms in Chicago before launching his own firm, designing and building a series of middle-class subdivisions and luxury estates along the scenic shores of Lake Michigan.

In his book *The MAGA Doctrine*, Charlie describes one project in particular his father contributed to: New York City's Trump Tower. Architectural work was contracted out to the Manhattan firm Swanke Hayden Connell, where Charlie's father worked as a project architect. Charlie describes his father's interaction with Donald Trump as remarkably positive. And yet the relationship with the firm ended in typical Trumpian fashion: with legal wrangling over delays. Documents show Trump was eventually awarded $1.75 million in damages, while the firm was conferred $250,000 in fees.

Charlie's mother, Kathy, was a petite woman with dark-brown curls that hinted at her Polish American roots. Her relatives on her mother's side had come to North America on crowded steamships in the late 1800s, escaping annexed Poland and the discrimination at the hands of the Russians, Prussians, and Austro-Hungarians that followed. Kathy grew up a half hour away from Prospect Heights in Downers Grove, a onetime prairie town turned bedroom community that had met the challenges of the region's rapacious growth from nineteenth-century farming hub to modern-day Chicago suburb with relative ease. After college, Kathy worked as a trader at the Chicago Mercantile Exchange, and when her children were older, she went back to school to get a degree in mental health counseling, eventually landing a job as a therapist. Charlie credits her with helping him develop compassion.

Kathy and Robert were moderate Republicans, newspaper readers, and voters. They were supportive of Charlie's growing interest in politics, alerting family members when their son made one of his first appearances on Fox News: "The first time, it was a big event and we had all of our relatives watch," Robert Kirk told a local reporter in 2013. ". . . Now, it's almost routine."

But they were not news fanatics. Charlie was the family anomaly.

If Charlie embraced the life of a modern-day Alex Keaton, extolling the virtues of the free market and glorifying Reagan to his classmates, his sister Mary—two years younger—presented as the family lefty. In high school, Mary was a quirky creative, interested in art and dance, and a big reader. She spent a year as an au pair in the Berlin suburbs, then graduated from the University of Illinois with a degree in art history. Charlie has referred to Mary, half-jokingly, as a "Communist." Mary has been dismissive of Charlie's politics, too. And once, to annoy her brother, one of Charlie's classmates says, she took a book he was reading about Ted Cruz and put it in the freezer. She supported Bernie Sanders in 2016, posting on her Facebook page a photo of a bird perched on a podium in front of the silver-haired candidate, writing: "I was the bird."

AS A YOUNG BOY, CHARLIE ATTENDED A CHRISTIAN ELEMENTARY school near home, founded by a group of local suburban families who sought a biblical-based education for their children. It was at Christian Heritage Academy, he would later tell audiences, that he met teachers who encouraged him to give his "life to Christ." Charlie was an antsy and energetic student, the kind who couldn't sit still, so much so that "if the kind of overlords-to-be were in charge of my upbringing as they are today," he once said, they would have diagnosed him with ADHD and medicated him. But Charlie says his father took a more laissez-faire approach and thought the best thing to do for his growing son was to keep him busy.

By the time Charlie arrived at MacArthur Middle School, he was playing football and basketball, attending band practice and Eagle Scout meetings. He was also developing a "fire for politics," distinguishing himself from many of his classmates. After a teacher trash-talked then-president George W. Bush in class one day, Charlie began to do his own research, boning up on the theories of Milton Friedman, the Nobel Prize–winning economist and right-wing icon who birthed Ronald Reagan's controversial trickle-down economics theory in the 1980s. The idea that giving tax breaks to businesses was the best way to help America spoke to young Charlie, who was close to his father and admired the work ethic and drive that had enabled him to build his architecture firm from scratch. Charlie also knew that when the economy faltered—as it did in 2007—it was businesses like his father's that were vulnerable. His family felt the recession, he would later say.

The 2008 presidential race further sparked Charlie's preternatural interest in politics. He debated climate change, the ills of entitlement programs, and the importance of fiscal responsibility in the school cafeteria with a select group of friends. As the election season heated up, he told one of his debating buddies, whom he sometimes referred to as Mr. Liberal, that he worried John McCain, the Arizona senator and decorated war hero, was about to lose. One year, in that young man's yearbook, he signed his note: "Future President Charlie."

Once Charlie arrived at Wheeling High School, he began to craft a political identity on a more public scale. But it was a slow process. His freshman year, he was seen by at least one classmate as an eccentric loudmouth with poor social skills. A lot of people found Charlie amusing, the classmate said. "Here's this crazy political guy. He'll never get anywhere."

But by the end of junior year, that impression was changing. That summer, Charlie signed up to volunteer for the U.S. Senate campaign of Republican state representative Mark Kirk, whom he was not related to, making phone calls, knocking on doors, and handing out literature, often in the sweltering heat, accepting the drudgery but also soaking up the energy and excitement of a tight race. Kirk was a pro-choice moderate who supported gun control positions Charlie did not hold—and he was a raging foe of the local Tea Party activists Charlie would soon align himself with. But he was also vying for the same swing seat once held by someone Charlie hated: Barack Obama.

In front of audiences, Charlie frequently gives the impression that he was a hardworking high schooler with a decent shot of getting into an elite American college. Classmates remember him differently. He once told his chemistry teacher that he did not believe in homework. As far as sports, he was captain of the varsity basketball and football teams, praised for his free throw shot, and considered one of the basketball team's stars. But neither of those teams was very good. Charlie's senior year, the basketball team won two out of twenty-four games. The football team won two out of seven. Incidentally, it was the Gatos, Wheeling's dogged soccer team, filled with athletes whose parents heralded from Mexico and Central and South America, that elicited admiration from the student body, regularly making the Illinois championships and earning trophies for the school's display cases.

When it came to extracurriculars, Charlie did excel as an Eagle Scout, spending part of his senior year building a wheelchair ramp for an elderly neighbor. He prominently displayed the almost finished ramp on his Facebook page. Yet being an Eagle Scout, his classmates said, was considered a relatively low-status extracurricular activity at a school with an award-winning speech and debate team and a talented Jazz Program that traveled around the country.

Wheeling was a heavily tracked school, and Advanced Placement and Honors classes were where high-achieving, middle-class white kids tended to cluster. Charlie did land in a few AP classes.

Increasingly confident about his politics and rebellious by nature, this is where he began to show off his politically pugnacious side.

He poked at liberal teachers with whom he disagreed, dismissing them as "Post-modern, Neo-Marxists" and began to treat them as not just ideological opponents but actual enemies. "It drove them nuts. And I found enjoyment in it," he says.

One time, when a teacher wrote on the board that guns kill people, he asked provocatively, "Do forks make people fat?"

On several occasions, Charlie has said that he was kicked out of class for saying unpopular things. But classmates who were there at the time have challenged that telling. As they remember it, Charlie was often told to pipe down, not so much because of his views, but because he was rude, making the atmosphere inside the classroom unsettling. Despite his later assertions that liberals are dead set on their ideas and intolerant of dissent, classmates said that Charlie had "a superiority complex" and did not tolerate disagreement. Still, they must have recognized something impressive about him. In 2012, his senior year, Charlie was nominated "Most Likely To Take Over The World."

IN LATE SUMMER 2011, AS HIS SENIOR YEAR WAS ABOUT TO START, Charlie Kirk, increasingly enthralled by opportunities to buck authority, saw an opening. District officials had just announced they were doubling the price of the twenty-five-cent sugar cookies that many students saw as the only decent thing on offer in Wheeling's cafeteria. Charlie launched a Facebook group protesting the price hike, exhorting his four hundred followers with daily rallying cries: "Do not buy the cookies. Do not buy the cookies." He adopted "Fight the Power," Public Enemy's militant call to arms, as his campaign's theme song, pairing it with a clip from the video. He threatened that anyone who didn't participate in his boycott would be "shunned." He goaded a Korean American student to

"Add ur Asian friends," urged freshmen to "pick up the slack," and told students who questioned the protest: "If you don't support it, leave."

By October, the boycotters had won, sort of. Cookies went back to being twenty-five cents, but they were now from a new distributor and not as tasty, students said. And Charlie had moved on to a new obsession: the national Tea Party movement, which was becoming a powerful political force in the Chicago area. Charlie had been following the movement since its genesis in February 2009. That's when Rick Santelli, a former trader turned CNBC business newscaster reporting on the floor of the Chicago Mercantile Exchange, let out a raucous rant against President Obama's recently announced mortgage bailout plan.

"How many of you people want to pay for your neighbors' mortgage that has an extra bathroom and can't pay their bills, raise their hand," exhorted Santelli. "President Obama, are you listening?" Hoarse with rage and energized by the traders who whooped behind him, Santelli continued: "We're thinking of having a Chicago Tea Party in July. All you capitalists who want to show up to Lake Michigan, I'm going to start organizing." And the rest is history.

Some contend the Tea Party movement was simply a reaction to Obama's bank bailout, his answer to a fiscal crisis that threatened to land the country in another depression, and the hard-fought Affordable Care Act that had narrowly passed in 2010. But many journalists on the ground saw it also as a dog whistle, motivated by a hate that simply couldn't be separated from race. At least some of the protesters who marched around their downtowns brandished handmade signs with disturbing racial imagery. *Obama's Plan: White Slavery* read one held up at a rally in Madison, Wisconsin. A sign at another gathering around that same time declared: *A Village in Kenya Is Missing Its Idiot: Deport Obama!* Animosity against the then president was particularly strong in the Chicago area, where monied GOP operatives harbored a deep resentment that this president had sprung from their own town. Obama, driven and independent, hadn't waited to be anointed by the local political powerbrokers. Instead, he had launched his political career by elevatoring up to the offices of the wealthiest Democratic donors. Then, he'd harnessed the internet and grassroots campaigning in innovative ways—a magic mix that landed him in the White House, but that also defied how traditional party politics worked in the Chicago area.

As much as Charlie hated Obama, he was in awe of his political prowess, how he had leveraged social media, politics, and on-the-ground organizing to win the Oval Office. The GOP had begun studying the Obama playbook, too. The big takeaway was Internet, Internet, Internet. But Charlie saw something his elders didn't necessarily see in quite the neon colors: it was also about the kids. Obama had given tens of thousands of young lefties a place to channel their pent-up political energy. Charlie would soon decide he wanted to do the same—for his friends on the right.

THE SPRING OF HIS SENIOR YEAR, ON THE STAGE OF A SMALL, darkened theater near his house, Charlie, in a pale blue oxford and crumpled khakis, clutched a bulbous microphone to his mouth. Swaying back and forth in a pair of dress shoes, he let it rip.

"We can influence the youth to understand the issues and make it okay to be conservative," he bellowed, a goofy, self-satisfied smile creeping onto his face.

Charlie was standing before a gathering of Illinois Tea Party activists, many more than three times his age. He was with Mikey Diamond, a fellow political junkie who attended nearby Buffalo Grove High School.

The cookie wars behind him, Charlie and Diamond, with the help of Diamond's then girlfriend Maria Krutikova, had launched a political youth group called SOS Liberty. Now regulars on the local Tea Party circuit, they careened into the suburban parking lots of hotels, steakhouses, and rotary club meeting halls, giving short talks about "fiscal responsibility" and spendthrift politicians. Sometimes they brought along a slideshow entitled "Visualizing the Debt," a teaching tool they'd designed over meals together at the local Chipotle and during brainstorming sessions in Diamond's basement.

"High schoolers all over Illinois are now starting to get our message," Charlie continued, as he stood there looking nervous but resolute.

From the other side of the stage, Diamond, short, with a bowl cut and a crackling Kermit the Frog voice, added his two cents. "When you hear the number fifteen, sixteen trillion dollars, what does this mean?" he asked, referring to the national debt. "It just sounds like a really, really big number."

Charlie jumped in after Diamond with a brief history lesson, his reductive version of how-we-got-here. He traced the nation's ballooning budget deficit back to the decision to go off the gold standard in the 1970s, then launched into a tirade about "baseline budgeting," a maneuver that allows communities to predict future spending, but that critics say paves the way for routine budget hikes, while discouraging cuts. Charlie was still an awkward teenager, his eyes anxiously darting around the room. But not yet out of high school, he already managed to command a stage. He had an attitude, one that said: "Look at me . . . I'm going places."

He was also already embracing the alarm tactics that would soon characterize so many of the speeches he gave to young people.

"We owe $600 billion to China," he began, stoking fears about China, something that would later become a regular habit. "China can manipulate our actions if they decide to. They can control us with our debt and that's a threat to our freedom and liberty every single day.

"We cannot sleep," he told the room. "We cannot let tyranny get farther in life."

Soon, the SOS Liberty group grew. More students from Buffalo Grove joined—the son of an Italian restaurant owner, an award-winning Speech and Debater, a high school baseball player who wanted to work on Wall Street. Members made kitschy videos with the help of a classmate headed to NYU to study film. One, titled *I believe*, featured shots of children playing at the beach, flags waving, and scenes of the New York City skyline. "Join us as we work to preserve the American dream for future generations," a group of teenagers in khakis, yoga pants, and jeans recited in unison. Charlie was at the center of the group, a red T-shirt hanging over his crumpled khakis, his winning smile exuding charisma. He was camera-ready.

Along the way, Charlie began developing ties with local pols: Tea Party leader Denise Cattoni, an animated mortgage broker with a special needs son, enraged by mortgage lending laws that pushed so many of her clients out of their homes; and Joe Walsh, a recently elected congressman representing Chicago's northern suburbs, who was an outspoken libertarian with a brash, in-your-face style. On top of that, Charlie published a piece in Breitbart News and landed an appearance with Diamond and Krutikova on none other than *Fox & Friends*.

Diamond's dad had driven them to the Fox News headquarters on Michigan Avenue in downtown Chicago to make the sunrise slot. Diamond and Krutikova had passed muster with pat answers and nervous smiles, but Charlie, gesturing like a political pro, had forcefully appealed to the camera: "We think it is time for our generation to step up to the plate and sound the SOS signal to Washington."

Krutikova says Charlie could be distant and arrogant during these early years, though the two were friends. His admiration for religious leaders surprised her. Sometimes during walks together around a nearby lake to reduce senior-year stress, he would cite

Bible verses or suggest she listen to Joel Osteen, a Texas televange-
list and self-help guru. But he didn't always act in ethical ways, she
says. Their senior year, when they were first building SOS Liberty,
she says Charlie used her Facebook password and started joining
conservative women's Facebook groups around the country, posing as her so he could then invite them to SOS Liberty's page and
publicize the group. At the time, she shrugged it off, chalking it
up to his passion for the cause. But in retrospect, she thinks it was
weird. She recalls that, towards the end of senior year, he also once
advised her to throw some classmates under the bus when she got
in trouble for posting a silly lewd comment on a classroom chat
board. She was surprised by the advice and did not take it. *That's
not very Christian of you*, she recalls thinking.

CHARLIE, ALREADY ENVISIONING A CAREER IN POLITICS, HAD HIS
ambitions set on West Point, the federal service academy that had
educated Mike Pompeo and Civil War generals Ulysses S. Grant
and Robert E. Lee. He planned to spend four years developing
physical and mental discipline, do his military service, and eventually go into politics. But he was deferred and eventually stunned to
learn he had been denied admission.

In the coming years, Charlie would cite a number of reasons
why West Point turned him down. One childhood friend remembers him blaming the denial on his celiac disease.

A few years later, he would complain that he had lost the slot to
a "far less qualified applicant" who had been "of a different gender
and a different persuasion."

"I kind of got the short end of the stick," he told a crowd in
2015, later insisting that he was being sarcastic. Another time he
denied having made the recorded statement at all, dismissing it as
"fake news." The year he graduated, no one got into West Point
from Wheeling. And when one student did, a year later, he was a

top student whom Wheeling's principal referred to as "simply an astounding young man."

Charlie accepted a slot at Baylor University, a medium-sized Baptist University in Waco, Texas, where drinking and sex outside of marriage were prohibited. It seemed like a decent fit. Charlie was openly religious. He did not drink in high school and told at least one friend he planned to wait to have sex until marriage. At the time conservative firebrand Ken Starr, who had been the independent counsel that investigated the Monica Lewinsky scandal, was president of the university, with a mission to raise money and the school's profile. Attending Baylor was a smart move for an up-and-coming GOP operative.

BUT GOD HAD DIFFERENT PLANS FOR CHARLIE. ONE AFTERNOON, shortly before his high school graduation, Charlie was speaking before a crowd of four hundred at a youth engagement event hosted by Benedictine University outside of Chicago. "Washington is spending your future away," he thundered from his perch beneath a basketball hoop. "Spending my future away, spending our children's future away. But you know what? We can still turn this around. We can bring this ship back up." His microphone cackled as he stared up at the gym bleachers, plaintively, already exhibiting the infectious speaking style he would continue to hone.

Bill Montgomery, a seventy-one-year-old Tea Party activist with a head of silver hair, was in the audience that day. Montgomery was a serial entrepreneur from nearby Lemont, a one-time quarry town of sixteen thousand located thirty minutes from Chicago. He'd owned a Cajun restaurant, run a small newspaper chain that specialized in local news, worked as a sales and marketing director for various pharmaceutical companies, and headed up a suburban printing company. Now the retired jack-of-all-trades had extra time on his hands.

As the crowd was thinning out, he approached Charlie and made a suggestion that would change his life. "You don't know me," he said. "But you can't go to college."

Montgomery was an incurable gadgeteer and Starbucks regular who favored thick print ties and usually had multiple phones in his pocket. He loved politics, particularly now as Tea Party activism had become all the rage among Chicago-area patriots like himself. A person could spend almost every evening attending rallies, talks, and meetings for new groups, old groups, or groups you wanted to start. Montgomery also loved mentoring young people and was always looking for fresh talent, a young person with solid conservative values to get behind and cheer on.

Montgomery would later tell Bloomberg reporter Julie Bykowicz that Charlie's speech was "practically Reaganesque," a high compliment for a lover of The Gipper. Montgomery saw raw political talent in Charlie, someone who might be able to help spread the free-market ideals he believed in. Soon he and Charlie were brainstorming inside area coffee shops. At first what they came up with was a loose idea, but it quickly took shape. He and Charlie would start a group that would seek to attract the next generation to conservatism, a kind of Moveon.org for the right. Or better yet, an ad agency for unfettered capitalism. They'd start local and then expand. Charlie would be the face of it; Montgomery would work behind the scenes. He'd capitalize on his printing experience to help the group produce eye-catching promo material and use his sales acumen to create buzz. Together, they'd stop the hemorrhaging of young people to the left, a sort of revenge of the conservatives. They would take to the road and grow the heck out of it. There was no telling how far they could go.

Charlie talked it over with his parents. Not going to college wasn't exactly part of their plan for him. But they agreed to a short-term deferral. A gap, not an abandonment. Classmates and friends were skeptical, though. They were certain he was making a terrible mistake. But Charlie was, as always, confident, certain that he didn't have to do what everybody else was doing. One friend said he had the impression that Charlie, always thinking about his political résumé, just didn't want to settle for a mid-tier college. Not going, the friend surmised, probably looked better in his eyes. It was unique. It was daring. And it would allow him to fast track up the ladder. Furthermore, Charlie was paying for college himself. And those who knew him knew he didn't like wasting money unnecessarily.

In the beginning, the plan was actually to enroll in January. But Charlie never did. The young man who launched the largest college recruitment effort in the history of the conservative movement, sharing with donors on a daily basis the indoctrinating terrors of campus life, would never actually experience that life. Charlie would become an expert, a go-to among donors who funded him, on something he knew less about than millions of his peers.

On June 5, 2012, two days after graduating high school, Charlie decided he would be using his $1,800 pool of graduation money to launch the group. During a talk he gave in Silicon Valley in 2015, Charlie recalls how they came up with the name. "I need something with pizzazz," he told Bill. "I need something that can really sizzle." They settled on The Turning Point, a moniker that would soon morph into Turning Point USA.

Charlie has mythologized this origin story. But in public tellings, he has left out a key detail that paints him in a less heroic light. As he was planning his new group with Montgomery, he was still affiliated with SOS Liberty. And on the same day he launched The Turning Point, Charlie posted an embittered resignation letter on SOS Liberty's Facebook page, alluding to disagreements group members were having with him about who was in charge.

Charlie accused them of "planning behind my back." Then, he announced he was going out on his own and invited anyone who wanted to join his new group under his leadership. "I will take the same passion and drive I have and create a bigger, better, smarter, more effective group," he wrote. The resignation felt to many like "a power move," according to one former SOS member.

That summer, as Charlie's friends packed their bags for college and wrote letters to their new roommates, he and Bill packed their own bags. They spent weeks zigzagging across the Midwest in Bill's tiny Thunderbird, hitting one Tea Party gathering after another, handing out business cards Bill had made for them, and looking for someone to underwrite their dream.

CHAPTER TWO

Birth of a
Libertarian Messenger

Young Cliff Maloney had discovered the evils of "collectivism" and now he wanted to do something about it. It was summer 2011 and luckily the twenty-year-old theater major was interning inside the Capitol Hill office of libertarian icon Ron Paul. Cliff had been turned on to Paul a few months earlier by a fellow classmate at the University of Pittsburgh at Johnstown, where he was also getting a degree in education. The classmate had told Cliff he needed to watch the veteran congressman eviscerate Rudy Giuliani during the May 2007 GOP presidential debates. The topic: American involvement in the Middle East, post 9/11. Paul, an anti-interventionist, contended that meddling in Middle Eastern affairs was bad policy.

"If we think that we can do what we want around the world and not incite hatred, then we have a problem," Paul told Giuliani. Leaning over the podium in a decidedly unfashionable suit, he sounded surprisingly practical and un-politician-like. "They don't come here to attack us because we're rich and we're free. They come to attack us because we're over there."

Cliff had finally found someone who spoke to his inherent belief that people needed to take care of themselves, and that when you meddle in other people's affairs and they meddle in yours, everyone loses. It was one of the prime libertarian values the then political neophyte would grow to hold dear, and one that had first occurred to him seven years earlier.

Cliff's first payday is seared in his memory. It was 2004; he was thirteen and he was newly hired as an afterschool onion chopper at Don's Deli in Boothwyn, a blue-collar suburb of Philadelphia, where plumbers and printing plant workers bought super-sized heroes and Philly cheese steaks for lunch and dinner.

A job was a source of pride in Cliff's household, not to mention the only way he could afford sports drinks, movie tickets, and, eventually, gas. His father, Cliff Senior, a tatted-up landscaper who showed up at school events with grass stains on his pants, was a "get-off-your-ass-and-go-to-work" kind of guy. Cliff Sr. had pulled his life together after serving three years in jail for drug possession. Cliff's "Granny," his father's mother, was an emergency room nurse. A hard worker, she was always willing to take people's shifts when they needed time off. And whenever Cliff's sisters or his cousins talked about a new boyfriend, Granny wanted to know one thing first: "Does he have a job?"

Cliff still remembers ripping open his first paycheck from Don's. "It was for practically nothing," due to an annual flat tax, imposed by the municipality. He might not have realized it at the time, but that was the moment he became a libertarian. It wasn't fair to work like that so the government could take away your hard-earned money and give it to someone else.

He would later tell me, "Even back then, I didn't trust the government."

CLIFF MALONEY WAS BORN IN 1991, CONCEIVED WHILE CLIFF SR. was on work release from jail. His mother was in her early twenties and already a mom to Cliff's older sister, whom she'd had at nineteen. After Cliff, two more kids would follow.

Cliff Sr. was Irish Catholic and sometimes had a hot temper. He was the inheritor of an addiction gene that had rattled the lives of other relatives and had nearly destroyed his own. But jail had been a wake-up call. He'd pulled his life together, banning beer from the house and building a landscaping business. Cliff Sr. was not afraid to sit in a folding chair at an AA meeting and admit he needed help.

Cliff's mother came from a line of Welsh immigrants who'd first settled in Pennsylvania to escape religious persecution in the 1600s. She was religious, but not precious about it, and had Cliff christened at the Methodist church on the corner because it was close.

"Let's just say my parents weren't researching churches," Cliff told me.

At the time of Cliff's birth, the family lived in a small brick multifamily in Upland, a scrappy pocket of ramshackle houses along I-95. Their neighbors were hourly workers—gas station attendants and supermarket checkout clerks. His mother whacked weeds for her husband's business, worked in the office at a local bakery, and eventually landed a job as a secretary for the school district, all while raising kids.

By 1996, there were four of them and the family had moved a few I-95 exits away to Boothwyn, not a high-class town but a step up from where they'd been. Here, dads tended to be on salary as electricians, mechanics, and maintenance workers. A lot of the moms worked for the school district. The Maloneys settled on a main drag, Meetinghouse Road, in a stucco house with a sloping yard and a well-worn basketball hoop. In the early years, before he could afford storage, Cliff Sr. kept his equipment at the house, filling the place with the reek of manure. Trains whizzed by every few hours on tracks across the street, bringing passengers and cargo to and from nearby Philadelphia. After a while, you didn't hear it anymore.

The four-bedroom on Meetinghouse Road was cramped, two girls, two boys, and there wasn't a lot of privacy. Someone had removed the door to the small second-floor bedroom Cliff shared with his younger brother and no one had ever replaced it. Things could get chaotic. Maloneys weren't afraid to speak their mind, and Cliff Sr. still had a temper now that he was sober. Once, Cliff says, he came home from work and kicked the family's one air conditioner off the windowsill. The kids had been running the thing with the windows open again.

At Don's Deli, the taxes the government pulled from Cliff's already puny paycheck weren't the only thing that bothered him. He was even more annoyed at the child labor laws that prevented him from working more than a few hours a day. Regulations like that did only one thing for a guy with an ounce of ambition: they held him back.

Despite his complaints, the deli was a place to soak up life lessons. First, you needed a friggin' lot of onions to make a cheese steak. Second, life for folks in Boothwyn, Cliff learned from Don's customers, was precarious. A lot of people lived paycheck to paycheck—if they were lucky. Otherwise, it was hand-to-mouth. This was not the future he had in mind for himself.

CHICHESTER MIDDLE SCHOOL, WHERE CLIFF SPENT HIS TWEEN years, could be rough. A lot of kids came to school hungry. Fights broke out. A mere 57 percent of eighth graders could read at grade level the year Cliff started. But the school did have a few teachers who would make a lasting impression on Cliff.

Every year, Mr. Tarves, his sixth-grade English teacher, played a few rock songs and read excerpts from novels, essays, and poems, then asked the students to guess what was poetry and what wasn't.

It was like a brain teaser. The answer: it all was. It was a light bulb moment for Cliff, the first time he had given any thought at all to the idea that art and culture might be a part of a person's life. That was the year he began to see he wasn't just at school to avoid truancy court.

Inside the school's auditorium, Ms. Pasternack produced the school's musicals taking middle school line blocking, stage etiquette, enunciation, and wardrobing as seriously as if she were producing a Broadway show in New York City.

In the fall of seventh grade, when students were choosing sports teams to join, Cliff heeded Ms. Pasternack's call to audition for theater tech instead. The idea of running around a basketball court after school struck him as a total nightmare. Six months later, Cliff had mastered the sound board, the light board, and realized he could sing. He was cast as the lead and was sliding across the stage on his knees as Ziggy Springer, a character modeled after Elvis in a musical about the 1950s called *Nifty Fifties*, while his mom and dad cackled in the audience.

For Cliff, the school musical was everything he loved: teamwork, multitasking, and a place to start with a chaotic nothing, face the fear of failure, and come out the other side with a product that was orderly and appealing. It also highlighted his ability to juggle, learn fast, and lead.

Cliff's theater geek career blossomed in high school. He performed in *Beauty and the Beast* as Gaston and *High School Musical* as Coach Bolton, and also joined the golf team because it allowed him to get on area courses for free. He remembers the team as subpar, but like many things for the young Cliff, he also viewed it as a life lesson on the world's pecking order and where he fell into it. Locally, the Chichester team shined as it was in a district populated by a fair number of down-and-out, drug-riddled communities. But when Cliff got to districts, his team was clobbered by the kids from Philly's monied suburbs where players had grown up honing their game at their parents' country clubs.

In high school, as in middle school, work took on a big role in Cliff's life. Freshman year, he landed a gig at a local billiards hangout, a dimly lit pool hall where he says he met a lot of "up to no good folks" who served as cautionary tales. Cliff started as a clerk, but by eleventh grade he was opening and closing the joint, running the Wednesday-night eight-ball tournaments, and playing free pool himself. He was also watching people whose lives weren't working. They could barely make their mortgages. What money they had from low-paying jobs or gigs peddling DVDs out of their trunks in the parking lot went to beer, weed, and pool hall slot machines.

Cliff was the closest thing to an authority figure at the pool hall and therefore a sounding board for complaints from patrons struggling with drugs, alcohol, and gambling addictions that seemed to be making their lives worse. "People bitching about shitty situations and not doing anything about them," Cliff says. He saw what he didn't want to be. "My family line is very obsessive compulsive." Everything in moderation, his great-grandmother would say— but moderation was not really a Maloney trait. His dad had been beaten down by drugs; his younger sister was slowly giving in to the opioids that were flooding the region and leaving in their wake an epidemic of overdose deaths and ruined lives. The key was getting into the right thing. You needed to channel your compulsion. To Cliff's mind, it just wasn't that complicated: "These weren't people that were stupid; they were just into the wrong shit." His shit was work.

CLIFF'S POLITICAL VIEWS EVOLVED FROM WHAT HE SAW AND HEARD around Boothwyn. But modern American libertarianism actually has its history in nineteenth- and twentieth-century Austrian economists and philosophers who came to the United States to share their ideas. Government is an extension of its people but can get easily corrupted if not kept in constant check, went the philosophy. Emphasizing personal responsibility as a path to freedom was a way to stay out from under the grip of an intrusive bureaucracy that yearns to entangle you in caring for others. These ideas are outlined in books by business journalist Henry Hazlitt, a relentless opponent of government intervention and a critic of Franklin Delano Roosevelt's New Deal; Ludwig von Mises, also a proponent of laissez-faire economics—or the idea that government should never intervene in the economy; and Friedrich Hayek, who contended in his seminal book *The Road to Serfdom*, an energetic ode to the free market, that when government did intervene, this involvement could easily lead to totalitarianism, as decisions are made by a small group of planners who impose their will on others.

Together, these thinkers offered a lean and often unforgiving view of what it meant to be in community. That view caught fire in the late 1960s and early 1970s among a small cadre of American intellectuals, pols, and uber-wealthy tycoons who were distressed by the Vietnam War draft, and by the way New Deal ideals were embedding themselves into modern-day American policy. They were further irked by President Richard Nixon's 1971 decision to set artificial wage and price controls to temper inflation and his abandonment of the gold standard—just the kind of economic tweaking at the hand of government they despised. So in December 1971, a group of them birthed the Libertarian Party. A few years later came the nation's first libertarian think tank, the Cato Institute. It was co-founded by Wichita, Kansas, billionaire Charles Koch, a co-owner, with his since deceased brother David, of one of the largest multinational conglomerates in the world. Ed Crane, a former California money manager who had run for student body president at Berkeley on a platform to abolish the student government—he lost that race—served as co-founder and

the institute's first president. The other founder was Murray Rothbard, an economist and self-proclaimed anarcho-capitalist.

In 1979, David Koch, excited about building their movement,
jumped into the political arena, running as vice president on the
Libertarian ticket, along with a presidential candidate by the name
of Ed Clark who positioned himself to the right of the Republican candidate, Ronald Reagan. The libertarian duo would lose,
garnering a mere 1.1 percent of the votes. But, around this time,
other monied arch-conservatives—including Joseph Coors of the
Colorado brewing family; Richard Mellon Scaife, an heir to both
the Mellon banking fortune and billions from oil, aluminum, and
real estate; and John M. Olin, an Illinois-based chemical and am-
munitions manufacturer—would begin pumping millions of dollars into a series of other newly forming nonprofit institutes and
tax-exempt foundations designed to spread the free-market gospel.

Today, a mere one percent of American voters are registered
Libertarians. But one in ten, most of whom vote Republican, identify themselves that way. As a rule, libertarians oppose entitlement
programs, because in their eyes, the only thing that incentivizes
people to take care of themselves is having to take care of themselves. Government help is government meddling. It makes things
worse. While—or maybe because—aging billionaires like Charles
Koch have spent years popularizing libertarian ideals, younger
magnates who have amassed their fortunes in retail and tech—
people like PayPal co-founder Peter Thiel, Whole Foods co-founder
John Mackey, and TechCrunch founder Michael Arrington—have
professed their allegiance to at least some parts of the philosophy.

In its purest form, libertarianism calls on corporations to pay
as little in taxes as possible. It opposes protective government measures designed to regulate corporate pollution, workplace safety,
and an employee's negotiating power over salaries and benefits. All
of this is not for greed's sake, purists contend, but in the name
of a free-market philosophy. Libertarianism not only protects its

followers from the burdens of helping others via government programs, it makes a moral virtue out of such tightfistedness. If you
are a poor libertarian, the ideology keeps others from helping you.
Which might sound like a bad deal. But Cliff would say, if you
think the government is helping you by encouraging you to rely on
handouts, you are getting suckered.

In struggling Boothwyn, Cliff was surrounded by people getting help from the government. He watched them wait for welfare
checks that were too small, or too late, or that never arrived. Assistance was sometimes pulled right out from under them—maybe
a law was changed or they were no longer eligible. He did not want
to end up that way. Government wasn't reliable. His parents sometimes struggled financially, but they were rulers of their own lives.
"My family had a really strong take on that. Don't rely on anybody.
You're on your own in the world."

Cliff's father's life offered another lesson. Cliff Sr. had the mis-
fortune of getting involved in the drug business in the 1990s, the
era of mandatory sentencing laws and expanding prison capacity.
Once a low-level offender got sucked into the system, there was no
way of shaking it off. You were going to jail, and once you got out it
followed you around. In a place like Boothwyn, where there weren't
many jobs to begin with, an ex-convict was close to un-hirable.
Cliff Sr. got around that by starting his own landscaping business.
But once he got up on his feet and started making a decent living,
government intervention came knocking. The Philadelphia suburbs had different rules for different municipalities, and as such
was a regulatory minefield. There were licensing fees, insurances
to pay, and permits—and if you didn't pay them, there were fines.

Cliff's kid sister offered her own lessons in how the government
hurt when it tried to help. By thirteen, already a spitfire wildcard,
she was having trouble following rules. She was missing school,
stealing the family car, and eventually landed in juvenile court.
Whatever the government did to help her or rein her in only made

things worse, according to Cliff. Once "she went into the system, it began eating her up." Eventually, Cliff recounts, she was addicted to heroin. There were court orders, mandated halfway houses, and bills for government-required services like treatment facilities and social workers. Bureaucrats could pretend they had solutions, but really they wasted your time and your money. And when your kid sister is an addict, all you want is respite from heartbreak. The government doesn't offer that. Cliff was unsentimental about it, but her continued travails left an indelible mark on him. Soon, he didn't just distrust the government, he really hated it. He didn't think it could be saved or reformed. It needed to be torn down.

When Cliff graduated from high school in May 2009, few were leaving the halls of Chichester for the Ivy League. Most students went to state schools or community college; some got jobs at the local Wawa, a regional convenience store. Cliff's older sister dropped out of high school and eventually enrolled in beauty school; his younger brother graduated and eventually joined the Air Force. Cliff had not been a standout student. But he liked school and admired many of his teachers. So, he took out a loan and headed for Johnstown, one of the University of Pittsburgh's satellite campuses, for a degree in education. His plan was to become a math teacher.

Cliff immediately dug into undergraduate life. He joined the campus theater troupe, singing his heart out in *Jesus Christ Superstar* and *The Wedding Singer*, playing a lead role in *Chicago*, and eventually a gay bellhop in *Lend Me a Tenor*. Cliff developed a name for himself onstage—and off, as one of the more active dorm residence assistants. Once he co-sponsored a campus housing dodgeball tournament and convinced a reporter from the student newspaper to cover it. Cliff, initially politically apathetic, was changing. He kept close tabs on Johnstown's thirty-six student senators and what he saw started to gnaw at him—the way people got elected saying they'd fight for sensible things like better campus lighting or expanded shuttle bus service to and from student housing and the mall. But the campus continued to be dark at night and there were never enough buses. Cliff eventually decided to do something about it. He would be the gatekeeper, the guy who wasn't going to let those things happen. To fix a broken system, you had to get control of it. In that moment, he might have found his calling.

When he ran for student senate president in spring of 2011, Cliff treated the campaign like an all-encompassing, professional-grade operation. He promised to bring high-speed wireless internet to Johnstown, and more importantly he vowed to keep that promise. Teams of volunteers plastered the campus with flyers, knocked on nearly every door, and flooded the parking lots to make sure the message reached commuter students, who made up a third of the three-thousand-person student body. On election day, he combed the campus himself in a suit and tie and asked for his classmates' votes. He won. The following year, he ran again, and beat his opponent—who had opted for an online campaign, not a glad-handing one like his—2:1. That time, the school clocked a higher voter turnout number than anyone could remember. Cliff was lauded for his uncanny ability to get out the vote.

Once in office, Cliff kept the suit on, wearing it almost every day. He saw the need to create order, just as he had during his pool hall days. Everything was too loosey-goosey in the Johnstown Student Senate. He fought for a sweeping series of changes. From then on, any candidate elected to the student senate had to work toward at least one specific initiative. Once elected, they should be held accountable to their voters. At the end of his first semester in office, Cliff sent his own "accountability letter" to the student newspaper. He and his senate colleagues had secured a university promise of additional parking near the Student Union, as had been requested, he wrote. He had done a total reorg to the senate committee structure so students would know to whom and where to go with their suggestions and complaints. And the wireless internet was on its way. By the time Cliff graduated, despite some glitches, all of Johnstown had wireless internet service. Cliff had lobbied the university president ruthlessly and made it happen, telling himself during one of their first meetings that he wasn't there to make the president look good. He was there to represent the students.

While Cliff was making a name for himself as a student leader, he was also becoming more outspoken about national issues. When that classmate had turned to him and suggested he watch a video by a Texas congressman named Ron Paul, who was running for president, it was during a heated lecture hall debate about the Iraq War. Cliff was strongly opposed—and vocal. "You sound like you'd really like him," the kid had said, comparing Cliff to Paul.

Cliff went back to his dorm room that night and devoured one Ron Paul YouTube video after another, learning all he could about the idiosyncratic OB-GYN from Texas who'd been serving in Congress since the 1970s. Cliff felt a connection with Paul from the get-go. He was real, with a tell-it-like-he-sees-it rhetorical style that made him seem like the farthest thing from a politician. As a fundraising tool, he and his wife had begun selling their family recipes in an annual cookbook. Not fancy dishes, but regular people food, with a twist: Grandma Paul's Special Meatloaf, Oreo Cake made with Cool Whip, Chicken made with Doritos. Like Cliff, Paul had working-class Pennsylvania roots and believed in people taking care of themselves. Cliff also admired Paul's absolute faith in free markets. A Ludwig von Mises groupie, like the oil and gas magnates who'd also fallen hard for libertarianism, he got totally burned up in 1971 when Richard Nixon started up with his inflation fixes. In 1974, the year Nixon resigned, when the downtrodden GOP was searching for a new way forward, Paul, seeing an opportunity to jump into politics, decided to run for Congress. He lost his first bid for his Texas seat but won in a special election two years later when the winner stepped down.

In 1988, Paul made his first stab at the White House running as a libertarian. At the time, the Libertarian Party still thought the way to push forth the philosophy was by luring people away from the GOP. Paul won a mere .5 percent of the vote. But he wasn't giving up.

When he ran again in 2008, Paul used a different tactic; he joined the GOP, but still played the outlier, crisscrossing the country to level with potential supporters about how bad he thought government really was. Cliff believed voters heard Paul's mistrust and could identify their own. He wanted to decriminalize drugs, get out of Afghanistan, and cut defense spending, the Federal Reserve, the Education Department, and the FDA. This was everything Cliff believed and more. Paul dropped out midway through the primaries, but only after the media started calling his young avid followers the "Paulites," a sign of his grassroots popularity. Now, the 2012 presidential campaign was about to get underway, and Paul was running again, his third bid for the highest office in the land.

One day, Cliff had an epiphany. He poked his head out of his dorm room and looked down the hall. His classmates were working on getting drunk, getting laid. None of them, he surmised, gave a shit about what was happening to the country and what this guy named Ron Paul was trying to do about it. *What is going on?* Cliff wondered. *How are people not like: This is it. We have to do something. How had no one else on his campus caught the bug?* That's when Cliff decided: *We have got to mainstream these principles.*

Summer was approaching. Cliff needed to be part of Ron Paul's operation. He reached out to Paul's staff and pleaded for a job. When he landed an internship in Paul's DC congressional office, he was stoked. But as soon as Cliff got there, he realized he'd applied for the wrong position. He was so new to politics that he didn't understand that congressmen were required to keep their administrative staff separate from their campaign operations. He didn't want to be sitting in a cubicle on the phone dealing with "Bob calling in because he's not getting his VA check." He wanted to be drawing on whiteboards, planning strategies, and fighting for votes, block by block, door by door.

Nonetheless, Cliff got to spend a lot of time around Paul, attending congressional subcommittee meetings, learning how to talk to DC insiders, and inhaling intern life on The Hill. Paul, the plain-spoken Texan, was even better in person. He was quirky but presentable, misunderstood but wise. A great-grandfather, he loved chocolate chip cookies and his family.

Cliff also discovered something else while in DC. He was not alone. There was an entire world of young Ron Paul acolytes, outsiders who had worked their asses off for him in 2008. And they were getting support from GOP power players in DC as well as a constellation of low-profile far-right donors who wanted to see libertarianism—and thus tax cuts and limited government—become mainstream. They were enraged and embarrassed by the fact that the Republican Party had lost to Barack Obama in 2008 and was at risk of doing so again. To them, it was a failure of immense, historic proportions. And they felt partly to blame. They'd failed to get out their message, to communicate how policies that delivered overwhelming benefits to the ultra-wealthy were good for all Americans of all income levels. And they'd particularly failed with young people. Obama was beloved among mainstream suburbanites, urbanites, even some rural voters. But he was also super popular among the young.

Resolved to recommit to their cause and desperate for some new ideas, these wealthy powerbrokers, whose own names rarely appear in the press, were doubling down on preexisting conservative organizations with nonpartisan-sounding names: Americans for Prosperity, the American Legislative Exchange Council, and the Heritage Foundation. They were also opening their pocketbooks to groups targeting the next generation, at unprecedented rates. If you had thoughts on how to sell their ideas to young people, they wanted to talk.

That's how Young Americans for Liberty (YAL) was originally born.

Their leader was a boyish-looking free-marketer from Texas A&M named Jeff Frazee. A true believer and workhorse who thought George W. Bush was too liberal, Frazee had latched on to libertarianism in college, attended the Libertarian Party Texas state Convention in 2004, and interned for Ron Paul a year later. Then he convinced the congressman to give him the national youth coordinator job for the 2008 campaign, and when Ron Paul dropped out, he gathered his young fans together to launch a youth group to spread Paul's ideology to young America. That summer, Cliff met Frazee in Paul's office and immediately the two hit it off. Cliff was exploring life in DC, Frazee was starting to think about YAL's future. He was aging out of the leadership job and looking for a replacement. Cliff's passion for the cause impressed him.

Back at Johnstown that fall, Cliff was fired up by his summer on Capitol Hill and emboldened by his connection to a political network made up of guys like himself, hard workers from places no one had ever heard of. He had seen enough from his cubicle in Ron Paul's office to realize how you get power: you have to build your own network, and then people start paying attention to you. So Cliff began to dedicate all his spare time and energy to building out a YAL chapter on campus. When you thought of YAL, you would think of Cliff Maloney.

YAL gave him a platform and a small budget, but the rest was Cliff. He was determined to spread the ideas Ron Paul espoused, as quickly and loudly as possible. His activism should be dramatic, larger-than-life, the kind of stuff that you might see on a stage. At one of YAL's first public events, Cliff pasted a roll of Kraft paper on a wall near the student union and wrote "We the People . . ." on it in black Magic Marker, using huge loopy letters designed to resemble Colonial-era calligraphy. It was a super-sized rendition of the Constitution, one you might find on one of the musical theater stages he had spent so many years on. Libertarians often referred to themselves as "constitutionalists," and pitched themselves as the real defenders of the freedoms the Founding Fathers had envisioned for the nation. Cliff was learning to see the Constitution as one of his best activist props.

Another time, his group organized a protest against U.S. intervention in the war in Syria. Half a dozen activists stood near the student union, brandishing large signs that read *Peace is Cheaper* and *Peace is Patriotic*, and handed out flyers insisting this was a nonpartisan issue. Cliff, wearing a bright red shirt, held his own sign: *Wars are Poor Chisels for Carving out Peaceful Tomorrows*, it read, quoting Martin Luther King, Jr. It was politics. And it was poetry. Mr. Tarves, Cliff's sixth-grade teacher, would have been proud. It didn't hurt that Cliff had also made the student paper.

IT DIDN'T TAKE LONG FOR CLIFF TO BECOME A YAL STAR. WHILE still getting his degree at Johnstown, Cliff was appointed Pennsylvania state chair. His job was to build chapters throughout the state, and over the next year he did it with discipline and panache. He was obsessive. He combed Facebook for campus politicos with libertarian streaks and then drove to meet them in person, putting thousands of miles on his used car. He called campuses nonstop, testing his pitches until he had one that worked. "Do you have leadership skills?" he'd ask a student he was recruiting, a leading question that often prompted the kid to start rattling off his or her skill set. Suddenly, the kid would be selling himself to Cliff. And wouldn't you know, he just happened to have something for him to lead, his very own YAL chapter.

In the spring of 2014, Cliff graduated from Johnstown. He had six weeks to kill before beginning a scholarship-funded master of education program at the University of Portland in Oregon. Then he received one of the best phone calls of his life. Tea Party activists were looking to make an impact in a congressional race out west, pumping tens of thousands of dollars into the victory efforts of a Ron Paul–endorsed candidate in Sacramento. Someone needed to manage the voter outreach effort. Was Cliff interested?

The candidate was an eccentric Russian émigré named Igor Birman who'd arrived in the States during high school. He'd gotten a degree from UC Davis and then one from Emory Law School and had been chief of staff for California congressman Tom Mc-Clintock, a Tea Party darling in his own right. If he won, Birman would be the first Soviet-born member of Congress. It was a perfect libertarian story line: Who better than a child of Communist Russia to sell the message of free-market absolutism? Cliff jumped at the opportunity.

It was a six-way primary in the Sacramento suburbs, a purple region where the parties fought bitterly over razor-thin margins. These "jungle races," as they were sometimes called, could be chaotic. Nominees were chosen in open primaries, which in this case resulted in one Democrat—the incumbent—running against Birman and two other Republican challengers, along with a little-known candidate running as a Libertarian and another as an Independent. The top two vote-getters, no matter their party affiliation, would face off in the general.

When Cliff showed up, Birman was polling below 3 percent, beyond a longshot. Then Cliff got to work, casing the country for young libertarians who could be his boots on the ground, calling, "text bombing," cajoling, and in Cliff's salesman-like fashion, selling them on a chance to make history. His tactics for recruiting volunteers for phone-banking and door-knocking were so effective that people drove for hours to come work for free all day and then sleep on the floor of the headquarters at night. On primary day, Birman won 17.5 percent of the vote, missing the runoff by a smidgen—a more than respectable showing for someone who'd entered the race almost as an afterthought. Word got out that young Cliff Maloney really knew how to move the dial. For years after, YAL taught the Maloney Four-Step—a recruiting process that includes contacting recruits via social media, getting them on the phone, getting them to verbally agree to do something specific, and then making sure they do it. Hardly rocket science. But it required persistence, which Cliff had in spades. And the honorific was cool, a great branding tool for an activist trying to make a name for himself.

After the June primary, Cliff went back home and started getting ready for his move to Portland. He'd had his fun with politics; now it was time to buckle down. But the political talent spotters had Cliff on their radar, just as they soon would young Charlie Kirk. Why go to school, they asked, when you can come with us and make a difference *now*? YAL offered to move Cliff to the national office and make him a regional director. The pay wasn't great, but they more than hinted that if things worked out, Cliff would be running YAL in no time, maybe even within a few months, as Frazee, already inching into his thirties, was ready to move on to help grow the donor bases of other conservative orgs. Cliff agonized over the decision. His mother pleaded with him to follow through with the master's program. Who walked away from a free degree and a steady job? Didn't he know how the world worked?

In fact, Cliff decided, he did know a thing or two about that. If his brief time in the political arena had taught him anything, it was that the world rewarded those who took charge of their destinies, not those who took the first handout they were offered. He declined the scholarship and took the job.

CHAPTER THREE

The New Son

On a bone-chilling afternoon in winter 2012, inside a suburban Chicago coffee shop, Joe Walsh, the Illinois Republican congressman and Tea Party activist, known for his brash declarations, leaned across a Formica table and told Charlie Kirk he had "the easiest fuck'n" job in the world, growing his youth group. Nothing opens up the wallets of far-right donors more than the threat of college kids being eaten up by their socialist peers. If Charlie could present himself as the young man who would close the floodgates, he'd be able to raise limitless cash.

Walsh, a former social worker turned free-market renegade, was Charlie's latest mentor. The two had met at Living Waters Assembly of God, a Chicagoland church thirty minutes from Charlie's house, where Walsh was campaigning for his congressional seat. Charlie, already a networking aficionado, was there bonding with members of the Christian right, whose support would soon become an important part of Charlie's rise to prominence. At first glance, Charlie seemed like a dork to Walsh, "a beanpole of a kid" with an awkward facial tic. But there was something about him people liked, and Walsh soon liked it, too. Charlie had a special charm. He grew on you. You'd take him out for dinner and he'd devour the food like he hadn't eaten in weeks. You'd give him advice on what to watch and he'd watch it. You'd invite him to an event and he'd come. Joe Walsh and his wife, Helene, were like a lot of people in Chicago conservative circles who met Charlie back then: eager to help a kid with boundless energy who supported the larger cause of saving America from Obama-ism.

The truth is the job wasn't quite as easy as Walsh suggested. Sure, a lot of donors had bottomless pockets and were willing to spend millions, if not hundreds of millions, promoting their conservative agenda, especially the parts of it that stressed lightly regulated free markets and rock-bottom tax rates. But the competition was fierce. It had been sixty plus years since the leaders of the modern conservative movement—anti-communists, corporatists, and captains of conservative culture, sometimes referred to as the "conservative elite"—had made their wishes known: to take back the country from members of the hated Liberal Establishment, admirers of Franklin Delano Roosevelt and his vision for an expansive government that sought first and foremost to protect its citizenry.

To build their army they had birthed dozens of conservative groups, many of them aimed at the young and each organized around a specific niche of the hard-right wish list. Fundraisers for these groups—political entrepreneurs, really—spent many weekends traveling from conference to conference and fighting for a spot on the conservative donor gravy train, which was estimated to disperse hundreds of millions of dollars through the right-wing universe every year. The two biggest events were CPAC, the Conservative Political Action Conference held every year at the end of February, and Restoration Weekend, a gathering of policy wonks, donors, and up-and-comers who gathered every November to plot America's future.

In between these events, energetic supplicants would aim to rub shoulders with donors at every possible opportunity. Palm

Beach was hot during the winter season. Manhattan was hot all the time. (Charlie would tell a friend that $10,000 was like lunch money for the average donor there, thanks to the high cost of living. So, it was wise to hit the island often.) Wyoming was hopping with deep-pocketed hunters at the height of elk season from September to December. Elevator pitches and five-year plans at the ready, those who succeeded in this world not only had to be slick and speak with conviction, they needed almost superhuman self-confidence.

Charlie Kirk had that confidence. Where it had come from wasn't entirely clear. But he wasn't just selling his support for slim tax policies or a commitment to free speech. He was selling a product he believed in fiercely: Charlie Kirk. As Turning Point USA grew, Charlie wanted young people to see his brand of conservatism and think it was cool—but he also needed the gray hairs to be turned on by his dream. And they were. Much like Reagan, who seemed to always be radiating an infectious optimism, Charlie radiated a can-do-ism that his supporters saw as refreshing and empowering. Donors wanted to be around this energetic spitfire, seeing in him a fighting future they could get behind.

Charlie sold them that future. One conservative fundraiser told me Charlie was able to position himself as a guy unafraid to "stick it to the libs." And the old-guard—filthy rich, but fearful that their whole worldview was being beaten apart by lefty academics and the kids they were indoctrinating—wanted a warrior, a crusader on the frontlines to represent their interests.

Leaders at other conservative groups grumbled that Charlie was more style than substance, selling a vision rather than creating one. They were doing the hard, behind-the-scenes work while he got the glamour, and they resented it. But you couldn't argue with the dollars. Charlie knew how to get the cash.

At the Leadership Institute, the far-right training school, instructors preached that raising money was a relationship game.

You didn't just beg rich people for money and then take off. You developed bonds with them. Charlie didn't need to sit in a Leadership Institute classroom to pick up this lesson. He seemed to have absorbed it through osmosis. He didn't just express gratitude to his donors, whom he called investors, he gushed—or according to some of his right-wing detractors, he shamelessly brown-nosed them.

IN AUGUST 2012, JUST A FEW MONTHS AFTER THE SUPREME Court upheld Obama's Affordable Care Act, a rage-inducing tragedy in these crowds, Charlie boarded a commercial flight with Bill Montgomery, his sidekick, and headed for the Republican National Convention in Tampa, Florida. Bill, a lover of the impromptu road trip, had convinced Charlie to go. Bill had tried to build other political organizations in the past, but this thing with Charlie looked like his final shot to create a lasting legacy. And if they were going to do it, they needed more cash.

On board, while Bill quietly managed his decades-old fear of flying, Charlie memorized the names and faces of the nation's top far-right backers, many of whom he hoped he and Bill would bump into that week. Charles Koch, Charlie would have learned from any photos or business magazine profiles he might have picked up, had a slim, towering frame, pearly white teeth, and affiliations with a host of organizations that planned to spend close to $400 million to defeat Obama that election cycle. Harold Hamm was a fracking giant born to Oklahoma sharecroppers and the youngest in a family of thirteen children. He was about to pump close to $1 million into Mitt Romney's election efforts. And the seventy-nine-year-old Sheldon Adelson, a Las Vegas casino magnate, motored around conferences in an electric wheelchair and was so politically influential he was known as the "Kingmaker."

Once in Florida, things got bumpy. Bill, in his haste, had booked a room at a Days Inn in Siesta Key, an hour and fifteen minutes away. Then, news broke that Hurricane Isaac was about to hit. Charlie and Bill worried road conditions might block them from Tampa once the convention started. Bill downed the Star-bucks coffees with cream and two Splendas each that he was known for mainlining and stayed optimistic. Luckily, the storm's path shifted, and despite slick roads, the actual damage was mini-mal. But after arriving in the city, the duo faced another glitch. Neither had understood that convention tickets were hard-fought commodities, acquired months in advance. Charlie thought the Republican National Convention was like a hockey game "where you could just buy tickets at StubHub," he recalled. Charlie, who has multiple versions to many of his stories, said a friend who was also at the convention ultimately obtained a pass for him. In an-other telling, Bill, ever the chatterbox, who had a pocket filled with homemade business cards, eventually finagled a free pass from some exiting visitors he had chatted up. Either way, the persistence paid off. The last day of the convention, in one of the stairwells, Charlie bumped into Foster Friess, a Wyoming-based growth fund manager and far-right donor extraordinaire.

"My name is Charlie Kirk," Charlie told the swashbuck-ling Friess, who wore a cowboy hat atop shock-white hair. "I'm a nineteen-year-old from Chicago, Illinois, the capital of com-munity organizing." Charlie was referencing Obama, who got his start organizing political campaigns in Chicago's mostly African American South Side. Charlie told Friess he dreamed of build-ing a powerful youth organization that could rival Obama's 2008 presidential campaign. He told Friess he was going to build it from the bottom up.

Friess was a politically incorrect born-again Christian who once told a TV reporter that women could avoid getting preg-nant by holding aspirin between their knees, thus keeping their legs closed. He was a big spender, known for once throwing a lav-ish, multiday birthday party in swanky Jackson Hole, at which he spontaneously donated a total of $7.7 million to his friends' favorite charities. And today was an emotional day for him. Earlier he'd heard former secretary of state Condoleezza Rice give a talk about her life growing up in Alabama under Jim Crow laws, where her family could not go to a whites-only movie theater or sit at the local Woolworth's counter. Like many Black Republicans, Rice did not see this as a sign of systemic racism, but a pesky annoyance to overcome with grit and patriotism. "It does not matter where you came from," she told the filled arena. "It matters where you are going." The speech had made Friess cry. Now, a spirited young man in an oversized coat jacket was also pulling at his heart strings. Like Condoleezza Rice, Charlie Kirk wanted to save the country they loved.

Friess had already blown nearly $1.7 million on the former Pennsylvania senator Rick Santorum's go-nowhere presidential campaign. (He'd been excited by the candidate's faith and family values platform.) But ever the optimist, Friess wasn't done donating. In fact, he was looking for some fresh ideas. And he was constantly haranguing the Republican Party elites about the need for new blood. A few weeks later, Charlie would receive a $10,000 check from Friess, who would go on to give the group millions more. Charlie, in return, would exemplify the Leadership Institute's caring and feeding technique by creating an eight-minute video-paean to Friess entitled "Only in America" for Turning Point USA's website. It was an ego-boosting technique that would become one of his fundraising trademarks.

Another time, Charlie would call Friess "one of the most amazing people God put on this Earth." The Foster Friess story is one of Charlie's favorites. ("I gave him my stairwell pitch, not my elevator pitch," he once quipped.) Perhaps he's so fond of the anecdote because it evokes themes that are part of his creation myth: grit, money, and famous people charmed by him. It also highlights a trait of which Charlie is exceedingly proud: when he spots an opportunity, no matter the stakes or the time pressure, he acts.

"It doesn't matter if you're building a business that's in paving or in finance, technology, food . . . you have to paint a vision," Charlie mused as he recounted the story of his group's beginnings during a podcast interview conducted by a Chicago-area entrepreneur, who would also become an early donor. During the interview, Charlie didn't hesitate to liken himself to entrepreneurial greats like Steve Jobs and the former CEO of Starbucks, Howard Schultz. "Just look at this design," he gushed, holding up his iPhone. "I mean, look, it's just so sleek, it's so beautiful. It's almost as if you feel like you're entering a different dimension, and it's a reflection of who you are. That's what Apple sells. They sell—they sell creating the future. I'll use a couple of other examples. Starbucks does not sell coffee, they just don't. They sell a vehicle for you to achieve what you want to achieve through energy or through fulfillment or through your favorite customizable, you know, drink. So every one of these major brands, from Howard Schultz to Steve Jobs . . . they painted a vision. So I painted a vision from day one. That's essentially what I said. And that we are losing our country."

In the fall of 2012, Charlie and Bill continued to cruise around the Chicago region in Bill's Thunderbird, hitting one Tea Party event after another, trying to find more heavy hitters to throw them some cash. It was Bill's job to convince the people in charge to put Charlie up onstage. At first, Charlie was more like the amateur opening act, working through his short schtick on the national debt, the ills of socialism, the problem the GOP had attracting young people. But soon he was giving longer speeches, perfecting his pace, and delighting the suburban Tea Party set—middle-aged real estate agents, retailers, and small business owners—with his repertoire of gags about corrupt Illinois politicians and dead grandmothers voting from their graves.

"The really cool thing about Illinois . . . We have term limits . . . One term in office. One term in jail" was one of his favorite jokes.

The crowds ate him up.

Bill wasn't a stranger to mentoring young talent. And Charlie was a worthy addition to his cadre of mentees—some of whom occasionally got themselves in hot water. Caleb Hull, a conservative media strategist, got in trouble for using the "n" word on a 2014 Twitter account that he then deleted. Another one of Bill's protégés was Mary Miller, a born-again Christian mother of seven with a cattle and grain farm who, in 2020, won a House seat representing Illinois's 15th congressional district, then stood on a stage and praised Hitler for his good rapport with young people. "Hitler was right on one thing," she told a right-wing group called Moms for America, giving a pat on the back to the mass murderer of six million Jews. "Whoever has the youth, has the future."

During the first winter of their partnership, Bill introduced Charlie to a Chicagoland jeweler named Mike Miller, a gregarious socializer who liked steakhouse dinners and trips to Las Vegas. Miller specialized in unique pieces made with luxury gems. That meant he had a robust Rolodex of wealthy clients. Mike liked Charlie, donated to his cause, and then began introducing him around.

Things really began to go Charlie's way at an evening fundraiser that Bill got Charlie invited to for Bill Prim, a retired police commander and immigration hardliner. Prim was hoping to secure the Republican nomination for sheriff in the Tea Party hotspot of McHenry County. That's where Charlie finally wrangled an introduction to Gary Rabine, a chatty bootstrapper who'd made his fortune in the rough-and-tumble world of cement paving and had the clout, contacts, and money to land Newt Gingrich and his wife Callista to speak at the event at his golf course in Woodstock, Illinois.

That night, Gingrich, the former House speaker who was now making a cottage industry out of his back-to-back speaking gigs, was in fine form. In a twenty-minute speech, he praised Prim for his "integrity" and for his plans to bring "modern policies and techniques" to McHenry's sheriff's office. To his fellow conservatives, Gingrich encouraged hope. The grim state of the DC beltway would improve, he told them. Conservatives "persevere through difficult times," he promised, adding, "I believe we will outlast Obama."

The speech was a highlight for Rabine. But just as exciting, he recalls, was meeting Charlie. After the party, they talked for hours. Charlie would eventually tell Rabine that he had decided to forgo college as he didn't want to study alongside campus elitists. Rabine, a devout Catholic from the Chicago region who'd never gone to college himself, understood. At forty-nine, he was a successful businessman with a series of companies that generated tens of millions of dollars a year. But he still had a vivid memory of an afternoon in 1981, his senior year in high school, when he was just a kid with a mullet. During study hall, a group of cool kids were rattling off the names of the colleges where they were headed: Michigan State, University of Illinois . . . Then one "smart-ass" turned to him: "Gary, what school you going to?" Rabine was the captain of the football team and a gifted wrestler. He'd thought about trying to get a wrestling scholarship, but his dad had told him he wasn't smart enough for college. Rabine told the group that he was going to work for the family landscaping business, maybe pave some driveways. "Really, Gary?" one of the kids poked. "So, you're going to be a ditch digger."

"It embarrassed me for about five seconds," Rabine once noted. "And I'll never forget those five seconds."

Now, thirty-three years later, Rabine had three college-educated kids. And their degrees had all been paid for by the long hours he and his wife, Cheryl, a former hairdresser with an unshakeable work ethic, had put into building their business.

But instead of learning in their college classes about the beauty of the capitalistic system that had catapulted him and Cheryl into the ranks of the uber wealthy, Rabine worried that his children were getting "twisted with this message that was totally against our fabric"—that "free enterprise" should go away, that it shouldn't be the "system of choice." He concluded that Charlie's mission wasn't just important. It was vital.

Rabine, like Bill Montgomery, collected mentees, doling out pearls of wisdom—about the importance of networking, developing a strong work ethic, and being responsible with your money. He also liked being around young people. He and Cheryl had even adopted a boy from Russia.

At his office a few days after meeting Charlie, Rabine set to work helping his newest pupil tighten his pitch. People were busy. They had minuscule attention spans. And they were unlikely to think a young man his age had anything to tell them. The pitch needed to be crisp, precise, and to the point. Shorter, shorter, shorter was the goal. Charlie practiced it over and over.

Superhuman drive was a trait that Rabine and Charlie shared. Rabine may have seemed like a regular Joe. He certainly wasn't a sophisticate. But his drive was beyond compare. And he was sometimes described as "the Elon Musk of road paving." As of 2018, Rabine had started twenty-five different companies, and in 2019 Rabine Group reported $111 million in revenue. His biggest national clients included Walmart, Lowe's, and Home Depot, whose co-founder, Bernie Marcus, a GOP mega-donor, he considered a friend.

A month after the Gingrich event, Rabine was preparing to speak at a Palm Beach shindig hosted by the Job Creators Network, a conservative advocacy group Marcus had helped launch. While the association's moniker cleverly suggested an advocacy group for trade workers, the network was looking out for the vested interests of those workers' bosses, serving as a sort of union for CEOs. The group's specialty: "education campaigns." One, in 2019, would grace Times Square after Congresswoman Alexandria Ocasio-Cortez questioned New York City's willingness to award the behemoth Amazon nearly $3 billion in tax breaks in exchange for opening a campus in Queens. "Thanks for nothing, AOC!" it read. An ad the Network placed in the *Wall Street Journal* in 2020 denounced COVID warnings that sought to protect American workers. "Dr. Fauci, We'd Like a Second Opinion!" it read. Other splashy national billboard ads have billed minimum wage hikes as "job-killing mandates."

Rabine was scheduled to share his business success story with members at the event, but he had a better idea. During a call, he told Marcus: "Bernie, I can speak like you want me to about my rags to riches story. But I got a kid that I'm mentoring right now that will be a way better story than mine. And I really want to get him in front of you and all these other people."

Marcus was not enticed. "Come on Gary, a nineteen-year-old kid? Are you kidding me?"

Rabine persisted and sent Marcus a video of Charlie giving a speech. "You let me know." A couple of hours later, Marcus reached out: "All right," he told Rabine. "Send the kid."

It was at this event that Charlie first encountered a politically plugged-in Palm Beach couple, Lee and Allie Hanley. The Hanleys weren't like Gary Rabine, who wore athleisure-wear golf shirts with his company logo emblazoned on them and proudly called himself a "hillbilly." They weren't like Bernie Marcus, who despite his deep pockets could be gruff. They were an always exquisitely dressed Greenwich, Connecticut, couple who summered on Fishers Island, the ultra-exclusive WASP enclave off the Connecticut coast, and wintered in Palm Beach at a Mediterranean-style home designed by the iconic architect Maurice Fatio.

Lee, the heir to a brick and petroleum fortune, was a Yale alum and track and field star. Hollywood handsome as a young man, he was gregarious and deeply invested in spreading his ideas about the superiority of Western civilization and Judeo-Christian values from his perch on half a dozen boards, including the Yankee

Institute, a libertarian think tank he helped found, and The King's College, a small Christian college in the Financial District of Manhattan that offered classes on Christian spirituality, and the philosophy of human sexuality through a biblical lens.

Even though the Hanleys had five children between them, they soon took Charlie under their wing. With the Hanleys championing him, Charlie Kirk became a familiar face around Palm Beach, where, on verandas and oceanside patios during the October to May "social season," fundraising executives from all over the world, including the Vatican, arrived in a steady stream, and millions of dollars were promised to conservative candidates and causes.

In November 2013, Allie Hanley invited Charlie to Restoration Weekend, the four-day seminar popular among wealthy, liberty-loving powerbrokers. At that point, it was being held every year at the Breakers, a lavish, turn-of-the-century Italian Renaissance–style resort not far from Mar-a-Lago. Restoration Weekend was the brainchild of a political apostate by the name of David Horowitz, a onetime Berkeley-lefty-turned-anti-Muslim-radical with an eponymous think tank, the David Horowitz Freedom Center. Horowitz was also an ace at spotting gifted protégés who could spread his far-right rhetoric deeper into the American conscience. One of his catches was Ben Shapiro, the Daily Wire founder. Shapiro had coined the oft-repeated phrase *Facts Don't Care About Your Feelings*, which would become the title of one of his multiple bestsellers, and which was at the time a snarky catchall for everything the young right thought was wrong with the young left. Now, Horowitz had opened his doors to Charlie, who was delighted to make himself available.

Meanwhile, Allie Hanley was busy opening up "the entire southern corridor" to Charlie. Like so many right-wing elders— from Montgomery in the Chicago burbs, to Horowitz, out in California—Allie Hanley had a thing for spotting just the right kind of talent, sprucing it up to her liking, and watching it grow. She'd been doing it for decades. In 1979, she held a luncheon for five hundred at her Georgian mansion in Greenwich for a handsome Republican presidential hopeful from California: Ronald Reagan. As charming as he was, Reagan didn't pass muster for Allie in the tie department, according to a *New Yorker* article written by Evan Osnos. When they'd met for the first time a few days before the event, Allie had taken stock of the candidate's brown necktie. When he and his wife, Nancy, showed up in Greenwich, Allie greeted the future president with a selection of options more suitable for the preppy East Coast enclave.

With Allie's influence rubbing off on him and a new stylish wardrobe, Charlie got the "makeover" he needed, Joe Walsh recalls. He replaced his outdated suits with expensive-looking sports coats, which he paired with starched white oxfords and cool streetwear sneakers or leather lace-ups the color of desert sand. Soon, he would don hip patterned socks and sport a voguish hairdo. His tic waned and the Chicago twang dissipated.

It wouldn't be long before the gangly kid from suburban Chicago wasn't just hitting up the rich for cash. He was hanging with them at their sprawling vacation homes, hunting and fishing with them, attending their lavish birthday celebrations, and having God-chats with them on their boats. One fundraising executive, almost twice Charlie's age, recalls arriving at a donor's beach house for a meeting and noticing Charlie pacing in the backyard on his cell. He was there as a houseguest.

Charlie would soon also be included in important strategy sessions with conservative powerbrokers desperate to overcome Obama-ism and take back Washington in 2016. In November 2014, Lee Hanley invited Charlie to come meet an esteemed pollster named Pat Caddell, a former Democrat credited with helping to get Jimmy Carter elected (among other impressive electoral feats).

A year earlier, Hanley had commissioned Caddell, now playing for the right, to dig deeper into a theory he had been developing for a while, that an increasing number of voters distrusted the federal government and the power-hungry elites who they believed were controlling it. Caddell heard in this mix of anger and dismay a political opportunity for the GOP to find an outsider, a populist candidate, and push him into the highest office in the land. Caddell's research even had a name: "The Smith Project," alluding to the 1939 classic film *Mr. Smith Goes to Washington*, about a small-town hero who is appointed to the U.S. Senate and then takes on a system rigged against the little guy.

Lee Hanley was circulating Caddell's findings to donors like billionaire hedge fund manager Robert Mercer and his daughter Rebekah. Also on the list: energy investor Toby Neugenbauer, political strategists like Steve Bannon, and the young man Hanley now knew with the most direct connection to college-going America: Charlie Kirk.

Charlie sat comfortably in the impressive living room of the Hanleys' mansion—a fantasy of a place, outfitted by the celebrated interior designer Keith Irvine and garnished with great works of art from Lee's collection—as his mentor laid out Caddell's technicolor vision. "Charlie, there's going to be someone that will barnstorm onto the national political stage in a way that we could never anticipate," Lee told him. "It's going to be someone who hates the establishment, hates Washington, D.C., smashes political correctness, and will probably be a businessman."

At the time, Charlie wasn't sure what that barnstorming would look like. But, no matter, he was going to be part of it.

Around that time, Lee and Allie Hanley would also host a candlelit dinner for Turning Point USA at their Palm Beach home. Charlie, like a teenage son who'd invited the gang home, ended up bringing along a bigger crowd than expected. Allie, who was accustomed to chairing million-dollar benefits, quickly arranged for more place settings, then told the room they would not be getting the portions they normally would, according to two people who were there. Allie, they said, carried herself like the veteran hostess she was—thrown off her guard for a second, but quickly recovering her composure. The party must go on. And anyway, Charlie was just a big puppy dog—it was hard to get too mad at the kid, especially since he was being carefully groomed to take the low-taxes, small-government ideas the Hanleys and their peers held dear and pitch them to the next generation of voters.

CHAPTER FOUR

From the Ground Up

While Charlie was traveling the country, winning over monied oil magnates and GOP socialites, his volunteers were back in Illinois, putting the dollars he was amassing to good use. The plan was to make a "full-frontal attack" on the liberal indoctrination of college kids by invading their campuses with free-market ideas. "Conversions would be the measure of success," Charlie told them.

By late fall 2012, Charlie had garnered a crew of about a dozen followers, whom he sometimes referred to as "young patriots," plucking some from his former high school political group SOS Liberty and others from the lively campaign of a local congressman by the name of Bob Dold, who had lost his rebid for Illinois's 10th congressional district seat. But Charlie had hung around long enough to pull the best and the brightest from the candidate's volunteer ranks.

Turning Point USA was now working out of a slate gray storefront in Lemont, Illinois that Bill Montgomery had donated. Next to the office was a sagging, two-story Colonial with boarded-up windows, a sad remnant of a more glorious past. The main drag—boastfully named Illinois Street—had been converted into an unsightly two-lane highway. It was hardly an inspiring venue for a group that sought to take over America. No one cared. They were building out an operation that was bigger than downtown Lemont, bigger than Illinois, and bigger than them.

Ever aware of his image, and in an effort to make his outfit feel like the Apple of conservative politics, Charlie would later refer to their first building as a garage. Those who were there at the beginning say it hadn't been a garage for years, if ever. Still, it buzzed with the high-octane energy of young men and women in their late teens and early twenties who got fired up by tax codes and what they saw as bloated line items in the federal budget. They showed up casually dressed in basketball shorts, yoga pants, and sweats—to pore over their laptops, edit videos, design literature, and plot their campus invasions, sometimes toiling well into the night, while downing pizza and subs. Among them were a star field hockey player who loved Chris Christie, a Guatemalan American community college student, and the son of Polish immigrants who arrived on American soil with one suitcase each.

They were guided by Bill Montgomery, who showed up in his button-down shirts and slacks, sometimes a tweed jacket, to strategize. The approach: they were salespeople, and free-market capitalism was their product.

Even for this unusually driven crowd, recruiting college students on campuses wasn't going to be easy. The competition was obvious from the get-go. Conservative youth groups had been around for years: the College Republicans since the 1890s, the Young Republicans since the 1930s. Young Americans for Freedom, one of the newer outfits, had already been around for more than fifty years, inaugurated in 1960 by conservative firebrand William F. Buckley, under an elm tree at his parents' sprawling estate in Sharon, Connecticut. But Charlie believed these other groups were stale and out-of-touch, privately labeling them "anemic." Their members did often look like illustrations from *The*

Official Preppy Handbook when they showed up around campus at election time to register young adults to vote. And their social media games were, to hear Charlie tell it, weak, as if they still hadn't figured out that young people now lived online. In short, Charlie believed the old guard had lost the spirit and passion to innovate. And he was fond of telling donors that that was why they should bank on him.

Still, these other groups did have a few major things going for them: budgets, alumni, and the institutional support of the conservative DC machine. Sure, you could plant a chapter of some new group no one had ever heard of and hope young people would join. But why do that when you could use the groundwork already laid down by these preexisting groups for your own liftoff? Charlie, with the help of Bill's sales acumen honed at the pharmaceutical companies he had worked for, understood that no matter what you were selling, you first needed to build brand awareness. And that's what Turning Point USA would spend its first few years doing.

The plan was to cozy up to other conservative groups with marketing material—catchy signs a conservative kid might want to hang up in his or her dorm room—churned out of the Lemont office at a rapid clip: *Socialism, You Make It They Take It* and *We Survived College Without Becoming Liberals*. The material would have Turning Point USA's logo on it and a link to the group's website, which was bursting with news articles and info on how to get more involved. It was a tactic that would eventually help TPUSA grow its own membership.

Back in Lemont, volunteers even came up with a chummy name for their campaign: The Free Market Alliance, suggesting they were a unified network, and these other groups were now under the Turning Point USA umbrella. Eventually, the leaders of these other groups would find themselves enervated by the whole setup. As far as they were concerned, there was no such network. And if there was, Charlie was certainly not running it; after all, he'd just arrived on the scene. Further, some would openly question the membership numbers Charlie claimed he had, insisting they were bloated. But that was still to come.

By fall 2013, Turning Point USA was distributing thousands of pamphlets with titles like *101 Ways Big Government Harms You* and *How America Broke Its Wings*, to debunk what the group called "every falsehood and misconception our youth are taught in high school and college." The pamphlets included graphs that claimed that out-of-control government spending on welfare, student tuition, and bad teachers was the real source of America's problems. So were the number of licensing requirements for hair stylists. The plight of America's overregulated barber industry was a favorite talking point of free-market think tanks, a clever way to frame deregulation as the savior of mom and pop shops, not oligarchs. But mostly the pamphlets taught young people how to fight back against the left's tyranny. *Indoctrination Prevention* was the ominous name of one twenty-three-page guide—with the zombie-like face of a student plastered on the cover. "They want to brainwash you," the pamphlet declared.

Young Charlie had just turned twenty, but was already exhibiting a sophisticated understanding of a strategy set forth by the forefathers of the modern conservative movement in the 1960s: that broadcasting the existential dangers of the oppressive left was the best way to collect followers. In 1964, the historian Richard Hofstadter observed the strategy and termed it "the paranoid style" of politics. The tactic was to convince people that there was a "gigantic and yet subtle machinery of influence set in motion to undermine and destroy a way of life."

"We must reframe this struggle as a moral struggle, as a transcendent struggle, as a struggle between good and evil," wrote conservative activist Eric Heubeck in a 2001 manifesto for the Free Congress Foundation, a right-wing think tank founded in 1977 by Paul Weyrich, who was also known for co-founding the Heritage

Foundation and Jerry Falwell Sr.'s Moral Majority. "And we must be prepared to explain why this is so."

Charlie and his fledgling group would soon make a name for themselves by using this strategy. *Think: It's Not Illegal Yet!* would soon be one of Turning Point USA's catchier slogans. It was a call to young Americans that this wasn't just about their politics; it was about something more personal: freedom. And fighting to get it back wasn't a battle—it was a war.

Just about anyone could start their own TPUSA high school or college chapter, and as early as fall 2013, TPUSA was reporting fifty different chapters. In addition to its growing army of volunteers, the group would soon hire paid office administrators to manage the production of swag, liaise with volunteers, and orchestrate campus events. Eventually, jobs would be posted online via ads on hiring sites like Glassdoor. The requirements were minimal; it was good to have a college degree, but not a necessity. What you really needed was a "passion" for spreading the free-market gospel.

Crystal Clanton, a petite, neatly dressed political science major from Marquette University, a small Jesuit college in Milwaukee, Wisconsin, fit the Turning Point USA type to a T. A standout volunteer and one of the first to come on board, Clanton had been promoted to the full-time, paid position of national field director, second in command to Charlie, in May 2014. Clanton had the kind of bootstrap story TPUSA donors loved. Raised by her grandparents in the modest town of Gurnee, Illinois, she'd been a conscientious high school student, making the honor roll and being crowned Ms. Gurnee 2011 in the local beauty pageant. The liberal elite might have looked down on beauty pageants as lowbrow and retrograde, but for many young conservative women, a pageant title was a vehicle for rising within the conservative movement, signaling industriousness, good looks, and old-fashioned values. Clanton wasn't just a beauty, though. She was also a true believer in the anti-Obama rhetoric that permeated area conservative circles. She'd been told by her grandparents that the president's policies were hurting hardworking Americans like them, and she believed it. Clanton's views did not make her popular in college. "I had no shortage of run-ins with the radical left," she would later write in a TPUSA pamphlet she helped produce.

Like Charlie, Clanton was hyper-driven, hardworking, and mature beyond her years. But unlike Charlie, she was a managerial whiz. As national field director, she built out a recruitment system and a national field operation that would eventually mimic the structure of a corporate sales team. Regional directors, usually recent grads (and paid a yearly salary of around $55,000), would eventually oversee field directors (paid an estimated $40,000), who would in turn oversee student campus leaders (who would eventually be paid $125 a week to run chapters, while attending school). Such compensation was necessary to lure students away from other conservative gigs that—thanks to generous donors—were also relatively well-paid. This was not always the case for progressive organizations.

Today, the DNC is noticeably tight-lipped about what it gives its college arm, but young members are not. In a September 2019 editorial for Tulane's college newspaper, Jackson Faulkner, the development director of the College Democrats of Louisiana, called the DNC's parsimony toward the College Democrats "a badly kept secret."

It was a reality, he wrote, that organizations like Turning Point USA used to their advantage when they launched "hateful" campaigns the Democratic clubs didn't have the resources to adequately combat. The College Democrats mostly rely on the Democratic National Committee for funding, even though the DNC didn't guarantee it a line item in its budget until 2018. Progressive student groups like the collegiate arm of Planned Parenthood and the Everytown for Gun Safety's student arm—Students Demand Action—have enormous support on many American campuses. But their tight budgets hamstring their efforts to counteract increasingly loud voices coming from the young right.

At TPUSA, though, money seemed hardly an issue. Supplies for campus activism events were at the ready for the asking—just a FedEx shipment away. Young employees were well-paid, but also offered insurance, paid leave, and flexible hours as long as they got the job done. Work-related expenses were billed to headquarters, often via a corporate credit card. For employees and some chapter members conferences were all-expense-paid affairs.

While the perks were good, the work was also intense. Field staff was expected to be on the road from August through June, clocking thousands of miles with boxes and boxes of TPUSA swag ready to be unloaded from the backseats and trunks of their cars.

The goal was maximum growth in minimum time. There were "I love Capitalism" chalk parties to organize where new TPUSA chapter members scrawled their love of the free market on campus walkways. There were Cookies for Capitalism handout days to oversee and most importantly young people to recruit. The organization put a huge emphasis on data collection, demanding that field workers take the name and email address of anyone who approached TPUSA tables or attended any of its speaking events, workshops, volunteering gigs, or conferences. Regional directors had to meet strict recruitment quotas based on the number of campuses in their regions, which were given kitschy names like the BlueGrass South, Hollywood Pacific, and Citrus Florida. They earned bonuses for good work and were penalized, according to more than one former employee, for falling short. Clanton, like Charlie, was deeply devoted to the larger conservative cause and her own role in spreading it. And like him, she could make enemies. One office worker told me she routinely assigned him time-intensive projects, like a pamphlet on why small government was good for women, didn't manage the project, then got annoyed that it wasn't to her liking. She "zeroed in on people" she didn't like, he said, then looked to find fault with them, so she could "write them up." Another co-worker said that Clanton's extreme ambition could make it hard for other employees to rise through the ranks, as if she perceived their success as a threat to her own job. Despite these gripes, everyone agreed Clanton was an organizational powerhouse and utterly devoted to the cause.

At first, in the office, especially when Turning Point USA was still local, many employees were geeky politicos. They were consumed by talk of out-of-control government spending and the over-regulation of Main Street. But as time wore on, Bill Montgomery's advice to first focus on branding efforts began to pay off, and TPUSA's staff and its college volunteer pool swelled with a new wave of converts, each class cooler and showier than the last. Boys with gelled pompadours, skinny jeans, and designer sneakers; girls with flowing hair, bare midriffs, and high heels. In addition to hosting speaker series and campus activism events, chapter heads were encouraged to offer movie outings and trips to gun ranges. The group's annual conference would soon garner a reputation as a sometimes out-of-control party venue with flowing booze and easy hook-ups. TPUSA was no longer just about politics. It was about life—like-minded people bonding over shared values and fun.

With the new, laid-back image, TPUSA attracted an eclectic mix: driven careerists, gym rats who showed up to the office in their workout clothes, and the occasional pothead. The environment could be cliquey, with higher-ups playing favorites and field workers who were conventionally attractive, in a Fox News sort of way, getting preferential treatment. "You could be a piss poor organizer and climb up the organization," one former employee told me. "A lot of it was about personality and optics; that meant more than your ability to organize." One field rep, a graduate of Liberty

University and aspiring model, needed to be told what capitalism was. This image-consciousness was not a weakness, though, but part of the design. There were still serious wonks on staff—poli sci majors who'd interned on governor's campaigns or held prestigious gigs in DC who saw TPUSA as their ticket into the epicenter of the new conservative movement. But most of the young activists who were gravitating toward Charlie's world seemed to know instinctively that for every one of those policy wonks, Conservative America was now looking for a young, preferably good-looking devotee who could build out the base on their campuses, on their Twitter feeds, on Insta and YouTube. After all, if you were going to reach into middle America and convert seekers, you needed to be sought after.

In summer 2014, Charlie fell in love with an attention-grabbing idea to speed up growth: a roll-out he called the Big Government Sucks campaign. It would include blanketing campuses in the fall with the in-your-face message on stickers, T-shirts, and signs as a means of drawing attention to the group and recruiting followers. When he shared the plan with his growing advisory council—which now included a Seattle tech entrepreneur, the CEO of a financial services company, and an attorney who represented Christian nonprofits—some loved the idea. But some were reticent about using "sucks" on a poster. Charlie was insistent. You needed to speak to college students the way they spoke to one another. And anyway, wasn't it time to challenge the left with something punchy and aggressive? He wasn't building a think tank, he was building a battle tank.

Clanton and her team got on it, developing a ten-week campaign with a different focus every week and activism kits with supplies to be packed up and shipped to more than seven hundred campuses. For Debt Awareness Week, they would hand out "Debt

Receipts," indicating how much students would be expected to dole out in their lifetime to pay off the federal debt. They set up games of debt pong on campus quads. This was a version of the frat-favorite beer pong, where in lieu of playing for drinks, you played to cut wasteful government spending. During Truth About Obamacare Week, they stormed campuses with pamphlets on the ills of universal healthcare, focusing on how likely it was that such care would get into the hands of "illegals." The grand finale was, of course, Big Government Sucks Week.

The Big Government Sucks campaign worked particularly well. Charlie was always game for a press appearance, and he was a great spin doctor. The campaign, he told journalists, "resonated" with students. It was "edgy" and "provocative." "And it's working," he bellowed to a reporter at CNS News, a conservative news site, likely flashing his trademark grin. Every bit of publicity helped TPUSA grow and raise more money.

Eventually, TPUSA developed its own style guide, spelling out for its graphic artists, copywriters, and party planners how to convey the group's message with a "staccato" tone and "bold," "clear," and "direct" language. The hard emphasis on easily digestible messaging was a conservative specialty, and a favorite of one of the most powerful and well-connected members of TPUSA's advisory council. Virginia ("Ginni") Thomas, the second wife of Supreme Court Justice Clarence Thomas, was tight with both Clanton and Charlie. In 2013, Thomas had founded her own coalition, Groundswell, to get conservative journalists, think tank leaders, and activists to communicate conservative talking points in a uniform manner. According to a 2013 article in *Mother Jones*, which reported on one of her secretly recorded meetings, Thomas and her cronies were dismayed that the right was "failing the propaganda battle." People needed to "write articles on a 4th grade level," members were told. At one gathering, in opposition to Obama's immigration reform, the group discussed a reductive talking point that was thought to be zippy and resonant: the president was "choosing politics over public safety." Group members had been pumping it out across the media landscape, and it was gaining traction, co-opted in conservative blog posts, tweets, and numerous articles. Soon, Charlie and his allies would be doing the same, coordinating their messaging with far-right celebrities, movement leaders—and eventually a new president.

CHARLIE HAD PROMISED TO BUILD THE MOST INFLUENTIAL CON-servative youth outfit in the country, and as far as he and his donors were concerned, he'd done it. By the end of 2014, TPUSA had more than 25 full-time employees and was reporting volunteer armies on 750 high school and college campuses. But perhaps most importantly, TPUSA was reportedly amassing the most comprehensive list of young conservative voters in GOP history, just in time for the 2016 presidential election. Getting names on clipboards was paramount. And field directors and chapter leaders would later tell me that signing up students on campuses could sometimes seem more important to their bosses than making sure those students were in fact conservative.

But no matter, TPUSA marked its arrival in the big leagues by planting a hundred volunteers and twenty-six staff members decked out in red golf shirts at the 2015 Conservative Political Action Conference, CPAC, held inside the Gaylord National Resort and Convention Center in National Harbor, Maryland. It was the ultimate confab for die-hard conservatives looking for a bird's-eye view of the future of the movement. To show them what young Charlie Kirk thought that looked like, TPUSA invested in a huge, high-profile booth, front and center near the entrance to the area known as CPAC Central. Their camp spanned the area of three regular-sized booths, with loud music, red carpeting, a free speech wall, and dozens of young, invigorated recruiters milling about.

And there was swag, so much swag, emblazoned with Turning Point USA's new favorite motto: Big Government Sucks.

THAT WEEKEND, AS CPAC PULSATED WITH TALK ABOUT YOUNG Charlie Kirk's rise to prominence, another upstart—Cliff Maloney, the convivial Ron Paul acolyte who had become a darling of libertarian powerbrokers ever since he had begun climbing the ladder at Young Americans for Liberty—was also gearing up to take a big leap forward. As the group's Northeast regional director, Cliff was opening YAL chapters and recruiting members at an unprecedented pace. Chatter that he was the guy to push libertarianism out into the campus mainstream was near constant.

A lot of Cliff's beliefs still corresponded with those held by Charlie and his group TPUSA, which shared at least some of YAL's donors. But outwardly, YAL catered to a young conservative with more of a rebel side. The legalization of marijuana and criminal justice reform, for example, were oft-touted issues designed to lure in young YAL recruits. TPUSA, on the other hand, increasingly presented as more focused on culture war issues. If you wanted to hate on the libs, TPUSA was for you. If you saw yourself as a political stalwart with your head in the policy books, YAL was likely more alluring. As a rule, TPUSA tended to focus on a young person's right to grow up and make a lot of money. YAL tended to focus on a young person's right to simply do whatever they wanted. It was two sides of the same coin, branded for different conservative cliques: the purportedly mainstream kids and the nonconformists.

Now, the hard-charging Cliff was hopping from one state to the next selling his brand of right-wing politics. He was also developing a bond with his idol Ron Paul's fifty-two-year-old son Rand, an ophthalmologist and junior senator from Kentucky who also held fierce libertarian beliefs. Rand Paul had swept into DC in 2010 on a Tea Party wave and was about to take his own stab at the White House. Like his father, Rand made Washington spending his bête noire, rallying against Senate Majority Leader Mitch McConnell and the party establishment and proposing as his first piece of legislation $500 billion in cuts. Part of his plan: slash food assistance for the poor by 30 percent.

Rand was an outlier in DC at a time when outliers were in. He had tight ties to the House Freedom Caucus, a radical throng of Tea Party activists intent on not being told what to do. They had just managed to run their longtime speaker John Boehner, an Ohio moderate, out of town. Replacing him was Tea Party ally Paul Ryan, a nerdy policy wonk obsessed with slashing any strand of the social safety net he could get his hands on. It was a monumental shift to the right for the GOP. And it was thought that Rand, with a growing base of young fans, might just be the young, charming buck who could use this shift to take the reins back from the Democrats in 2016.

On the last day of CPAC, Rand, with his boyish locks and a slender red tie, paired with casual slacks, took to the stage, striding confidently out to greet his fresh-faced fans.

"I believe that America has much greatness left," Rand crooned, his voice oozing the confident Kentucky swagger that was making him a hit with young people like Cliff. He scanned the packed auditorium, passionate, defiant—and unlike his father, young.

"We must believe in ourselves, believe in our founding documents, believe in the economic system that creates more stuff for more people than at any time in recorded history."

From the edge of the stage, a throng of students brandishing *Stand with Rand* signs jostled to get a close-up of their new hero. They were mostly members of YAL. Rand would go on to win CPAC's straw poll, his third win in three years. If YAL's free-market renegades, now some of the most impassioned members of the GOP, had a royal family to represent them, it was the Pauls. Charlie Kirk might have been on the political ascent. But it was the liberty kids, it turned out, who owned the moment. And soon Cliff would, too. In April 2015, Rand announced his bid for the U.S. presidency, naming Cliff Maloney as the campaign's youth director.

That spring and summer, Cliff, donning a sleeveless velour vest with Rand's name stitched on the chest, toured the country's campuses to recruit young people to Rand's camp. Once again, his theater years came in handy. He knew how to infuse a moment with high-stakes drama, urging young people to join the Rand bandwagon if they hated war, hated taxes, hated the hypocrisy of big-spend Washington elites. Sometimes, flashing a mischievous-looking smile, he would shout to the young crowds that had gathered to meet the candidate: "Any fans of freedom in the house tonight?" Then he would offer up palm cards and info on the next Students for Rand meet-up. By the end of the summer, Cliff had planted close to four hundred Students for Rand college chapters. And he had only just begun.

But it was not to be. After placing fifth in the Iowa caucuses late on a frigid February night, Rand dropped out in a fog of disappointment. Political autopsies would later blame the Trump train and the nation's rising fear of terrorism, which rendered his anti-interventionist stance ill-suited for the times. Cliff was deeply disappointed, but his career was by no means over. Instead, he would be rewarded for his loyalty. Jeff Frazee, his buddy and boss, was moving on. By spring, Cliff had a new title: he was YAL's new president.

That summer, with his barreling frame and baritone voice, Cliff took the YAL reins with enthusiasm, exuding a level of high-minded gravitas rare for a twenty-something. He touted YAL as an efficient machine that pushed "principled ideas," and it worked. By the end of 2016 YAL boasted that it had trained more than 2,000 youth activists nationwide.

Occasionally, YAL chapter leaders had to swat off TPUSA

kids trying to poach their members, but Cliff didn't mind. He professed an appreciation for Charlie's energy and made sure to attend TPUSA's now legendary fundraisers, where, after listening to Charlie speak, donors would soon be known to rise from their tables and promise hundreds of thousands of dollars to the cause. Cliff went for obvious reasons. Any org leader worth his or her salt knew to always go where the big money was. He also spent a lot of time in Texas, chasing oil money—and once had to swim in a donor's cold water pool in used golf shorts. Anything to bond with the investors.

On the ground, Cliff liked to motivate his team, military style. Training was called boot camp. Planting a chapter was called an invasion. Members were called campus soldiers for liberty and were expected to act like they were part of a well-trained militia. Unlike TPUSA's activism events so often designed to stoke the libs, YAL's activism efforts appealed to students' common sense. Liberals weren't to be mocked; they were to be converted. Libertarianism, after all, was a vote for self-determination. Who didn't believe in that? It was also about right and wrong, as much a philosophy as it was a political idea. To emphasize this one year, at his bi-annual gathering of like-minded investors, the longtime libertarian Charles Koch quoted Frederick Douglass (who would have had a thing or two to say about a gathering of rich powerful white men trying to figure out how to sell an anti-populist ideology to the masses): "I would unite with anybody to do right and with no one to do wrong."

Cliff liked to believe he would unite with anyone, too. And YAL made a point of not putting young people off with some of its less popular, fringe ideas. At least at first. Most of the pamphlets YAL tended to hand newbies avoided the vision of a state in which private enterprise was allowed free rein and government regulations and social safety net programs were slashed beyond recognition.

Although Cliff did not sell YAL as a fun factory in quite the way Charlie did with TPUSA, he did use his background in set design to drum up creative ways to engage students with the issues. He directed student activists, whom he referred to as "actors," to set up "unionized" hot-dog stands where hot dogs cost $25 and the lazy workers took frequent breaks. Students at the University of Illinois handed out pot brownies—home-baked brownies not with pot in them but plucked from a large pot—to protest the War on Drugs. It was a cheeky appeal to students who were pushing for the decriminalization of marijuana. At the University of Pittsburgh, student members advocated for prison reform by putting on prison garb and standing behind fake cell bars. And YAL was a big tent as a result. It welcomed an eclectic mix of right-wing rebels, geeky politicos, Christian-homeschoolers, and free-thinking stoners, among others.

While Cliff liked to present YAL as more high-minded than other student groups on the right, he did not discourage blurring the lines in order to make a point. One YAL tactic was to instruct campus volunteers to set up tables in high-traffic areas without bothering to get the necessary permits. If campus authorities shut them down, YAL would instigate a free speech lawsuit—with the help of a Koch-affiliated conservative legal foundation, Alliance Defending Freedom. Cliff was proud of these efforts. When YAL won settlements, he publicized the hell out of them, going on air himself to celebrate and writing them up in his annual report for investors to see their money hard at work in the battle against the silencing left. Some students said the pressure to get themselves arrested and then sue their own college while still in school was intense; they worried that these stunts could be detrimental to their futures. "I didn't really think they cared that I was actually in college to get my degree," Seven Surack, the former chapter leader at one of Indiana University's regional campuses, told me.

Still, Cliff's allure continued to draw new recruits to his army.

He won them with bro hugs, electrifying conference speeches, and bourbon rounds near the YAL Arlington headquarters. The inner circle at YAL was a close-knit group, and Cliff brought his buddies in. Justin Greiss, for example, a friend from Pennsylvania, was his director of mobilization, helping to support recent graduates by securing them jobs inside the liberty movement. Staff members worked together and lived together near the office in crowded houses they gave sassy names to, like Casa de Liberty and Liberty Lounge. They also partied together, holding often all-male drinkfests where they griped about the dearth of females. While the hardworking, hard-partying atmosphere at YAL headquarters was exhilarating for some, others said YAL could feel like a backward fraternity, with guys making lewd jokes and talking trash about women. There were other complaints: Cliff was a climber, "an attention hog," a guy who always made it about himself. Cliff would later respond to these raw critiques with his own. Quoting baseball great Babe Ruth, he wrote to me in an email: "The loudest boos come from the cheapest seats." Some hires also complained of Cliff's bullying side. And rumors swirled that he often got overly friendly with female underlings, making the casual work-around-the-clock atmosphere not challenging and fun, but uncomfortable.

Cliff rarely showed vulnerability, except when it came to his ballooning weight. All the drinking and schmoozing over meals with DC power brokers and fat-cat donors began to take a toll on his health. Not to mention the Chick-fil-A fare he ate on the road in between conferences and during fundraising trips. When Cliff saw a clip of his hero Ron Paul opining about personal responsibility— a libertarian rallying cry—and keeping one's weight in check, he took it to heart, embarking on his own multiyear, 120-pound weight-loss journey. Several staff members joined in solidarity, sticking to low-carb diets of chicken breasts and broccoli, at least when dining with their boss.

Cliff may have depended on his staff for a social life, but work was his priority. He was an ambitious guy who had risen up from a little house on a Pennsylvania thoroughfare to the hallowed halls of DC. He was the boss. And he didn't let people forget that. This clarity of purpose, he believed, was the best way to make a name for YAL, and for himself.

"I'm all for being against the left, but you have to have something to stand for. What's the prescription for the problem you are trying to solve?" he once told the *Washington Post*. In Cliff's eyes and the eyes of the "investors" who supported him, he was the prescription.

CHAPTER FIVE

The Kid Is Gone

A s the 2016 election season neared, Lee and Allie Hanley, the polished political duo that had taken such a shine to Charlie, paired up with Robert Mercer, the hedge fund billionaire, and his daughter Rebekah to find the next American president. The esteemed political strategist Pat Caddell had told them to look for an anti-establishment everyman who could appeal to the needs of disgruntled America. And they were hoping once found and elected, he could represent their interests in the White House.

In 2014, they convinced themselves they had found him in a geeky senator from Texas by the name of Ted Cruz. Cruz was a Princeton grad with a preppy, pearl-necklace-wearing wife named Heidi, who worked at Goldman Sachs. Forget that Cruz typified the kind of out-of-touch elitism that so often turned off voters. The Hanleys and the Mercers believed they understood what anti-establishment looked like to the American electorate.

Expert, if not intimidating entertainers, the Hanleys began inviting Ted and Heidi to White Caps, their medieval-style castle on Fishers Island. Charlie would eventually begin hanging out with Cruz, too, hunting with the Texas gun-lover and award-winning college debater, and inviting him to speak at Turning Point USA events. He even featured Cruz at a 2015 CPAC event he organized, shortly before Cruz announced his presidential run. And he started selling Cruz's biography *A Time for Truth: Reigniting the Promise of America*, as a fundraiser for his organization, with at least some copies packaged with a letter extolling the virtues of the Texas senator, an act of co-branding that would become a Turning Point USA specialty.

Eventually employees for Turning Point USA would be asked to support Cruz, too. Payden Hall, who was working for the nonprofit in spring 2016, told *New Yorker* investigative reporter Jane Mayer that Ginni Thomas, wife of Supreme Court Justice Clarence Thomas and one of the most powerful behind-the-scenes figures in the hard-right establishment, called her at a personal phone number, asking her to distribute Cruz signs before Wisconsin's 2016 GOP primary. This, after Clanton had emailed Hall at her work address to let her know Thomas would be reaching out to make the arrangements. When two hundred signs showed up at the home Hall shared with her sister, it made her uneasy.

For their organizations to maintain nonprofit, tax-exempt status, youth groups like TPUSA, Young Americans for Liberty, and Young Americans for Freedom can educate as part of their mission, but they are not permitted to intervene in political campaigns for or against candidates. It's a distinction that tax-exempt nonprofits on both sides of the aisle can get fuzzy about, as such groups are often supportive of candidates who support their agenda. Further, what leaders of these groups can and cannot say about political figures, so as not to violate IRS law, but maintain their free speech rights, can be challenging to decipher. But TPUSA seemed to many to be particularly flagrant about its allegiances. Staff members maintained top positions inside local Republican clubs. Speakers at Turning Point USA–related events routinely denounced key figures in the Democratic Party, and political figures facing upcoming elections sometimes took the stage. In July 2014, Bruce Rauner, then the Republican candidate for Illinois governor, spoke at a Turning Point USA fundraiser. Charlie would later boast that he and his "closest friends" had knocked on tens of thousands of doors and made 100,000 phone calls on behalf of Rauner, who went on to win the governorship. That same year, Rauner's family foundation cut Turning Point USA a $100,000 check. A year later, the foundation plopped another $50,000 into the nonprofit's coffer. It looked, even to a casual outsider, that Turning Point USA was clearly engaged in politics—and benefiting from that engagement.

In spring 2019, Charlie would officially launch Turning Point Action, a 501(c)(4)—or social welfare organization—ostensibly to address this issue. A 501(c)(4) is allowed to engage in politics, thus Turning Point Action was permitted to publicly endorse candidates and partisan causes. But the two organizations could look remarkably similar to outsiders, as they shared some of the same leaders and strikingly similar logos. And journalists were frequently confused about which organization was involved in which causes. It was a reality that, in the Turning Point world, was inevitably seen not as a Turning Point failing but as yet another sign of an "activist press" that just didn't get it.

BY SPRING 2016 THE HANLEYS AND THE MERCERS HAD LEARNED what must have been a tough lesson. They may have wanted Cruz as their next president, but their money and sway couldn't make it so. They lost their dream candidate to a political process that didn't always bend to their will. After winning the February caucus in Iowa, which had taken down Rand Paul, Cruz endured a series of his own bruising primary defeats. His coffer near empty, he dropped out that May, just as Donald J. Trump was leap-frogging to the front of the line.

The nation's Mr. Smith, it would turn out, was not a corny Texan who wore cowboy boots and velour vests. He was a crass real estate tycoon with a genuine chip on his shoulder about the fancy people who shunned him and his gilded lifestyle. The Hanleys proved adaptable and promptly switched their allegiances. Donald Trump might not have talked like a standard country club Republican, but that didn't scare them off. Soon they became convinced that not only was he capable of wooing the disenchanted everyman all the way to the White House, but that he, if supported, would do their bidding.

As for Charlie, who had once referred to Trump as a "pure demagogue," he was not yet ready to cozy up to the blustery businessman. In fact, in March 2016, he let on that he was "cheering for a slowdown of the Trump train." Charlie did not yet share Trump's obsession with "illegals" and while he, too, worried about China's influence, he didn't seem to share Trump's level of outsized fear that China was "raping our country," either. Further, Charlie was also still holding fast to his own obsession, one the candidate did not share, over the nation's ballooning budget deficit. Trump was also a thorn in the side of the nation's evangelical leaders. And Charlie, a skilled calculator of where power concentrated, was increasingly bonding with them.

But in spring 2016, Trump released a list of Christian right–sanctioned conservative judges he would consider, if he were elected, to replace the vacated Supreme Court seat held by the recently deceased Antonin Scalia. The move was seen as an effort to fortify his power base, and eventually the votes of tens of millions of conservative Christians. And in June 2016, Trump and his team gathered with hundreds of their leaders in a hotel ballroom in Times Square. Accounts of the lively meeting—and one held earlier that day with a smaller group—suggest the towering New Yorker, a man skilled in the art of a deal, was ready to negotiate. Trump promised that if elected, he would get busy "freeing up your religion," and then unveiled an evangelical executive advisory board to assist him.

One of the eleven people appointed to that board was James MacDonald, the then well-connected founder of the evangelical megachurch Harvest Bible Chapel in suburban Chicago, which Charlie had attended and where he occasionally gave spiritual pep talks. MacDonald would eventually be consumed by a management scandal that would cost him his job in February 2019. Also appointed to the board: Jerry Falwell Jr., the president of Liberty University, whom Charlie would soon develop a tight spiritual bond with. Falwell, too, would eventually flame out, in his case amid a sex scandal.

During the August 2016 Republican National Convention in Cleveland, where Trump was officially anointed, Charlie, too, had his debut. The de facto leader of young, conservative America was asked to speak. When Charlie rose to the stage in a crisp blue suit, an American flag pin attached to his lapel, he gave an impassioned spiel about young people and the Grand Old Party. He did not mention Trump. Further, he admitted to a *Wired* magazine reporter that he was not the biggest "fan in the world."

But behind the scenes, Charlie was inching closer to the candidate. And it was at the convention where he was introduced to Don Jr. Charlie, who was increasingly being touted as a savvy social media operator, told Don his online presence needed work and he offered to transform it. But Don was slow to take the special shine to Charlie that seemed to overcome so many others. He was skeptical about bringing the upstart onboard. "We don't know what the hell we are doing," Don told Charlie. "We don't need someone else who doesn't know what they're doing." But Charlie somehow eventually won him over. Soon after, Charlie took a leave of absence from his role at TPUSA and joined Jr.'s cohort on the campaign fundraising trail. By the end of the summer, Charlie Kirk wasn't just supporting Trump—he was in his inner circle.

Earlier that summer, Trump's once wayward son had formed a fundraising trio with two of his rich Texas buddies—a raven-haired money manager and fellow University of Pennsylvania graduate named Gentry Beach and Tommy Hicks Jr., a private investor. They were a ragtag team. Don, UPenn classmates told journalist Emily Jane Fox, was infamous for crawling his way home from parties drunk, his pants soaked in his own urine. Hicks pled no contest to a misdemeanor assault in high school after he and two others injured a fellow student at a party, and Beach had seen some trouble with the IRS. Now the trio, who'd bonded on hunting trips in Scotland and Hungary, were hunting for dollars. And Charlie was part of the crew.

During twenty-hour days, Charlie, knapsack strapped to his back, carried Don Jr.'s bags and fetched his Diet Cokes and Red Bulls as they hopped—often via private plane—from Michigan to Florida to Texas to Louisiana to woo donors sometimes at $50,000-per-person fundraisers. During one June trip, Don Jr. raked in $8 million.

Once, while driving to a meeting in New Orleans, Charlie recalls Gentry Beach noticing him staring out the window distractedly and issuing a sharp correction. There was no downtime on the trail. "What are you doing, Charlie? Why are you not working right now?" Beach asked him. "What's preventing you from right now calling three donors and raising money? If you want to be excellent you have to work like it." Charlie was careful to never again let his focus slip for long. A few weeks before the election, according to a story Don Jr. recounts in his book *Triggered*, Charlie helped organize a stopover for Jr. at a Florida State University frat house. When he, Jr., and Hicks arrived, there were hundreds of college kids, some of them already drunk, shoulder to shoulder in the backyard. "It could get a little rowdy," Charlie warned his boss. He was right. Shortly after, Don recalls climbing up on a backyard picnic table and launching one of his fiery tirades into a microphone from what looked like a karaoke set. But soon a group of skimpily clad coeds began clambering onto the table to get close to him. Charlie was alert and attentive. When he saw Jr.'s trapped expression, he quickly began scanning the area for an escape route, away from the increasingly out of control crowd. Charlie found one and gestured to a fence behind the table. They made a run for it, climbing over and racing to their waiting car.

On the eve of the election, Charlie, sporting a rumpled oxford, sequestered himself in Don Jr.'s twenty-fifth-floor Trump Tower office with Hicks, Beach, and Jr. Don fielded radio calls, while Charlie manned his Twitter feed. It had been a long day, and even as precinct reports began flowing in that the real estate mogul from Queens was doing better than expected, a lot of campaign insiders didn't think he was going to win. But Charlie had faith. And when news came at 2:30 a.m. that Trump had pulled off a miracle and secured the Blue State of Wisconsin—a telltale sign that he'd take the whole country—anxiety reverberated through the concrete tower. What now?

At least one person was thrilled about Trump's twist of fate. Since the day he decided to forgo college to start Turning Point USA, Charlie Kirk had been on a crusade to dethrone liberal America. And now here he was, a modern-day William F. Buckley, riding the Trump train he had once hoped would derail. Only twenty-three years old, Charlie had a direct line to the most powerful man in the world.

That winter, after recuperating from his sleepless nights on the trail, Charlie sauntered into a Las Vegas steak house and headed for a table of middle-aged men and women who were eating steaks and downing bottles of wine. There was Mike Miller, the Chicago-area jeweler who'd been one of Charlie's earliest financial backers, rubbing shoulders with Joe Walsh and his wife, Helene. In return for Miller's early support, Charlie had taken him along on his ride up through the far-right ranks.

Walsh, who'd spent countless hours chatting with Charlie about their libertarian dreams, told me that after a few months in Trump World, his young friend was unrecognizable. Charlie ordered with abandon—devouring steak and multiple hors d'oeuvres—and gabbed over everyone. "'Don and I did this. Don and I did that,'" parroted Walsh to me. "'We got Trump elected. Did you see me on TV, Joe?'" The congressman was dismayed. Six months ago, Charlie had been like a son to Helene and him. Now, he was obnoxious, self-absorbed, and fully supporting a president who went counter to so much of what he and Helene both believed in. "We didn't know what he stood for anymore," said Walsh.

The next day, Walsh bumped into Charlie at a bar. It was the old puppy-dog Charlie again, pleading for his mentor's advice on what to do, how to proceed, now that Trump was president. Walsh says he warned Charlie to stay true to his principles and not hitch his wagon to any political figure, let alone one whose views were so counter to his own. But it was obvious to Walsh that Charlie, however conflicted, had his own plans. Now that he'd gotten this close to the president, he seemed to believe it was his fate to get closer still.

Back in Chicago, driving home from O'Hare Airport, Walsh turned to Helene with a pained expression. "The kid is gone," he said.

PART II

CHAPTER SIX

"Coming Out Conservative"

G o home Racists!" bellowed a young white man in dark
faded jeans, a lumberjack shirt, and a scraggly beard. He
cupped his hands together to form a bullhorn, continuing, "Get a good look at your fellow racist students, right here!"

The young man, later identified as a grad student named Oli-
ver Baker, was objecting to a TPUSA volunteer table on the quad
at the University of New Mexico campus in Albuquerque, where
a handmade Magic Marker sign advertised an Affirmative Action
Bake Sale. The pricing of the baked goods:

Asians: $1.50
Caucasians: $1.00
African Americans and Hispanics: $0.50

It was the fall of 2017 and there was a new American president in the White House, one with a flagrant disregard for civility,
decorum, and government protocol. Trump, with his arsenal of
politically incorrect digs, was a kid at heart—a mean-spirited kid,
who was emboldening an entire generation of young, disaffected
right-wingers who felt like outsiders on their campuses. Well, they
were insiders now, and they were ready to rumble. In this new
environment, TPUSA's playbook—the carefully designed political

pamphlets, the debt pong tournaments, and the Cookies for Capitalism handouts—seemed like quaint relics of a bygone era. Young college conservatives were embracing the us-against-them game, adopting some of the same brash tactics that had worked for the president as he wormed his way into the White House.

Cruelty, homophobia, and overt ethnic stereotyping were now tropes of everyday political discourse, as right-wing student activists performed "Coming Out Conservative" celebrations, mocking members of their campus's LGBTQ communities. They held Free Speech Ball Days, rolling enormous beach balls across their campus quads for students to write whatever they wanted on them. "Go Home Illegals"? Sure! Why not? The more offensive the comment the more powerful the point. These days liberty seemed to mean the right, above all else, to be a jerk. They built Trump border walls out of cardboard. And they organized the aforementioned Affirmative Action Bake Sale, which was, on this particular day, being manned by one of TPUSA's most popular regional directors, a University of Colorado dropout named Will Witt, a frat-boy-handsome activist—TPUSA's favorite kind—in shades and a backward baseball cap.

Witt had begun batting for the right a year earlier, not long after he claims a University of Colorado teaching assistant gave him a lecture on "white privilege," telling him that his mere presence as a white man was oppressive to the Black student sitting next to him in class. Outraged, he joined his campus TPUSA chapter, took the president post, then eventually decided he needed to take his fight on the road. He dropped out of college. Harnessing his confidence, his charm, and his new role as an employee at TPUSA, where he quickly landed a full-time job, he set out to tell conservative college kids around the country that silence was not an option.

On that day, Witt was accompanied by a few new recruits whom he was coaching as they sought to plant a chapter on the Albuquerque campus, a commuter school of sixteen thousand, dotted with adobe-style structures typical of the region. The idea behind the stunt was to sell baked goods at different prices, depending on the customer's race, as a way to protest admission policies that sought to diversify campuses. The fact that UNM didn't use a race-based selection process didn't seem to matter. The sale was designed to agitate, and it was serving its purpose.

While UNM may not have utilized affirmative action in admissions, the practice was common at colleges around the country, helping draw students from a variety of different backgrounds. And it was controversial, unpopular even, in progressive states like California, which had in 1996 passed a proposition banning affirmative action at public universities. (A 2020 ballot initiative affirmed that most California voters still didn't support the practice.) But despite these findings, college students rarely expressed open opposition to the policy, which right-wing activists attributed to campus pressure by the "PC Police" to keep quiet. Some researchers, however, had a different idea: that there was actually a "hidden consensus" among students about the enormous benefits they derived from diverse learning environments. To test this hypothesis, researchers at Dartmouth and Stanford surveyed eight thousand college students and faculty members—between late 2016 and early 2018—asking them who they would choose to admit to their schools from an eclectic pool of applicants. They overwhelmingly chose candidates with high academic merit who would add diversity to their campuses. Did young Americans want to learn in environments that represented the makeup of the country? It would seem that was a yes. And judging by how students reacted to Affirmative Action Bake Sales, there was something else many wanted: to avoid openly offending their peers of color with insults and allegations about why they were there. For right-wing activists this aversion to offending was an issue of free speech. For a lot of students, it was something else: common decency.

That afternoon, one of Witt's volunteers, an olive-skinned girl in skinny jeans, held up a *Socialism Sucks* poster like a shield as a flock of angry kids—"The left-wing mob," in TPUSA-speak—approached, to join the heckler in condemning Witt and his cohorts. "Go the fuck home," one shouted. A student on roller skates whizzed by, stealing a sign and shoving some pens and stickers off the table with her arm.

Witt, hands tucked inside his pants pockets, his shades now resting on the top of his baseball cap, smirked as the chants of racism continued. His underlings, including the young woman in jeans, were staying strong but feeling the burn. They would later tell him how discomfiting it had been to stand there and absorb such harsh treatment from their classmates. But that was what he was there to teach: calm and stamina in the face of the enemy. And anyway, for Witt, now a veteran at these campus culture war games, the hecklers only affirmed what young conservatives were taught at the Leadership Institute, the far-right training academy where many of them now took classes: they'll call you racist whenever they don't have anything smart to say. Still, Witt, who could only take so much push back, was ready to call it a day. He began boxing up the TPUSA swag, leaving another volunteer to film the mob. This was called "weaponizing your phone"—another Leadership Institute lesson. Such clips played well on Twitter and YouTube and made for good lib-shaming, especially if you could catch the opposition using foul language or even violence. Such footage was also visual bait for aging donors who were horrified by what Charlie called "the intolerant left." As one fundraiser told me: "Nothing scares a conservative grandparent more than the thought that their poor innocent grandkid is going to get indoctrinated in college and turn into a gay communist, BLM activist, antifa member."

AMERICAN CAMPUSES HAD LONG BEEN HOTBEDS OF POLITICAL strife. But thanks to a steady stream of content now being captured on video, craftily edited for maximum shock value and shared on-line, it's no wonder these donors felt threatened. From their per-spective, campus libs had been torturing right-wingers for years, making one impatient demand after another. In the 1960s and 1970s, civil rights, gay rights, and feminist student activists had coalesced into a broad social movement. In the 1980s, they rallied against Ronald Reagan, and in the 1990s demanded environmen-tal justice and curriculum reform. They wanted more classes that focused on women's studies and African American studies and the study of Native Americans. It was the beginning of the "PC po-lice." And as far as a lot of right-wing benefactors were concerned, there were too many rules. Just as the libs in DC, infatuated with corporate regulations, wanted to constrain what businesses could and could not do, conservative donors contended that liberal kids wanted to constrain what the donors' children and grandchildren could and could not say, learn, even believe.

And now, as far as these donors could tell, things were getting worse. Today's young left-wing protesters were no longer just out-siders banging on the campus gates with their disparate demands. They were insiders, manipulating from positions of political power, and forcing the arms of institutional leaders who were bending to their will for fear of retribution—or worse, violence. They were calling for the removal of statues they deemed offensive and seek-ing to change the names of buildings commemorating former slave owners. They were demanding a more "honest" treatment of his-tory, what donors would soon be calling Critical Race Theory, or CRT for short. And they wanted a more "inclusive" exploration of art and literature. In the eyes of these conservatives, that meant disrespecting national heroes and obsessing about authors and art-ists from, as their president put it, "shithole countries."

Tales of intolerance abounded. In November 2017, Oberlin College in Ohio was sued after students were accused of libel-ing a small-town bakery (they had accused the owners of racial profiling in the wake of a shoplifting incident). A jury awarded the bakery $44 million in damages. A judge later reduced the award to $25 million, and in 2022 an appeals court upheld the judgment.

In March 2017, word spread that out-of-control protesters outside a campus auditorium at Middlebury College in northern Vermont, had jostled a liberal political science professor so severely that she suffered a concussion, after the professor attempted to moderate a Q&A with Charles Murray, author of *The Bell Curve*, a controversial polemic on race and intelligence published in 1994. The *Wall Street Journal* editorial board dubbed the protesters "the Mob at Middlebury."

That same month, at Evergreen State College in Olympia, Washington, Bret Weinstein, a professor of evolutionary biology who had protested a white Day of Absence to commemorate African Americans' contributions to the progressive institution, became the target of student harassment so alarming, he says he feared for his safety and eventually resigned his post. By going public, Weinstein positioned himself at the center of a campus-wide controversy over race and became a cause célèbre among conservative commentators like the hot-tempered Tucker Carlson.

These incidents—taking place at some of the nation's most notoriously liberal campuses—didn't mean that every campus in the country was overrun by "social justice warriors," as right-wingers had come to call student protesters on the left. Nor were these events nearly as clear-cut as some of the media portrayed them. Documents unsealed in September 2021 indicated that one of the bakery employees in the Oberlin incident—the son and grandson of the two owners, no less—had made racist comments online regarding Black people. And at Evergreen, the Weinstein incident had not happened in isolation, but was in fact part of a much larger wave of racial unrest at the school that involved, among other things, the alleged targeting of Black students by campus police.

All the same, these handily packaged examples of an American "cancel culture" gone rogue, videotaped and widely spread online, were providing excellent fuel for a conservative uprising that had started after Obama's victory in 2008 and been reignited upon Trump's election. Together, they created the perfect environment for near constant fearmongering among right-wing influencers, projecting a message that college kids were totally out of control and dangerous. This hysteria was exactly what young right-wing groups needed to raise money from fearful donors. And that donor money, in turn, was necessary to keep training and employing the young influencers. When Charlie Kirk told donors that college campuses had become "islands of intolerance," they believed him—and the checkbooks came out.

In the months after the August 2017 Unite the Right rally in Charlottesville, Virginia, which engaged a mob of confederate-flag-waving white supremacists and resulted in the death of a thirty-two-year-old paralegal, a nation already deeply disturbed by the Trump ascent focused its anxiety on openly racist nationalists, Neo-Nazis, and militia members. The Proud Boys, the anti-government Oath Keepers, and the loose coalition of incels, trolls, and meme-makers on the online forum #4chan who referred to themselves as Groypers were now America's premier boogeymen. They were a collection of disgruntled outsiders who tended to blame their discontent on government as a whole and any group they saw as left-wing darlings: immigrants, women, people of color, and members of the LGBTQ community. But the real sign of the far right's growing power was not the presence of these loud and strident extremists, who populated the internet's underbelly. It was the increasing omnipresence of ostensibly mainstream conservative groups, like Turning Point USA and others within the larger conservative movement, who were not outliers, toiling on their own, but well-funded establishment insiders who claimed mainstream status—all the while spewing content that could be mean-spirited, misleading, and scary. *I'm Pro Choice. Pick Your Gun*, read a TPUSA poster propped up on tables across American campuses around this time. Beneath those fighting words were three photos: a Glock 27, an AR-15, and a 12-gauge rifle. Another favorite among young conservative activists: *Gun Control Means Using Both Hands.*

If temperance and civility had once been a core value cherished by the American conservative and admired by the right-wing country club set, those days were gone. An appetite for brash sensationalism and confrontational politics popularized by right-wing radio stars like Rush Limbaugh and Glenn Beck had gone viral, and young Americans were leading the charge, as a resentful and raving president helped to super-charge the campus environment and make this kind of bullying cool. The nastier and more offensive you could be, the more likely you were to be heard. Never mind that Trump's interest in the kind of skeletal government young conservatives tended to embrace was limited, at best. His policy initiatives would soon include farm subsidies, trade regulations, and government spending hikes—all policies Charlie and his crew swore against. It didn't seem to matter. For young people who wanted to own the libs one showdown after another, Trump was the president they were looking for. And groups who adapted his in-your-face tactics were the new normal.

These groups, thanks to a well-established funding pipeline, were also drowning in cash. Even before Trump arrived on the scene, conservative donors had been pumping tens of millions of dollars annually onto campuses in their efforts to win over young people. And more alarmingly, they were grossly outperforming their counterparts on the left, according to researchers for Generation Progress, a left-leaning advocacy group that had sorted through years of tax documents in an effort to clock the right's increased power and pull among the nation's young.

In 2014 alone, Generation Progress found that the five top-spending conservative organizations that offered programming to groom young activists—including the Charles Koch Institute, the Federalist Society, and the Young America's Foundation—spent $77 million, more than the $36 million spent by the five largest progressive organizations targeting young people, including groups such as the Feminist Majority Foundation and the public health and social justice group Advocates for Youth. These comparisons told only part of the story. The truth was the left simply did not have the well-coordinated educational infrastructure the right did. And large progressive activist organizations supported college students on a piecemeal basis, with ad hoc grants and leadership training. But they did not have the kind of robust budgets, common among groups on the right, earmarked just for campus outreach. These funding and networking disparities made it difficult for left-leaning college groups to launch comprehensive campus opposition campaigns and to offer clear alternatives to the messaging coming at students from the right.

In recent years, a few progressive donors had begun to take an interest in campus organizing. In 2013, San Francisco hedge fund billionaire Tom Steyer launched NextGen Climate, pumping millions into an effort to mobilize young people around climate change. By 2016, after Trump's election, Steyer reimagined the group as NextGen America, and by 2017 was amassing a paid army of impressively organized young people to register voters on their campuses and to door knock for Democratic candidates in the 2018 midterms. Everytown for Gun Safety, a gun-control advocacy group, founded in 2013 with seed money from former New York City mayor and billionaire benefactor Michael Bloomberg, would soon also double down on young people. After the February 2018 mass shooting at Marjory Stoneman Douglas High School in Parkland, Florida, the group would pledge $1 million in grant money to support student advocates and grow its campus arm,

Students Demand Action for Gun Sense in America. It was an effort to mimic what the NRA had been doing for years. But these were relatively new efforts and they were hardly the norm.

Further, stealth tactics employed by right-wing campus groups rendered the left's job even more challenging. Their presence was ubiquitous, by design, but could often be deceiving. The sixty-four-year-old Intercollegiate Studies Institute, with $16.5 million in its coffer in 2017, for example, posted pamphlets on bulletin boards inside campus buildings advertising its free offerings. The group's name made it sound like an inviting haven for young intellectuals looking to expand their knowledge of history and philosophy. Funded by some of the Christian right's wealthiest benefactors, its goal was much more narrowly focused than that. Its free classes, videos, and podcasts focused on faith's role in the Constitution, the future of conservatism, and the perils of living in a "Woke World." One class challenged ideas around the separation of church and state. Others emphasized the cultural superiority of Western Civilization. The seventy-one-year-old Foundation for Economic Education, often referred to as FEE (with an estimated $8 million in net assets in 2017), might easily appeal to a curious student interested in a more in-depth exploration of different economic models. But its hundreds of free classes promoted one distinct kind of economic model: libertarianism, the austere philosophy that shuns consumer protection measures and union organizing. The Fund for American Studies—which spent over $11 million in 2017—is not an apolitical academic institute, but an education center whose central goal is to "win over each new generation" to its extreme anti-government ideals that are billed on the group's website as "the principles of limited government, free-market economics and honorable leadership." And the Institute for Humane Studies, at George Mason University in Fairfax, Virginia, is not a human-rights advocacy group, but another peddler of libertarianism.

A common strategy among right-wing activists on college

campuses was to pass themselves off as commonsense moderates, then subvert expectations by eventually introducing more right-wing ideas. Students showing up for a documentary about global warming or a panel on the Second Amendment might discover they were suddenly facing highly produced programs designed by well-funded think tanks pushing climate change denial or extreme gun rights.

Recent grads employed by the vaguely monikered climate-denying group Collegians for a Constructive Tomorrow (CFACT) often showed up outfitted in hiking boots and lumberjack shirts to recruit students—making them unrecognizable from typical tree-hugging Bernie fans. They led group hikes, beach cleanups, and "eco-summits." And it was during those casual get-togethers where they introduced ideology deemed both radical and danger-ous by a wide swath of Americans—for example, that "the global warming narrative is all about government control" and "the sci-ence behind climate change is not settled."

Other right-wing groups took a brasher approach. In 2017, the anti-choice activist group Created Equal presented college stu-dents on their way to class with video images displayed on large Jumbotron screens of bloody fetuses, crushed heads, tiny fingers and feet. Activists clutched microphones and called out to class-mates that the solution to unwanted pregnancies was not to "dis-member and decapitate innocent children."

Also, in 2017, gun advocacy groups were going after college students with their own innovative strategies designed to broaden support for firearms. In addition to online campaigns that featured hot, gun-toting coeds, these groups were focusing a notable part of their activism on recruiting young women on their campuses. They promised a new brand of feminism: empowerment via weaponry. Conservatives had long insisted that reports of campus sexual as-sault, violence, and aggression were grossly overplayed by the left to instill unnecessary fear in young women. But now, conservative groups were exploiting those fears to sell guns. In addition to its pro-gun college workshop NRA U, the National Rifle Association also offered a college version of its "Refuse to be a Victim" program that taught young college-aged women "personal safety strategies" to protect themselves from the "dangers" of campus life, including sexual assault. The program did not expressly teach about firearms, but it did handily introduce young women to a lobbying group whose aim was to curry support for them.

In addition, gun rights advocates like Antonia Okafor, a Black twenty-something Texan whose parents hailed from Nigeria, were appearing in NRA ads targeting millennial women. In her 2016 ad, Okafor proclaimed: "I am not the victim you need me to be." Soon after, she began touring campuses as a paid rep for Gun Owners of America, telling students, "Gun rights are women's rights" and selling firearms as feminist tools of equity and empowerment.

The advocates' push seemed to be working. In 2017, a senior at Kent State in northeastern Ohio showed up on campus the day after her convocation ceremony in a white minidress, with a graduation cap that read *Come and Take It*, and a black AR-10 hanging from a strap around her shoulder—scaring the hell out of her fellow students. Destroying campus unity and the wholesome activities that brought people together seemed to be the goal. That same young woman soon got a nickname from her supporters: "Gun Girl."

Students for Concealed Carry was also going gangbusters, launching campus carry initiatives through laid-back, flip-flop-wearing dudes who manned campus quad tables expounding on "liberty" and the sanctity of the Second Amendment. By fall 2017, campus carry advocates, with the support of the larger pro-gun movement, had clocked victories in eleven states. Laws differed, but at some schools, students could now carry weapons to class.

Online newspapers—*The College Fix*, founded in 2011, and *Campus Reform*, a then eight-year-old arm of the Leadership

Institute—fed the rage machine, stoking demand for content that depicted liberal students and their administrators as out of control and intolerant. The Young America's Foundation spent generously in 2017 to bring Fox News personalities, Breitbart editors, and conspiracy theorists like Dinesh D'Souza face-to-face with young audiences in campus auditoriums. If they managed to kick up some controversy—as when Ben Shapiro, the editor of the far-right political website the Daily Wire, gave the finger to a roomful of progressive protesters in Madison, Wisconsin—all the better.

Because being offensive was no longer something you had to apologize for. It was cunning and cool. It was sticky. It drove engagement.

WITH TENSIONS RISING AROUND THE COUNTRY, AND MANY PROgressives experiencing increasing fear and rage at Trump's presidency, it wasn't hard to catch an angry assistant professor or usually mild-mannered lefty student driven mad by TPUSA's more aggressive stunts. And TPUSA chapter leaders and staff members were at the ready, watching for outbursts, provoking them if they could, and capturing them on their iPhones. Their videos were quickly slapped together for maximum impact, given sassy titles, and sent out into the cyberworld, where, if all went as planned, they went viral. Circulating online in late 2017 was the video of an anti-Trump grad student at the University of Illinois who grabbed a TPUSA member's phone—after the student hollered at him: "No one is scared of you fifty-year-old man. Don't you have kids to look after?"—then threw the phone across the lawn, cracking it. It was, it seemed, designed as a visual reminder that liberals were violent.

Another video that went viral in 2017: a PhD candidate at the University of Nebraska who was so turned off by the mere presence of a TPUSA recruitment table on her campus that she made

her own sign—*Just say no to Neo-Fascism*—and posed in front of
the table with her middle finger in the air. Later, the ponytailed
TPUSA activist reported she had felt unsafe.

There were plenty of lefties who sputtered their frustrated rage
and dismay at these student activists, including a student at Western Washington University in Bellingham who howled in disbelief at the sight of a large pro-Trump sign. The man brandishing
the sign mockingly responded: "This is apparently an art major.
She's an art major. Art is really going downhill." It was a scene
that may have struck MAGA lovers as funny. But close to a year
into Trump's presidency, millions and millions of Americans could
relate to the woman's sense of utter despair.

Turning Point USA's Affirmative Action Bake Sale in September 2017 was not the only conservative happening stirring
up controversy at the University of New Mexico. In the wake of
Trump's election, the school, which had long prided itself on its
diverse student body, had become a target of right-wing activism.
Just eight months earlier, in January 2017, UNM's Republican club
had hosted alt-right provocateur and former Breitbart News editor Milo Yiannopoulos for a rowdy evening of entertainment and
insults. Then, too, tempers flared. Five hundred attendees arrived
for the event, while a thousand protesters marched outside, clutch-
ing signs that declared *Immigrants Are Welcome. Fascists Are Not*
and *Go Home Milo.* Dozens of local police officers in riot gear were
also on hand to keep the peace. During his talk—"America Deserves Borders"—Yiannopoulos posted the ICE hotline number
up on a large screen and encouraged students to "purge your local illegals." He told the room that Muslim values and American
values "were incompatible" and insulted several women in hijabs,
telling them: "You're wearing a hijab in the United States of America. What is wrong with you?"

Also making their presence known on the UNM campus were members of CFACT, the national climate-denying youth group, helping students stand up "against the green lie." The national group was bringing its campaigns—"Keep Calm, Climate Changes," for example—to campuses around the country in its efforts to squash "liberal hysteria" about the Earth's health and share "cold, hard facts" about the environment, according to glossy pamphlets the group distributed. Wind farms, students around the country were told, were inefficient. What passed the efficiency test? Coal.

As for Will Witt, he would not return to UNM again that year. Soon after the bake sale, the charismatic upstart was hired by Prager University, a far-right "education" site that produced eye-catching five-minute videos designed to preach the right-wing gospel in deceptively simple terms to young web dwellers looking for quick answers to culture war conundrums. Some of PragerU's favorite video offerings were self-explanatory: *There Is No Gender Wage Gap* and *Why You Should Love Fossil Fuel*. Others, less so. *He Wants You* was a peppy defense of men who leered at women.

PragerU was founded in 2009 by Dennis Prager, a seventy-one-year-old Los Angeles talk-radio star with a mop of chalk-white hair and vitriolic feelings about Obama (he once criticized him for not being masculine enough), along with a former Hollywood producer named Allen Estrin. PragerU had the financial backing of Dan and Farris Wilks, two billionaire Christian right fracking giants who also bankrolled the Daily Wire. Executives boasted that its videos had received millions of views. By 2021 that number would skyrocket to billions, PragerU would allege, as the site increasingly became a teaching tool for other right-wing youth groups who aired PragerU videos during their campus get-togethers.

Witt was hired by PragerU to produce his own content: three-minute man-on-the-street videos, online versions of the agitating activism he had been doing for TPUSA. In one of his most popular, Witt dressed up as a sombrero-wearing Mexican with a fake mustache taped to his mouth and a poncho. He rambles around UCLA's campus, shaking a maraca and asking students: "Do you find this outfit offensive?" The liberal students respond just as he hopes they will, and sure enough, he catches it all on film. "Cultural Appropriation!," one young woman cries, as Witt rattles his maraca. Last time I checked, the video had been watched close to two million times.

The technology was new and the high-octane discourse was, too. But pushes to radicalize young conservative Americans, to rile them up and encourage them to view their left-leaning peers with deep-seated ire, that was not new. It was the result of a well-honed strategy that had been long in the works. The nation was reaching alarming heights of hysteria, and the college campus was bearing the brunt of it, as well-trained soldiers for the right executed a plan crafted years earlier.

CHAPTER SEVEN

"Tired of Losing"

O n a July evening in 1964, hundreds of young conservatives poured into the Cow Palace, a massive, high-ceilinged venue fifteen minutes from downtown San Francisco, for the Republican National Convention. They spilled onto the arena floor and crowded the bleachers, there to rally behind their hero, an Arizona senator named Barry Goldwater. Goldwater was a brazen, cowboy-hat wearing, department store heir who had ripped through the primary season with pugnacious panache and was poised to take the presidential nomination, despite efforts by moderates in the party to stop him. He was a force of nature, rich but rough around the edges, privileged while still pumping up populist ire. He opposed big government, civil rights, and journalists. His message was sharply divisive; many on the left lambasted him for growing a movement bolstered by racists. But young conservatives loved him.

The thundering sound of pipe organs rumbled through the stadium. Balloons poured down from the rafters. The crowd roared and the insurgent candidate, dressed in a chalk-white button-down, a dark blue suit, and a matching blue tie, arrived on the mammoth stage to raucous chants of "We want Barry!"

As he accepted the Republican Party nomination for president of the United States, Goldwater launched into one of his classic bold and mythic riffs, mesmerizing his audience of fourteen thousand. Even critics recognized his oratorical power. "The good Lord raised this mighty republic to be a home for the brave and to flourish as the land of the free," he began, his reedy voice rising and lowering with every word. "Not to stagnate in the swampland of collectivism. Not to cringe before the bullying of communism. Now, my fellow Americans, the tide has been running against freedom. Our people have followed false prophets. We must, and we shall, return to proven ways—not because they are old, but because they are true."

Forty or so minutes in, he landed his famous kicker, the one that seemed to set the stage for so much of the fiery rhetoric that would come in his wake. "Extremism in the defense of liberty is no vice," he roared. His fans, sometimes referred to as Goldwaterites, roared back with clamorous cheers. "And let me remind you also," he continued. ". . . That moderation in the pursuit of justice is no virtue."

Some historians have since called that convention the Woodstock of the Right, when the buttoned-up GOP officially brushed aside the Nelson Rockefeller wing of the party to embrace the political allure of populist resentment. It was the official beginning of the modern conservative movement, mostly powered by young, zealous crusaders who would revolutionize not just the party, but the entire nation: injecting into American politics an unabashed ire against elites that would become a siren call for the right, and whose beginnings can now seem, sadly, almost quaint.

National progressive politics, as imagined by Franklin Delano Roosevelt in 1933, had guided the nation safely out of the Great Depression, through the trials of a Second World War, and into a civil rights era that was granting Black Americans increasing freedoms. But for these newly energized conservatives, progressive politics symbolized all that was wrong with the country: a big-government ethos that they were certain was discouraging hard work, rejecting traditional values, and relying too heavily on government handouts. What the left called social safety nets these right-wing activists called entitlements. In their estimation, programs that helped the poor actually helped the lazy and were paid for by the hardworking and industrious.

That fall, the Goldwater-ites campaigned tirelessly for their fiery idol, going door to door in swing states, phone-banking, and plastering Goldwater signs everywhere they could. But on election night, they faced a devastating defeat. Their feisty Arizonian lost to Lyndon Johnson in the general election by a bruising 16 million votes. Crushed, but unwilling to give up, they vowed to keep fighting, eventually forming a political force to be reckoned with, now referred to as the New Right.

That same year—1964—was also a big one for a group of energized student activists on the left. Members of the group, known as Students for a Democratic Society (SDS), had taken to the streets to protest racism, economic inequality, and eventually the Vietnam War. They had a manifesto, were launching chapters on hundreds of campuses, and would soon become an integral part of the free speech movement at Berkeley and beyond that was challenging regulations on where and how students could stage political protests. Culturally, SDS became a symbol for left-wing mobilizing. Its members defined our very image of the sixties, coining phrases like *Make Love Not War* and *Hell No, We Won't Go*, and contributing to the iconic vision of the young, protesting hippie and the counterculture lifestyle that came of age in the 1960s.

But by 1969, SDS itself had all but flamed out. Disagreements about the Vietnam War and concern over radicalized activists who were advocating violence turned off many supporters. Tensions between disparate factions made it all but impossible to settle on a unified set of goals, and perhaps more importantly a plan forward.

The group was unable to co-opt the establishment in DC or to translate its activism into actual legislation.

This was not so for the Goldwater-ites. Lesser known by the American mainstream, but no less committed than SDS and undoubtedly more organized, they headed for Washington, D.C., after Goldwater's defeat, where they would go on to change the face of American politics forever. Once there, they banded together with like-minded donors, and set out to build a political infrastructure independent of the Republican Party, but with hopes of one day infiltrating it.

One Goldwater-ite, Richard Viguerie, the son of a Houston oilman with full-rimmed glasses and a geeky, white-toothed grin, was already in DC. He would launch a small, unassuming marketing firm and introduce campaign mailers, a then-novel concept, into the political system. Viguerie would transform the way conservatives talked to their constituents and birth the Republican Party's most potent twentieth-century asset: the single-issue voter, a treasured lever-pusher who could be lured to the polls by inflammatory mailings about baby killers, tax and spend Democrats, and guns stolen from the hands of their owners by a tyrannical state. Today, he is sometimes referred to as the movement's direct-mail wizard.

Paul Weyrich, the devout Catholic who coined the phrase "Moral Majority," helped to architect the powerful coalition of anti-communists, free-market capitalists, and evangelical Christians who would make up the movement's future power base. Weyrich founded some of the movement's most useful organizations, which have allowed American conservatives to wield power well beyond their numbers, often in secret. They include the American Legislative Exchange Council, also known as ALEC, a political networking group funded by far-right business scions that drafts sample state bills, then instructs legislators on how to pass them. These bills have, over the years, softened unions, weakened environmental regulations, and gashed social safety net programs. To focus on federal policy, Weyrich co-founded the Heritage Foundation in 1973, the conservative movement's most influential public policy think tank. And to keep everyone in conservative circles on the same page, Weyrich helped found the Council for National Policy in 1981 with movement icons Howard Phillips and Tim LaHaye. CNP is a consortium of far-right power brokers, media operatives, religious leaders, and uber-wealthy corporatists who gather in secret three times a year to coordinate their activities out of the public eye.

There was also Morton Blackwell, a nerdy 1964 Goldwater delegate from Baton Rouge. He was one of the architects of the annual Conservative Political Action Conference, the now massive conclave of right-wing organizations that was founded in 1974 so conservatives could network outside of the official Republican Party structure. He would also become Ronald Reagan's youth director during his 1980 presidential campaign. But Blackwell's most significant contribution to the movement was his insistence that as the young movement gathered followers, those followers would need to be trained. Eventually, Blackwell would become the man to provide that instruction, launching the Leadership Institute (LI) in 1979, enrolling political naïfs in intense, days-long workshops and churning out ruthless operatives schooled in the magic art of what Blackwell called "political technology."

By the 1980s, if you were a mover and a shaker inside the GOP, you had gone through the school, attending at least one of the dozens of programs Blackwell offered—today, they include everything from get-out-the-vote workshops to direct-mail seminars, crisis communications crash-courses and in-studio lessons on presenting your far-right ideas on TV. Since its founding, some 200,000 young conservative activists have enrolled.

With a $24 million coffer in 2020, up from $19.4 million in 2010, a state-of-the-art TV studio, an online news outlet, and

seventeen hundred campus partner organizations, LI has facili-
tated the speedy growth of hundreds of college and high school
youth groups, fine-tuned their outreach efforts, tightened their
conservative messaging, and created firm bonds between activists, donors, think tanks, and DC insiders. The students trained
by Blackwell go off to work for bigwigs in the party: Reagan, the
Bushes, and most recently Trump. But they also become bigwigs
themselves. Mike Pence, Tucker Carlson, Dinesh D'Souza, Karl
Rove, and Laura Ingraham have all filtered through the Leadership Institute's doors. Mitch McConnell calls Blackwell "My
Professor."

Today, the eighty-eight-year-old Viguerie has a low-key political presence, only occasionally giving talks. Weyrich died in 2008
in a northern Virginia hospital, but the eighty-two-year Blackwell
continues to hold sway.

So, on a July 2018 weekend, I went to meet him.

BLACKWELL, NOW PLUMP AND SQUAT, WITH RUDDY SKIN AND
wisps of white hair sprouting from his balding head, was sitting at
a desk in his cluttered office on the top floor of the five-story building in Arlington, Virginia, where the Leadership Institute is now
headquartered. Sun streamed in through the windows, down on
piles of folders and the knickknacks that overflowed on his desk: a
jar of peanuts, a Styrofoam coffee cup, a mini Model-T car, and an
overflowing Rolodex. He seemed innocuous enough with his low,
gravelly voice and slow, deliberate speech. But his insistence that
"moderate Democrats are now an endangered species" signaled
to me that his decades-long dedication to demonizing the enemy,
in ways that seemed to bear little resemblance to the truth as I
understood it, had not subsided with age.

Blackwell is famous for torturing his political foes and encouraging his acolytes to do the same. His legend has been culled—and

can be defined—through the parables he tells his students. In one, he likens a political campaigner who is facing the release of information he or she does not want to go public to a young dog whose tail is to be clipped, a common practice among some breeders. If the damaging information is about your candidate, you want to cut the tail off all at once. Get the pain over with quickly. But if you have dirt on your opponent, you want to cut the tail off snip by snip. The goal: to inflict as much pain as you possibly can.

Blackwell almost always uses the word "opponent" when referring to what his students understand to be the asshole Democrat you are trying to squash. And that is by design. Because his outfit is a tax exempt 501(c)(3) nonprofit, it isn't allowed to engage in partisan politics. So, he insists with a straight face on the absurd claim Charlie makes about TPUSA, and that some left-leaning 501(c)(3)s also claim: LI is nonpartisan.

During our hour-long chat and another conversation I had with him months later, Blackwell, no stranger to the extended monologue, assessed his own contribution to American political life.

For years after the Goldwater defeat, he had worked hand in hand with other young conservatives to turn the failed coup into a permanent political force on the right. His buddy Richard Viguerie, who was at the time building up his direct-mail business, hosted regular Wednesday-morning breakfasts at his McLean, Virginia, home where he and Blackwell and a rotating cast of conservative luminaries would discuss the future of the movement. Blackwell was obsessed with the nature of their loss—or more specifically, why all the youthful Goldwater energy, what Blackwell called "solid Goldwater pedigree," had not been enough to win. As far as he could tell, they had been morally superior, and they had had energy. But that had not equated to victory.

The foundational question for Blackwell was simple: What did the left have that the right didn't? When you put it that way, the answer was obvious: hippies, civil rights marchers, and antiwar protesters. In other words, a robust tradition of grass-roots activism.

"We were tired of losing," Blackwell let out, sounding like a man who has told this story hundreds of times before. "At our gatherings, we decided what had worked well for the political left, we wanted to work for us." Blackwell believed in his heart of hearts that what he was dedicating his life to was more than a job, more than passion. It was "a moral obligation." He was going to save the country. He launched his first set of Leadership Institute classes in a hotel near the White House. Soon his good friend Larry Pratt would take the helm at the newly formed Gun Owners of America and would become one of LI's most influential allies. Twenty students attended the school's first iteration. A promising kid from Kentucky named Mitch McConnell was one of them. As for Pratt, he would show up from time to time, too, to share with Blackwell's disciples his worldview, which he also took to conservative radio. During an interview with daytime talk show host Bill Cunningham, Pratt said of a New York congresswoman who worried that a GOA member might want to harm her: "You know, I'm kind of glad that's in the back of their minds. Hopefully they'll behave."

At the Leadership Institute, the idea was to teach the real, nitty-gritty political tools young conservative activists didn't learn in their poli sci classes, the granular details of organizing a political network, executing a campaign, and understanding the nature of power, which Blackwell tells his students isn't about popularity or access—power is getting what you want. But perhaps more importantly, Blackwell wanted to teach certain core values that he communicated through his oft-repeated sayings. Activists had to have an unflagging commitment to the movement and, according to one LI trainer, be willing to "bleed for the cause." They needed to value fidelity over all else. And they needed to possess a cutthroat spirit, an understanding that politics wasn't play, it was war. "Winners aren't perfect," Blackwell told his protegees. "They make fewer mistakes than their rivals."

Blackwell has a near bottomless ambition that has kept his school thriving, growing, and expanding. He is still an RNC delegate and still comes up with tricks designed to punish his enemies. At the Republican National Convention in 2004, Blackwell made it his mission to remind voters of the controversy then swirling around Democratic presidential nominee John Kerry. The much-disputed claim was that at least one of Kerry's Vietnam combat awards—which included multiple Purple Hearts—was garnered improperly. So Blackwell bought adhesive bandages with purple hearts on them and handed them out. He also still feels responsible for the young people he trains, many of whom now roam the Capitol, and distress for those who don't come train with the group. It "tears" him up when he sees a conservative activist make "some stupid mistake that he or she could have avoided if he or she were willing to come and sit down for two days and learn a whole lot of political technology."

When our talk came to an end, I was ushered downstairs, where the real action was. Inside a stuffy third-floor classroom, the air barely circulating, were two hundred or so of Blackwell's college-aged students, dressed in belted khakis, gray linen suits, and flower-print skirts, now crumpled from hours of sitting.

It was Saturday and Arlington was hopping with the Hill's summer interns grabbing brunch, shopping, and getting their hair blown out for late-night bar hopping. But Blackwell's trainees— jacked up on coffee and powdered donuts—were powering through his now legendary weekend crash course, intaking everything they needed to know to become warriors for the right. Blackwell does limited teaching himself these days, delegating instruction to a dozen or so members of his full-time staff, part-time staff, and the occasional conservative who stops by from time to time to give back.

Holding court in the front of the room was David Blair, a young hunting aficionado from southern Illinois who is the school's director. He is tall with a broad frame and combed-back hair. And that afternoon he wore a dark, boxy suit typical of beltway newbies and a Stars-and-Stripes tie that matched the flag he was standing next to. In a testament to Blackwell's sway, Blair was plucked in 2016 to be the Trump campaign's youth coordinator after Blackwell had a brief phone conversation with LI alumnus David Bossie, Trump's 2016 deputy campaign manager. Blair enjoyed an office in Trump Tower and, rumor has it, occasional rides on Trump's Boeing 757.

Now, Blair pointed at a large screen displaying a photograph of two young women sitting behind a folding table on the quad of Georgia College & State University. *The Network of Enlightened Women* read a handout lying on top of the table. Despite the deceptively liberal-seeming name, NEW is actually a conservative women's outfit founded in 2004 by a female UVA graduate.

"What is wrong with this table?" Blair bellowed to his young comrades, pointing at the screen.

The table in the photo was largely empty, save for a lone bowl of candy and some sloppily placed material. And Blair could hardly contain his disgust. "This is an ineffective recruitment table," he boomed.

The subject of this lecture was "tabling." In activism lingo, "tabling" is code for setting up a folding table on a campus quad to advertise your group—what TPUSA and YAL chapters were constantly doing and what Witt had been doing at UNM. To the casual observer, this may seem like pretty mundane stuff. Not here. "Tabling" at the Leadership Institute—like canvassing, messaging, and postering—was treated like a competitive sport, taught with the kind of exacting precision Olympic-level gymnastic coaches might use to delineate complex floor routines. How you stood, what you wore, the expression on your face—all

of it was of utmost importance and could make the difference between success and failure, winning recruits or losing them to the
other side. And everyone inside the classroom seemed to know
that.

"They are sitting behind the table," a young man in the front
of the room quipped, pointing out a "tabling" faux pas. Recruits
were always supposed to be standing so as to be more readily able
to interact with passersby.

"The sign is too low," came another voice from the back. Signs
were supposed to be eye-level, simple, legible, and inviting.

"It looks messy," Blair jumped in. "It looks like a *man* put that
table together." He shook his head in dismay.

Soon, a photo of a table deemed "Highly Effective" popped up
on the screen behind Blair. It was for a Right-to-Life group and
featured a large poster board. On it was a display of several bloody
fetuses. Despite the gruesome photos, the table had a near festive
vibe. It was overflowing with handouts: plastic cups, coolers, stickers, pamphlets, and pens—all promoting the pro-life group. The
four women standing by the table were beaming.

Blair and his students couldn't say enough positive things
about the display.

"They have free stuff."

"It's colorful."

"It's near stairs, maximizing foot traffic."

"No one is sitting," Blair let out. "Do you sit behind the table?"

The room erupted in a resounding "No."

"If you want to sit," Blair pecked, annoyed at the very thought,
"go to lunch."

Near Blair was a large bowl of candy and piles of conservative
classics. There was Russell Kirk's *The Conservative Mind*, which
speaks the orderly language of the cultural conservative. And there
was the 304-page biography of Ronald Reagan, *How an Ordinary
Man Became an Extraordinary Leader*, by one of his most faithful

acolytes, Dinesh D'Souza. When a student made a good point about tabling or grasped some finer point of sign-making, Blair would toss out a book or a piece of candy as a reward, sometimes with exaggerated force. When a flung piece of caramel narrowly missed my head, one of the students mockingly scolded Blair: "Don't hit the reporter."

Blair was one of several instructors that weekend, culled from a circle of hyper-engaged politicos with a yen for imparting knowledge on the younger set. The class—a prerequisite for any of the other LI classes—is notoriously comprehensive and sometimes mind-numbingly boring, covering everything you need to know about building your conservative campus club to running the youth operation for a GOP presidential candidate. There is practically nothing Blackwell has left out.

Lectures were each generally under an hour long and crammed with factoids, strategies, and tips of the trade. Some included nuts-and-bolts stuff—everything from where to put a bumper sticker on a supporter's car (driver's side, front, so passing cars can see it) to how to make a political event look bigger (cordon off enough space for fewer people than are scheduled to attend), from how to get students to come to your events (offer pizza) to how to get volunteers to join your campaign (give them impressive titles they can put on their résumés).

During another Blair lesson, students were taught how to deliver "a last-minute barb" to an opponent—be it a city council member, a congressional candidate, or a presidential hopeful—a few days before an election. First come up with something you have been hounding the candidate about from the beginning: they love taxes or the NRA hates them. Then, launch a negative flyer campaign, he told them. And one night after dark, send your team out to tape those flyers on poles around the district. Ideally, this should be done on the eve of the election, with a particular focus on the candidate's neighborhood and the neighborhoods of his or her top officers, Blair told the room. That way, they will wake up the next morning and panic.

"They look up the street, down the street . . . and they see all these signs," Blair told the room, his voice betraying a mischievousness. "What you want them to do is overreact. You want them to freak out and think they need to go around and take all these down—or even better try to respond to it." This will keep them from their primary job of getting their voters to the polls, giving your candidate a competitive edge. And "you're not doing anything illegal," he assured his students.

At LI, attendees learn tactics, but also a special language—all terms plucked from the Blackwell dictionary. "Three a.m. Types" is the common moniker for the movement's most reliable young soldiers, willing to wake up early and stay up late, anything to further the cause. People who join your campaign as volunteers "bandwagon" onto it. At a meet-the-candidate event, the volunteer who organizes photo-ops with the candidate is called "the pusher." The one who stands next to the candidate and brings the person in for the shot is "the puller."

There is the Abe Lincoln Four-Step—a multitiered process for maximizing votes that Abraham Lincoln purportedly came up with during one of his elections and that Blackwell described in a *National Review* opinion piece in 2012:

- Obtain a complete list of voters.
- Ascertain with certainty for whom each will vote.
- Have the undecided spoken to by those in whom they have the most confidence.
- On Election Day, make sure every Whig gets to the polls.

The Abe Lincoln Four-Step was not to be confused with YAL's Maloney Four-Step, designed to get young activists fired up enough to volunteer on their campuses or for campaigns. That entailed: contacting them online, getting them on the phone, eliciting a promise from them, then hounding them until they followed through. Blackwell's trainers also taught the Leesburg Grid, a diagram that helps campaigns craft winning messaging about their candidates and negative messaging about their opponents.

Sitting near me was a young man in scuffed-up boots and a straw cowboy hat, his shoulders slumped over. There was another young man sporting a thin, red tie whose eyes were wandering to a wall of windows, and a trainee sitting in one of the middle rows who had on a pair of dress shorts—"The balls of that guy," another student would later remark to me, explaining Blackwell's thoughts on presentability. If you couldn't dress the part, you could hardly be expected to act the part.

It mattered. That weekend the trainees were being watched. Many of them were recent grads—finishing up at small, community colleges, prestigious Christian universities, Ivy Leagues, and large state schools. They'd learned about LI through their campus involvement with Turning Point USA, YAL, YAF, and other conservative groups. They'd caught the political bug and were now looking for jobs. Some would be singled out as promising, based on their participation that weekend and how they fared on a seven-page final that tested their general knowledge on the names of various governors, Blackwell's legendary adages, and political strategizing techniques. One sample question: When tabling, what do you do when bleeding heart liberals come and argue with you? Argue back, of course.

Those students deemed promising would get a reward: an opportunity to stay that week for yet more instruction to prepare for a fall job as a campus coordinator for the Institute, helping conservative youth groups affiliated with LI build their campus presences. Others still in college were simply looking to gain experience for the conservative groups they ran or the fall 2018 campaigns they hoped to volunteer for. Getting in with Blackwell and the young people in Blackwell's circle was important. One day, you, too, might be asked to go work for the president.

Classes at LI lasted well past midnight, at which point the students descended into the cramped basement dorms to crash in bunk beds. The following morning, they'd do it all over again. Classes, lodging, deli sandwiches, and the pizza they downed in between sessions were all offered to them for a small fee. Most paid their own way to get to DC, although scholarships were also available.

In one late-night class I visited, the students were divided up into groups and asked to pretend they were the youth coordinator for Dave Smith, a Louisiana congressman running for a Senate seat. The youth coordinator needed to deal with a "crisis" related to a series of campus "mock elections." Mock elections are like straw polls, a savvy way for campaigns to generate excitement around a candidate on a college campus, according to Blackwell. And if your candidate wins, they provide good publicity for the real election. In our classroom scenario, the youth coordinator heard an untrue rumor that her own campaign team had rigged a mock election. Now, one of her volunteers was about to take the rumor to the press, resign from her post, and join the opposing camp.

The students were asked: What is your solution to this crisis? What is your plan of action?

I wandered around listening to the students as they brainstormed for close to an hour. A group in the kitchen was leaning toward letting the whole thing blow up on its own. Another group proposed taking swift action.

"Take it to the higher ups," a young man in boat shoes and a charcoal gray suit offered—hardly the kind of proactive, take-charge solution Blackwell expected of his disciples.

"That's not a plan," scoffed a young man in a checkered jacket and cowboy boots. "The plan is what are you going to say to the higher ups?"

The group grew silent.

"The way we package this is extremely important," commented a junior from Colorado Christian University.

Someone suggested talking to the volunteer.

"Internal investigation?" offered another.

"Write a press release?"

"You know, there is a decent chance none of this is true."

Eventually the groups presented their plans, incorporating various strategies they'd learned so far at LI. They would use press releases, employ Three a.m. Types, trust no one, and try to verify.

I found the whole exercise confusing and uninteresting, but the students were charged by it, turned on, deeply committed to developing winning mindsets and using smart strategies to turn things in their favor. Blackwell's kids were beginners, but already acutely impacted by his lessons on the nature of power and the political technology needed to grab control of it.

There was an ethos in the building that well represents the greater ethos of the young far-right movement: those with any talent who work hard, sacrifice, pay attention, and follow instructions will be taken care of, well-paid, and mentored. They're in.

With his well-trained staff on the job, Blackwell himself didn't need to stick around for the entire weekend of training sessions. He'd left the building after our talk to attend to his garden at home—planting daylily seedlings he was cross-pollinating on his office windowsill. This was a longtime hobby when he wasn't growing his conservative flock, and it struck me as similar to his interest in developing young conservative activists. He'd chuckled a bit dismissively at my observation when I'd mentioned it in his office. I was a classic reporter, looking for a metaphor. He most certainly taught courses on dealing with the likes of me. But he was willing to play along.

The difference between his daylilies and his students, he told me, was that when it came to the young people, "I'm not cross-pollinating."

CHAPTER EIGHT

"I Hate Black People"

In October 2017, TPUSA's envelope-pushing ethos was put to the test when photos of a student activist wearing an adult diaper, sucking on a pacifier, and sitting in a play pen on the Kent State campus in northeastern Ohio went viral—and not in a good way. The diaper incident—or "Diapergate" as it came to be called—was a silly jab at campus lefties and their supposedly infantile obsession with "safe spaces." But it backfired. The joke was soon on TPUSA and hence, Charlie.

The organization was ruthlessly mocked for days on Twitter for the ridiculously childish activism event with doctored memes—some featuring Charlie wearing a diaper himself. A very public controversy also ensued between the group's headquarters and the Kent State chapter leader Kaitlin Bennett, an acid-tongued gun-rights advocate who seemed to be constantly edging her way into the spotlight. Headquarters blamed her for going rogue. Not so, Bennett claimed. The event had been okayed by higher ups. And now to save their asses, her bosses were throwing her under the bus. Things got heated. Bennett resigned in a rage—and the chapter was disbanded—but not before she posted an online letter in which she called TPUSA a "shithole of an organization" and Charlie a "college dropout who hires some of the most incompetent, lazy, and downright dishonest people I have ever encountered."

"P.S.," she ended the letter. "If you need a safe space after everyone hears about this, I still have the diapers."

It was hardly worth a lot of ink given that the #MeToo movement was exploding (the *New York Times* had just broken the Harvey Weinstein story), record-breaking fires were raging in California, and Trump's Muslim travel ban, spurred on by the president's political advisor Stephen Miller, was continuing to draw harsh criticism from human rights lawyers. Miller, himself, was cause for concern for anyone left of his former boss Jeff Sessions. A young nationalist who harbored untold ire toward the undocumented, he was now architecting Trump's agenda, and helping to write his incendiary speeches, including the president's dark inaugural address when he vowed to stop the "American Carnage" that had been the Obama presidency.

But the mainstream media, perhaps looking for a distraction from dismal beltway happenings—and eager to bear witness to at least one right-winger's comeuppance—ate Diapergate up, insisting that this was the beginning of the end for TPUSA. "The so-called diaper incident may end up being TPUSA's undoing," read a piece in *Salon*. An article in the *Independent* was titled: "Turning Point USA: How One Student in a Diaper Caused an Eruption in the Student Youth Organization."

The truth was, it hadn't. TPUSA was raking in the big bucks, and controversies like these didn't turn off donors, but instead often spurred them to give more. That year, TPUSA was about to amass close to $8.2 million, up from $4.3 million in 2016.

Still, Charlie was furious about Diapergate. For an image-conscious guy who worked hard to cultivate the right look, the right associates, and the right powerful, good-looking people around him, the debacle must have been embarrassing. But he told his underlings that TPUSA would be better at monitoring campus events in the future and moved on.

As for the media-driven story line that Charlie and his non-profit were on the way down, it tacked to a similar one pushed forward during the 2016 presidential election cycle about Trump: that he was an idiot and constantly on the brink of collapse, rather than a remarkably driven rich guy who was being supported by some of the most politically powerful donors in the country who would do just about anything to get him elected.

Surviving Diapergate was no isolated incident, but rather another example of how Charlie, like Trump, had a "Teflon" effect. The media, the Twittersphere, and TPUSA's young detractors did not in fact have the power to easily take him down, even when he and his followers were embroiled in embarrassing debacles.

Still, the number of those debacles was mounting at a rapid clip.

A year earlier, shortly after Trump was elected, TPUSA had launched a McCarthyesque Professor Watchlist (really a webpage, but an influential one) that featured the names and faces of professors who were said to promote "anti-American values"—say, by denouncing the NRA after yet another deadly shooting or renouncing racial inequities. The list's very existence had a chilling effect, particularly since many of the professors on it were Black, Hispanic, and/or members of the LGBTQ community. But what made it all the more alarming was the fact that their names were making the rounds on right-wing news sites and eventually landing in online chat rooms where alt-right actors, neo-nationalists, and white supremacists were foraging for victims to troll. Professors were receiving harassing phone calls, and in some cases death threats. After a Black sociology professor at Trinity College in Hartford reposted a provocative, and arguably inappropriate, Facebook post denouncing racial bigots with the hashtag "#LetThemF***ingDie"—dozens of callers left messages on his cell phone, using the "n" word repeatedly, howling "I know where you are!" and threatening to rape his wife and kill him and his kids. In one message left on his voice mail, the caller declared: "I hope you get what's coming to you . . . especially if you're a n*****. Go f*** yourself."

The professor was put on voluntary paid leave and forced to move with his family to an undisclosed location.

Matt Lamb, the TPUSA employee responsible for launching the Professor Watchlist, who is now an associate editor at The College Fix, a "right-minded news and commentary site," insisted to reporters at the time, and then to me more recently, that TPUSA should not be blamed for the harassment. "I would say it's really awful. But I would not characterize it as fair to say that Turning Point is responsible."

Lamb was right that the Professor Watchlist wasn't solely responsible, but riling up people who liked to get threatening was becoming a popular pastime for the far-right power broker. And a growing group of multimedia actors in the pages of Breitbart News, the Daily Wire, and on the Fox News shows of blustery media personalities like Tucker Carlson were now cluttering the web with a hysteria playbook that depicted American liberals as angry agents intent on taking down white people. TPUSA was just beginning to find its footing in this new world of political agitators via its social media accounts and those of its growing cadre of young ambassadors who would soon bombard Twitter, Facebook, YouTube, and TikTok with its increasingly inflammatory content, fueling an already-brewing us-against-them online mentality. This type of content had both helped get Trump elected and was helping to calcify dangerous divisions within the country in a way that would eventually tee up the deadly storming of the Capitol on January 6, 2021.

That December, the American Association of University Professors pushed back against the Professor Watchlist with an online campaign denouncing the project. And eventually, even a spokesperson for the Charles Koch Foundation took issue with the site, insisting that condemning professors for their speech was not in fact part of the conservative platform the foundation supported. But in keeping with TPUSA's skill at withstanding public criticism, the watchlist continued to grow. By the end of the year, it had over two hundred names on it.

A few months later, in February 2017, another TPUSA controversy erupted, this time when student journalists for campus news outlets began uncovering the group's latest power play: to secretly recruit TPUSA-friendly candidates inside student government races, in some cases in violation of student campaign rules. (Michael Vasquez, an investigative reporter at *The Chronicle of Higher Education*, would eventually uncover the story and introduce it to the mainstream press.)

In a series of January 2017 texts leaked to *The Lantern*, the student paper at Ohio State University, a TPUSA staff member was caught offering up $6,000 ($2,000 over the regulated limit) to a slate of handpicked student government candidates. In the text, the TPUSA employee explained the intent: to take out the other candidates, "without them knowing what's coming."

In a recorded phone call, another TPUSA staff member elaborated on the plan: to run the candidates as moderates, then, once elected, they can "start to get more conservative." Evoking the stuff of Netflix college dramedies, the staffer summed up her mission with: "A Trojan Horse is the best way to put it."

The effort, it turned out, was part of a large, well-organized TPUSA initiative—known as the Campus Victory Project—to eventually seize power over the Student Government Associations at all the nation's Division I schools.

"Most SGA's have been controlled by the left for decades," a report sent to me by a former TPUSA advisory board member noted. That meant hundreds of millions of dollars in student fees were spent pushing "a coordinated radical progressive agenda." Once the student governments were in its hands, the report noted, TPUSA expected its elected officials to implement a set of select policies that included defunding progressive organizations and blocking popular boycott and divestment efforts.

In multiple cases, student candidates outed for involvement with TPUSA were pressured to step down. But project founders at TPUSA had no intention of giving up efforts to turn student elections, which were opportunities for young people to see representative democracy at work, into lessons on rule-breaking, subterfuge, and the influence of dark money on the electoral process. By the end of the 2016–2017 school year, TPUSA was reporting wins on more than fifty campuses. And it was just getting going.

Around that time, another controversy was also brewing at TPUSA headquarters. If these other incidents couldn't take down the conservative youth outfit, this new scandal, it would seem to the group's many enemies, would surely do the trick.

In December 2017, investigative journalist Jane Mayer reported in *The New Yorker* that Crystal Clanton—the hard-charging national field director who now oversaw a staff of eighty-five, and whom Charlie had once described as "the best hire we ever could have made"—had sent a nauseating text to one of her charges. "I HATE BLACK PEOPLE. Like f**k them all," it read. ". . . I hate blacks. End of story."

Clanton, like Charlie, was beloved by higher ups. They praised her for her maturity and her poise. But Clanton's detractors had less flattering things to say. So, when Mayer, a feared yet deeply respected journalist and author of the 2016 book *Dark Money: The Hidden History of the Billionaires Behind the Rise of the Radical Right*, began poking around, it's not surprising that there were some Clanton-haters willing to spill the beans on their boss. Not only had Clanton been the reported author of a distasteful message, Mayer learned, but she had also reportedly fired a Black employee on Martin Luther King Jr. Day. The employee was the only Black field director the organization had when she was hired. And she told Mayer that while she saw white employees "mistreated, as well," she "felt very uncomfortable working there because I was Black." When asked by Mayer about the text messages, Charlie told her that the organization "took decisive action within 72 hours of being made aware of the issue." And Clanton told her via e-mail that she had "no recollection" of the messages and no longer worked for the organization.

Clanton did not respond to my requests for comment. But a new version of her story arose in 2021. At the time, she was scheduled to graduate from law school at George Mason University in spring of 2022, and she was being considered for a prestigious clerkship with William H. Pryor Jr., the chief judge for the U.S. Court of Appeals for the Eleventh Circuit. According to court documents reported on by Bill Rankin at the *Atlanta Journal-Constitution* in January 2022, when Pryor was considering hiring Clanton, which he has since done—she is scheduled to start in his court in 2023—he was told in a letter by Charlie that Clanton was the victim of a former employee who had "created fake text messages" to be used against colleagues. This employee sought to "malign Crystal's reputation," Charlie wrote, and has since been fired. When asked by *The Washington Post*'s deputy editorial page editor Ruth Marcus to explain the different stories, Turning Point USA spokesperson Andrew Kolvet "declined to make Kirk available or to provide any other response." As for Charlie, he seemed clear who was to blame for all the confusion: "I can assure that the media has made serious errors and omissions," he wrote in his letter to Pryor.

The racism allegations didn't stop with Clanton, though. Soon after Mayer's *New Yorker* piece, a series of Twitter posts unearthed by a reporter at the *Huffington Post* revealed that other TPUSA employees had exhibited a distasteful comfort with bigotry on their social media feeds. One tweet had come from Troy Meeker, a budding GOP firebrand. In 2010, as a teenager, the young Meeker had announced to his followers that he was going to get "KFC with my n****s." He is white. Another uncovered tweet came from TPUSA employee Shialee Grooman, also a GOP darling and a former intern for Arizona congressman Trent Franks. She had declared, in 2013: "All I get is n***** dick." She was in high school. The tweet was one of a series of other offensive tweets the twenty-two-year-old had typed into existence around that time. They included: "I love making racist jokes" and "If you're a race other than white I promise to make racist jokes towards you." Just a few years later, in 2016, Timon Prax, an Ohio field director turned Midwest regional director, had used Twitter to mock members of non-Christian religions—in particular Muslims for their "love for goats" and Jews for "always counting pennies."

Once again, the mainstream media began to fantasize about Charlie's demise. Would his donors cut him off? That did not turn out to be the case. Inside the organization, according to one former campus chapter leader, there was an accepting nonchalance— that the "uptight libs" are always looking to flag someone as a racist.

"The criticisms don't really stick because if MSNBC runs an article about, oh Turning Point is bad, your average conservative donor is just like, well, duh, it's MSNBC," a former regional field director told me. The former campus chapter leader told me that conservatives in the movement tend to react one of two ways when one of theirs is accused of racism. "When they see some big conservative being labeled a racist or there's racism in the organization, they say: 'Yeah, sure, there are conservatives who are racist, I get it.' So they just ignore it. And some of them, of course, are like: 'Oh, sure, they're racist. That's fine, so am I.'"

As for these young people, they quickly found cover. Soon after leaving TPUSA, Clanton was hired by Ginni Thomas, the wife of Supreme Court Justice Clarence Thomas, who was also on TPUSA's board of advisors at the time and served as a den mother of sorts for the youth group. Thomas and her Supreme Court husband were so sympathetic to Clanton's plight that they invited her to come live with them. Clanton did, for nearly a year. As for Timon Prax, the antisemitic tweeter, he, too, got a helping hand from a TPUSA friend. Gary Rabine, the Illinois pavement magnate who had introduced Charlie to many of his early support-ers, snapped Prax up as a social media director. Antisemitic tweets were apparently not a deal breaker for Rabine. And Grooman went to help out Kelli Ward, an Arizona Republican with strong ties to TPUSA and its staff, who in January 2019 became the chair of the Arizona Republican Party.

IN A PALM BEACH BALLROOM IN DECEMBER 2017, CHARLIE GATH-ered his "investors" together for a buffet brunch to celebrate TPUSA's more savory accomplishments. His board of advisors was now flush with prominent multimillionaires as well as suburban Il-linois supporters of more modest means. Not all were there that day, but his roster now included Tommy Hicks, the Texas hedge fund executive and Don Jr.'s BFF whom Charlie had traveled the country with raising funds for Trump's presidential campaign; oil magnate and former Texas secretary of state George Strake Jr.; John A. Catsimatidis Jr., the twenty-four-year-old son of the bil-lionaire grocery store giant who ran for mayor of New York City in 2009 and 2013; Charlie's old friend Mike Miller, who owned the jewelry store back in Illinois; and Adam Brandon, a conserva-tive movement insider who now sat at the helm of the Koch-allied FreedomWorks.

Charlie was enormously proud of his organization and eager to share the year's accomplishments. Thick, color brochures high-lighted the year's purported successes: more than 200,000 student activists recruited on more than 1,200 campuses. Online, the group was pushing out content at a rapid clip. Two million videos were viewed each day, 20 million viewers were being reached on social media weekly, and there were now 100 TPUSA staff members charged with spreading the right-wing gospel to America's youth.

As far as a lot of investors were concerned, TPUSA didn't have a bigotry problem. If kids were posting "racist stuff" or "anti-gay stuff"—as one former donor put it to me—that was a management problem, and it could be fixed with better supervision and oversight. Anyway, Charlie wasn't out there trying to alienate Black and Latino voters. In fact, Charlie had been talking to his supporters for years about the need for the Republicans to grow their diversity base. The Republican brand needed work. It was saddled with an "old, white guy" image that could turn off voters of color who, in his estimation, had good reason to embrace a conservative vision for America, one that cherished self-reliance, traditional family values, and faith.

Charlie also understood something that seemed lost on the Democrats, but not on Trump, who would improve his showing with both Latino and Black voters in 2020. You could be accused of racism and still grow your support among people of color.

Now, despite the allegations against his workplace—or maybe because of them—Charlie Kirk was about to launch a high-profile effort to do just that.

CHAPTER NINE

Conference Crusaders

Warring with angry campus leftists, socialists, and PC patrollers was by any young conservative's estimation exhausting. And by summer, most were more than ready to take a break from the enemy and regroup with people who understood what they believed and how much they sacrificed during the school year.

Their less politically-engaged peers were busy landing jobs at ice cream shops and corner CVS stores, and starting internships at tech startups and hedge funds. But for a certain breed of young conservative, summer was conference season—time to work, play, train, and guzzle booze with like-minded souls.

In July 2018, as the days grew hotter, hundreds of these weary high school and college warriors poured into hotel ballrooms, wood-paneled conference halls, and breezy summer resorts for three-, four-, and sometimes five-day events held by Young Americans for Liberty, Turning Point USA, and countless other groups. They refueled for the coming school year, learned new tricks of the trade, and reminded themselves that they were not alone.

Conference culture was not new. Ever since Buckley had gathered his followers together at his family's home in suburban

Connecticut to launch Young Americans for Freedom, conferences had become the lifeblood of the young conservative movement. They were seen as an integral part of the community ethos that the Leadership Institute and the right-wing's cadre of generous donors saw as crucial to luring persuadable youth away from the clutches of the socialist left.

Still, for years, such gatherings had been relatively staid. Not anymore. Conferences were now rowdy, raucous, high-energy affairs with big breakfasts, fancy balls, and star-studded speakers—much of it free, all of it designed to raise up as many warriors for the right as possible. If the atmospheres didn't exactly reflect the seriousness of the far-right's mission to crush the left, the lavish figures being spent to assemble the flock under a single roof did. Conservative youth groups routinely spent more than a million dollars a year on these events. In 2018, Cliff's Young Americans for Liberty Foundation told the IRS it had spent $2.4 million on them.

Variety was key. Like a Pornhub for politics, the conference circuit offered something for everyone, a way to lure you into the movement through whatever far-right obsession, sometimes referred to as your "issue," turned you on. Perhaps it was defending your right to nestle a deadly AK-47 between your fingers (attend the NRA's Youth Education Summit, a weeklong activism bonanza for high schoolers) or the thrill of fighting in utero baby killers (hit the annual National Teens for Life convention for lectures on how to peddle the pro-life position to Gen Z atheists and tackle pro-choicers on TikTok). Or maybe it was Reagan's trickle-down economics that got you going (for that you could travel to the Reagan Ranch in Santa Barbara for an annual high school event, held by Young America's Foundation, or hit up their DC-area gathering, where in 2018, you could watch ConservaWorld comedian Steve Crowder mock "global warming alarmists," Barack Obama, and "fat . . . feminists").

Right-wing youth conferences were safe spaces for conservative kids; places for them to freely laugh at jokes more widely found offensive, and openly vent, away from the wrath of angry lefties chastising them for their resentments. If I wanted to see these kids at their most unguarded, and truly understand what made them tick, I knew I needed to attend at least a few of these unbridled affairs. So I did, taking in over a dozen over the course of my more than four years working on this book.

ON A DRIZZLING EVENING IN JULY 2018, I STEPPED INTO A CAR-peted lobby at a Sheraton in Reston, Virginia, for YALCON, the Young Americans for Liberty annual conference. It was a year and a half into Trump's stint in the White House and the president had just launched a trade war with China, which YAL's free-trade allies inside the Koch network were spending millions to publicly oppose with newspaper ads and interviews.

Cliff Maloney, YAL's twenty-seven-year-old president, had spent the last few months voicing his own political opinions on Fox News and on Twitter. But he'd mostly avoided mention of Trump, so as not to alienate potential YAL recruits who might support the polarizing populist. Rather, Cliff made a habit of focusing on more vague libertarian enemies, ones a college kid with even a passing interest in politics was likely to also oppose: draconian drug laws and the "endless wars" Cliff frequently reminded his audiences we had been in since his own birth in the 1990s.

"People don't want government telling them what to do," he would often opine. "They just want to be left alone." It was likely not lost on Cliff that "being left alone" was a central goal of his twenty-something target subject.

Prior to now, I'd not actually met Cliff in person. But I'd watched his frequent appearances on the conservative-leaning talk shows that had helped him grow his influence and his own group's size—YAL reported 27 chapters the first year it launched, in

2009. But by summer 2018, Cliff said the group was supersizing its influence. It had looped in 700,000 social media followers, and was now distributing half a million pieces of "educational" material, annually, much of it produced by the libertarian think tanks, foundations, and advocacy groups YAL was now closely partnering with. And when I reached out about meeting, he was game. Unlike Charlie, who now berated the liberal media ad nauseam for its roundly negative coverage of his group and its antics, Cliff was still eager for media attention. Despite my assertion that Cliff and his young allies were a lot more powerful than people realized, libertarian politicos like him were still often seen as more peculiar than pertinent. And despite the caliber of his world-famous donors and the depth of his ambitions, Cliff was no household name.

During the conference, Cliff would spend at least some of his time sequestered inside the "Green Room"—a Hollywood-esque term his conference organizers used for a room where he hung out, shooting the shit with libertarian bigwigs like Congressman Justin Amash from Michigan's 3rd congressional district; and John Stossel, the bombastic TV personality who, I would soon learn, was a YAL conference regular. I had grown accustomed to youth group leaders making themselves scarce during crowded events. So Cliff's backroom perch didn't surprise me.

More surprising was the news that I would be closely supervised by YAL's communications director, Pooja Bachani, a chatty Boston University grad wearing a polka-dotted dress, who met me in the lobby and briefed me on my schedule. As a rule, the PR people I encountered during events were too busy to spend all day with me. So I usually enjoyed free rein to wander about and report on my own. Not today. Bachani was just one of a fleet of YAL employees who were charged with making sure the event went off without a hitch. Conferences could take months of planning. There were venues to book, speakers to invite, and seats to be filled (what

Cliff called "herding cats"). And once the conference got going, it was important to cater to the special needs, wants, and diets of the VIP influencers in attendance—who sometimes traveled with paid staff, family, and personal pastors.

Bachani stuck me inside a darkened ballroom where I joined hundreds of young YAL acolytes who were viewing *Off the Grid*, a thirty-five-minute ode to the life of northern Kentucky congressman Thomas Massie, a conservative libertarian. The grainy documentary exalted the quirky MIT grad who'd built a solar-powered family farmstead on twelve hundred acres of land. The beautifully shot snore of a film, produced by Free the People (a libertarian media outfit founded in 2016 that would clock $1.2 million in revenue in 2018), was a testament to the energy and money going into efforts to sell libertarianism. But it was also a bird's-eye view into how out-of-touch adherents could sometimes be. Watching Massie on his lawn, shaping rocks with a chisel, may have had a folksy appeal, but it hardly seemed like a sexy ad for a movement that sold itself as renegade.

Later, I listened as the impeccably dressed broadcast personality John Stossel, another idol in these parts, outfitted in an expensive-looking suit, regaled the ballroom with his libertarian conversion story; how he'd started on "the other side" as a "typical business-bashing consumer reporter" with the "liberal media elite," then slowly came to love the free market and its treasures. "Air-conditioning, computers, cars, flush toilets." Stossel paused and nodded his head in awe. "Wonderful stuff."

Eventually, I was able to lose Bachani and wander around the meeting area outside the main ballroom, a maze of tables topped with posters proclaiming popular libertarian adages like *Don't Hurt People and Don't Take Their Stuff*, "I [heart] Ayn Rand" buttons, and pamphlets denouncing "shady union bosses" and the "bloated regulatory state." There were also plenty of books. One crowd pleaser: Charles Koch's *Good Profit*, a business primer that outlined the successful management strategy behind the corporate giant's many EPA– and OSHA–sanctioned energy companies. Nearby, tidily dressed representatives from various far-right think tanks clutched clipboards and called out icebreakers to passersby, whom they sought to lure deeper into the movement with offers of paid internships, fellowships, and jobs: "Do you love liberty?" "Do you love the Constitution?" "Do you believe in freedom?"

At one table were members of the NRA's collegiate arm, promoting a "Second Amendment" workshop that debunked "anti-gun myths." It could be brought free-of-charge to your campus, along with an NRA representative for an evening of conversation, lots of free food, and a complimentary membership to the gun-rights groups for anyone who attended. At another table was a group with a deceptively science-y name, the Co2 Coalition, offering a glossy brochure that called on young people to ignore global warming. "Humans cannot exist if we treat every possible risk as real and catastrophic," it declared. And at a station representing the Koch-backed Grassroots Leadership Academy, an up-and-comer named Matt Hurtt (he'd first run for office at age nineteen) reminded me what the whole day was about. "We grab them while they are young," he said cheerfully, gesturing at the eclectic, milling crowd. That's when their opinions were still impressionable, I was told. The crowd, I would soon learn, was made up of Christian homeschoolers, self-declared anarchists, and young policy wonks, among others. Some gave off a studious, straight-laced vibe. Others reeked of marijuana.

Many of them would spend the rest of the afternoon perched at conference tables furiously taking notes about leadership, chapter growth, and Hayekian social theories—everything they needed to understand to become compelling representatives of the anti-government cause. On their breaks, I approached several of them to find out what had brought them here. A pimple-faced clarinet player told me he was trying his darndest to bring libertarianism to Vassar, a bastion of progressive cool. A former online gambling addict from nearby George Washington University would later tell me his passion for liberty had replaced that vice. And a straw-haired stoner from Indiana shrugged that he mostly wanted to know where he could discuss legalizing drugs. He'd once flirted with anarchy but now saw it as too extreme.

When it was time to meet Cliff, I was escorted to the "Green Room." He was seated behind a large round table, his hair short and tightly cropped—not a military buzz cut, but rather the clean look of a man who meant business. I was immediately struck by how much thinner Cliff looked, compared to his TV appearances—his pudgy cheeks and oversized chin were gone. I would soon learn he had lost 120 pounds, the result of a low-carb diet he'd been on for months. Now, not yet thirty, with his broad shoulders and elongated forehead, Cliff gave off an authoritative aura. His squarish gray suit didn't read chic like the slim-fitting ones Charlie Kirk now wore, but it suggested that Cliff Maloney had left his pool hall days behind him; he was a force to be reckoned with.

Cliff greeted me with cheery gusto. And I was immediately struck by his easygoing, affable style as he launched into a series of engaging anecdotes about his childhood, his weight-loss journey, how YAL was different from other groups, and how he thought the Dems were faring in Trump-era Washington, D.C. He viewed Vermont senator Bernie Sanders and the outspoken congress-woman Alexandria Ocasio-Cortez as threats because "they had convictions and principles" that they stuck to. He admired that, even if he disliked their politics.

Cliff had a strategic plan for everything, I would soon discover, including my visit, which had been carefully orchestrated to give off just the right impression. I was a liberal-leaning journalist thinking about writing a book about young, right-wing activists. To his mind, that made me just the kind of person who needed to know what he was up to. The days were over for YAL to be just another student group competing with other groups for attention, throwing campus-activism events and handing out flyers, he told me. YAL, under his tutelage, was about to transform. And what luck, I was there to witness it.

Cliff's big idea was to dig into the political process, for real. He wanted to turn his "campus bodies"—in other words, the young libertarian students YAL chapters were constantly recruiting—into campaign workers for state legislative races. The plan: train them, then send them out into the field to knock on doors for "liberty-loving" candidates. This was no petty operation, Cliff assured me. The long-term goal was to elect 250 libertarians—most of them running as Republicans—by 2022, starting with the upcoming 2018 midterms. The project even had a catchy title: Operation Win at the Door.

Cliff admitted that he had drawn some inspiration from Next-Gen, Tom Steyer's progressive youth activism outfit, and another relatively new progressive group called Run for Something, which had popped up in the wake of the Trump presidency and assisted mostly young candidates in the nuts and bolts of campaigning. But Cliff said his group was going to be bigger, more energized, and better organized than either. His operation was one-stop shopping: recruit the candidates, then help them get elected, and eventually, I would later learn, keep them on a short leash and closely monitor—and direct—their legislative activities.

At the time, Cliff's plan struck me as a bit outlandish, even a little unhinged. But that was before I learned that Operation Win at the Door was a collaboration with some of YAL's richest donors—and their political networks. In 2018, Young Americans for Liberty Inc. would report raking in $5 million and spending $1.8 million of that money on the Operation Win at the Door effort. The money would largely be coming from Koch network allies.

"Whether it's 110 degrees, or whether it's snowing [with] three feet on the ground, our people are going to be out knocking on doors," Cliff declared, a satisfied smile spreading across his face.

THE FOLLOWING EVENING, AFTER DARK, THEIR BANGED-UP LAP-tops now locked away in their rooms, YAL's young acolytes gathered in the hotel ballroom to wolf down dinner and giant slices of cake. Though they cleaned up nicely, the YAL kids—with dark, ill-fitting suits, beards and ponytails for many of the men, bland office wear for many of the women—were decidedly less glamorous than attendees at TPUSA conferences. TPUSA activists favored cool jeans and colorful suit jackets for the men; high heels, pricey handbags, and stylish skirts for the women. The sartorial shortcomings of the average young libertarian were such an annoyance to one higher up, he told me he'd even considered offering how-to-dress workshops.

That night, the ballroom was dim save for the neon strobe lights that swept across the floor. Suddenly, arms rose into the air. Nostrils flared and a slow rhythmic clapping began to ricochet off the walls. The scene was part military, part cult, as an unintelligible grunting morphed into baritone chanting: "President Paul . . . President Paul . . . President Paul!"

Then, seemingly out of nowhere, there he was: Ron Paul, the 2008 presidential hopeful with his signature cap of silver hair and bushy eyebrows that resembled upside-down smiles. This was the eighty-two-year-old Texan whose young followers had risen up, after his devastating primary loss ten years earlier, to launch Young Americans for Liberty, the very organization now hosting him at their annual conference. Today, he wore a button-down checkered shirt and a maroon tie, and addressed the crowd in his nasally, Kermit the Frog voice. "Oh. Very nice, very nice. Thank you very much for that very nice welcome."

Staring intently out at his fans, Paul launched into his assessment of the nation. It was bankrupt. Americans were less free than ever before. Everything was just "a big mess." And the job of those in attendance was to "stop them." "Them" being progressives who wanted to complicate the tax system, tweak the monetary system, and keep American troops in the Afghan War, which we had no business being in. We were "fighting for our liberties," he said, the wrong way, by "killing a lot of people."

The kids listened intently as Paul went on to paint a grim portrait of a country in terrible decline. Paul was known for his rambling speeches, but tonight was a particularly rambly one. He waxed about the horrors of food industry regulations, which violated his right to eat and drink whatever he wanted, and recommended that everyone in the room read works by Murray Rothbard, an anarcho-capitalist with Holocaust denier associations.

As hard as it was to believe, this retired gynecologist was YAL's premier guru, the Joseph Smith of their eclectic libertarian church. Paul had risen to power first as a congressman in Texas, then as a presidential candidate in 2008 and 2012. (He also ran briefly in 1988 on the Libertarian Party ticket.) Sometimes referred to as "the godfather of the Tea Party," he was infamous for his obstructionist votes in Congress and had detractors on both sides of the aisle. The late-night TV host Jon Stewart once joked that Paul was like "the thirteenth floor" of a hotel because his party pretended he didn't exist. But to YAL's soldiers, he was beloved for being an underdog. Like them, he was trying to sell a free-market message few knew they needed to hear. Their stage was the American college campus. His was all of America.

When Paul was done, Cliff, sporting a pink tie that matched the color of his ruddy cheeks, catapulted onto the stage to thank him. Tonight, Cliff exuded the seemingly contradictory mix I would come to see as essential to his character. There was the boyish excitement that often overcame him when he was in the presence of one of his heroes, coupled with the canny smile of a guy who's been at this game for a while and knows that beneath the pomp, it's just politics.

Cliff loved Paul. He had the deeply principled, twelve-term congressman to thank for bringing him into the movement back in 2011, when he interned in Paul's DC office. Paul had nurtured Cliff's career and looked out for his well-being. Cliff would later tell me that he wanted other young men and women to love his political mentor—to have that magical moment when Paul's calls for "philosophical and political action" woke them up inside, too. Even if Paul was getting up there in years, he was still an icon, emblematic of a worldview Cliff was devoted to spreading. That's what YALCON was for: connecting the elders with the next generation.

This was Cliff being sentimental. Yet what had gotten the twenty-seven-year-old political operative ahead was his tactical side, his ruthlessness. He wasn't running a feel-good outfit; he was running a military operation. And while speeches entertained, he considered them the "dessert." His troops also needed their "vegetables"—Cliff-speak for training, training, and more training.

Cliff liked to make it clear that his events were strictly invite only. The kids who attended weren't off the street, with a passing interest in politics. YALCON attendees had been handpicked for their drive and their potential. But they didn't necessarily have the political gut needed to make it in his world. And that weekend, the most senior of them—campus leaders and state and regional directors—would spend hours face-to-face with political veterans whose job was—as Cliff put it—"To beat the stupid out of everybody." Trainees would take part in "persuasion workshops," where they would practice selling libertarianism to fellow classmates, sometimes using a bag of Doritos as a stand in, absorbing which sales tactics worked and which didn't. They would get tips on how to cold call new members and "text bomb" them in an effort to entice them to meetings. They would learn about "confrontational politics" (the idea that refusing to compromise is always the way to stay pure, even if that means things getting politically uncomfortable). They would be taught "the Maloney Four-Step," the recruiting process that Cliff had pioneered in Sacramento. And for recent state chairs, there would be a heavy emphasis on meeting steep quotas. Once on the job, they would be paid according to the number of chapters they opened, members they recruited, and events they held (this was sometimes referred to as "your metrics"). But even before the school year started, newbies were expected to open as many as four campus chapters, using Facebook, among other tools, to collect the names and contact info of students who fit the YAL profile.

"We're not idiots. This is how we get people here," Cliff told me at the end of the weekend, referencing his roster of popular speakers. "But ultimately, this is a training event. It's not a hype event. We invite four hundred people, and it's exclusive, and you pay for their meals and their hotels. And then you teach them what they need to do and how they need to do it to build the movement."

YALCON WASN'T MY ONLY RODEO, SO TO SPEAK. OVER THE FOUR years that I researched this book, I witnessed the recruitment and training of young people into the ultraconservative youth movement in hotels and convention centers all across the country. In Newport Beach, Alexandria, Arlington, Williamsburg, Memphis, Charlotte, and Palm Beach, I sat on white leather couches set up on crowded conference floors and listened as young attendees raged about the "ruthless silencers" who had driven them over the edge and into arch-conservatism. These attendees were fed up with the "Femi-Nazis" who called rape at the drop of a hat. They were sick of being censored, told what to say and how to say it.

I sat in packed lecture halls and learned what an effective

meme was ("news with a joke wrapped around it," a right-wing social media influencer, who would eventually be kicked off Twitter, told the room). I learned how to understand power (it is better to be "feared and respected" than "loved and manipulated")—this came from a Maryland mayor who may have been quoting Morton Blackwell but was certainly channeling Machiavelli. I sat by glimmering pools and on hotel bar stools and heard about the benefits of psychedelics and weed gummy bears and how a certain breed of twenty-something conservative kid just came to conferences to party, even if that meant subjecting themselves to a few screaming righties ranting about "bat crazy" Democrats.

I heard Fox News commentator Tucker Carlson grouse about socialists and inept federal bureaucracies. I heard Trump ally Rudolph Giuliani wail about how Democrats wanted to execute him. And I heard Dennis Prager—who'd landed on the conservative youth map in 2009 after launching PragerU—posing pressing questions like "Is America Racist?" ("No," students were told online.) In person, Prager told them that the left was "a cancer in Western civilization." At that particular event, Prager also howled about how the lefties had destroyed football, art, and American schools with their distaste for tradition, patriotism, and faith. How well you could whip up a crowd at these conferences mattered if you wanted to be asked back. And judging by the roars of the MAGA-hatted audience that night, Prager hit all the right notes.

Conferences had their own flavors. But if there was a common denominator between them—beyond a love of the free market and a hatred for liberals—it was the party atmosphere. Wander around any conservative youth conference and it's not uncommon to find wine corks in the women's bathroom and drunk twenty-somethings at the pool. Late-night hotel bacchanals, attendees told me, were a big draw. And after hours, the vibe at the host hotels could mimic out-of-control spring break with no one in charge.

"I don't throw up when I drink like ever," one young Texan

confessed, during a podcast interview about conservative youth culture. "That was the first time I did in like five years." He was discussing his conference life and the various levels of inebriation he has felt at different events. The throwing up had happened at a winter Student Action Summit hosted by Turning Point USA, the group known for having some of the wildest conferences of all.

In 2018, the *Washington Examiner* reported that a young woman attending a Student Action Summit, a year earlier, claimed she had woken up in a hotel room with someone "groping her and shoving his hands down her pants." Asked by the *Examiner* to comment, Charlie Kirk said that his organization had addressed any and all allegations, kicking men out of the conference when necessary. "We have never not dealt with an issue," he told the paper, adding, "I get very passionate about this because the implication is somehow I've swept this stuff under the rug. That's bullshit."

In 2021, a young woman alleged in a series of lengthy tweets that in 2018, when she was a 17-year-old college student, an influencer at TPUSA's Young Black leadership Summit had sexually assaulted her after plying her with alcohol. The woman said at least one conference leader wanted to "keep it quiet and just handle it internally." Two years later, when she eventually spoke with Candace Owens, the right-wing personality who sponsored the event, Owens told her she knew nothing of the complaint and urged the young woman to report "her allegations" to the police. The woman did not. Turning Point USA did not respond to requests for a comment on the incident.

It was an open secret that these events could be magnets for older conservatives trolling for hookups, multiple young attendees told me. On a shuttle bus from Palm Beach International Airport in 2019, a sixty-eight-year-old man heading to TPUSA's student summit handed me his business card and told me he was looking for his "Republican Goddess." At another TPUSA conference, Wes Goodman, a thirty-something Ohio state representative who catapulted into office on an anti-LGBTQ platform, allegedly sent a text to a young man attending the conference, telling him he was horny and asking him to come up "to have some fun" with him, according to an article in the *London Daily Mail.* The young man declined. Goodman did not respond to requests for comment from the *Daily Mail.* According to documents uncovered by the *Washington Post*, Goodman had also been accused of fondling an eighteen-year-old college student in a hotel room in 2015 during a conference hosted by the Council for National Policy, a powerful network of right-wing activists founded in 1981 by a group of conservative Christians that included Paul Weyrich and a storied Southern Baptist pastor and homeschooling advocate named Tim LaHaye. Neither Goodman nor representatives for the Council responded to requests from the *Washington Post* for comments.

For years, YAL managed to steer clear of bad press and seemed, from the outside, to be one of the cleaner, safer conferences to attend. But I would come to realize that there might have been a good reason why I was constantly chaperoned during my reporting at YALCON in 2018—and every other time I would meet with Cliff. This shadowing was likely not, as I'd assumed, just his team's way of highlighting his importance while saving Cliff's time and energy for the important job of selling Young Americans for Liberty to his donors and VIPs.

In fact, by summer 2018, the organization itself was no stranger to sexual harassment allegations. And neither was Cliff. According to interviews I later conducted with nearly a dozen people who had close ties to the organization, Cliff had an overly aggressive side—an aspect of his personality that won him some serious enemies, particularly among women, who often felt they were limited in whom they could turn to, to complain.

Women told me that young attendees at YAL conferences often traveled in packs, and older female members made a habit of keeping a watchful eye on the younger recruits, instructing them not to circulate around the conferences by themselves so as to avoid being targeted by unwanted male advances and/or harassment. They said they tried to avoid being alone in rooms with male colleagues, even at the office. There was even a special nickname for these types of men at Young Americans for Liberty: Creepertarians.

One woman told me that, in 2018, during a YAL internship in the events department, another intern she was dating had "become physically abusive." But she continued to work in the same office with him because she didn't feel like there was anyone she could tell. YAL board chairman Jeff Frazee says he was unaware of this incident.

Another woman told me that Cliff hit on her at a YAL party in 2019 in Austin, Texas. The woman, who was working as an audio engineer at the time, claims Cliff "cornered" her on the balcony and "kept repeatedly propositioning me to go to the office with him" to see his "podcasting set up." It was midnight. The woman says she declined. Frazee confirmed that YAL received a complaint from the woman about Cliff's conduct and spoke to her about it. Cliff did not respond to a request for comment.

As it turned out, these allegations were only the tip of the iceberg. While Cliff was building his Win at the Door operation, a state chair named Addyson Garner was about to start building something, too: a safe space for female colleagues at YAL to reinvent themselves as activists. It was time to speak up about what it was really like for women in YAL.

CHAPTER TEN

Candace's Conversion

By August 2018, Charlie's life had taken on celebrity-like proportions. He had an L.A. publicist who traveled with him almost everywhere. He was about to start dating a beauty pageant winner—a onetime Miss Arizona. He had a favorite couch in the West Wing. And he was calling conservatism "the new punk rock." As to the racism allegations that had plagued his organization, he now had a powerful rebuttal: an electrifying Black YouTube sensation named Candace Owens.

The twenty-nine-year-old, renowned for her storytelling skills and her mix of Fox News bluster and Oprah-style self-empowerment, was now miraculously by Charlie's side almost all the time. With her high cheekbones and pugnacious personality, she could play both seductress and acid-tongued critic, online and off, telling a group of conservative donors that summer that she had "a fire burning in my belly" for the conservative cause. To her online critics, her tweets were brutal. She once called conservative media personality Tomi Lahren a "vile human being" and told Chelsea Clinton that Bill and Hillary were "trash parents." "No one thinks Lena Dunham is happy," Candace said to a crowd in Bozeman, Montana. "She doesn't shave her armpits." She was perfect for the Trump era.

Candace occasionally rubbed her elders the wrong way with her inexorable hunger for the limelight—with her avowed desire to be "the most famous Black conservative anyone has ever met!," as she told the wife of an advisory board member at a small Chicago area fundraiser when Charlie was introducing her around. Nonetheless, she would soon become a favorite on the far-right talk-show circuit, as well as TPUSA's "director of urban engagement," and then its communications director, an out-of-office job that allowed the words "Turning Point USA" to appear below her name on her numerous TV appearances.

For Charlie, finding Candace amounted to a political rebirth and a rewarding punch in the gut to his critics who kept insinuating that he was racist. For Candace, forging a partnership with a conservative movement that had historically had a discomfiting if not downright hostile relationship with the Black community was a somewhat risky move. But it was easy to understand why the Republican Party had gotten behind Candace. With the electorate so closely divided, the GOP didn't need a majority of Black voters to take a swing state like North Carolina or Florida. They only needed to turn a few percentage points. And they were betting that a dynamic communicator like Candace could help get them there—during the upcoming midterms, during the 2020 election, and beyond.

On an April evening in 2018, on a carpeted stage at UCLA with a microphone in hand and Charlie by her side, Candace was on full display. She was sporting a provocative, albeit cryptic TPUSA T-shirt—"*Hate Us, 'Cuz They Ain't Us*" it read—with chic wide-bottomed black slacks and a pair of gold pointy-toed high heels—amounting to a fashion mix that only she seemed capable of pulling off: upscale, downscale, and in-your-face aggressive.

For weeks, she and Charlie had been stopping off at campuses around the country together as part of their "Hard Truth Tour," telling American college kids the truth about racism (that it didn't exist) and, in some cases, mocking them over their efforts to make their campuses more inclusive. *Silly, silly people.*

At Stanford, Charlie told the crowd that he had tried to grab a coffee in a campus coffee shop, but they were doing diversity training and had closed early. He'd been cranky all afternoon. "They picked the wrong day . . . ," he said, his voice trailing off, referring to the training and chuckling to himself. Candace leaned forward and chuckled into her microphone, too.

If students wanted to play "Oppression Olympics," don't bother, he told the group a few minutes later. Candace would win. Candace nodded, knowingly. "I'm great at that event. I'm like the Olympic star when it comes to Oppression Olympics."

"Candace grew up in poverty," Charlie explained, telling the crowd that his new sidekick had "more uncles in prison than not in prison," an alcoholic father, and a host of family members on public assistance.

Candace smiled at the crowd, as if to say, *True. True.*

Today, at UCLA, inside an auditorium decorated with Turning Point USA banners, they were meeting with the campus Republican club. Most attendees were dressed casually in the standard student wardrobe of T-shirts and jeans, though a few showed up in pricey suits that seemed out of place in Southern California. In the back, hecklers frequently erupted when Candace spoke. (Later, she would dismiss them as BLM activists, though there seemed to be little indication that they were representatives of any ideological subgroup. They just didn't like her.)

Though she clearly had more poise and charisma than Charlie—and was four and a half years older—Candace let Charlie take the lead. He was paying the bills; it was his show, after all. His talk was pure white bread, praising the United States and its "benevolence." America was "charitable," "generous," "productive," "aspirational." The list went on and on. As he spoke, a chant of "U.S.A., U.S.A." broke out from the first few rows.

Charlie fed on the energy. He knew how to work the crowd. And those protesters, they weren't a nuisance. They were the most important members of the audience. What was the point of having them here if he wasn't going to rile them up?

As a group, American Blacks, he asserted, were the richest Blacks in the world. So stop complaining, seemed to go his thinking. "Blacks in America have done better than Blacks anywhere across the world." It was unclear what data he had used to arrive at this assertion. But since he was the one onstage, running the show, he didn't have to say.

From the back of the room, an angry voice went up. "America is the only country that has had four hundred years of slavery. Let's talk about that."

Charlie was ready for it.

". . . Just so you get the facts straight, America was the first western country to abolish slavery and fought a war over it," he shot back, either completely unaware—or simply not caring—that he was flat-out wrong. By the time America granted freedom to enslaved people in 1865, all the major imperial nations—Britain, France, the Netherlands, and Spain—had already moved to do so, some more than three decades prior. It didn't matter to Charlie; the way he saw it, it wasn't a crime to speak your own personal truth, even if the silencers were really stuck on their supposed "facts."

"But look folks, it's okay to hear something you disagree with every once in a while," he quipped with a smug smile. A few minutes later, Charlie put his microphone to his lips again for another dose of cultural poison. "Just because you're offended, doesn't mean you are right."

No one in the back seemed to appreciate the advice.

Tensions were rising, the room now immersed in just enough

of Charlie's acid-laced assertions for Candace, the gifted rabble-rouser, to jump in and inject her own thorny barbs. Layers of story on top of Charlie's layers of lies.

"Here's what I want to say," Candace let out, as if answering a question, although none had been asked. She brought the microphone up to her lips, then abruptly launched into her own personal assessment of race relations in the United States.

". . . There is an ideological Civil War happening," Candace began. "Black people that are focused on their past and shouting about slavery and Black people that are focused on their futures." Candace scanned the room, as if laying down a challenge for all Black people to abandon the illusion that white liberals care about them. It was a searching, hungry look.

". . . What you are seeing happening," Candace continued, "is victim mentality versus victor mentality."

Charlie, from his perch beside her, pointed proudly at Candace. He liked the vision, too, the imaginary story that his new partner in crime was unfolding before them. "That's great, by the way," he furrowed his brow and took a swig of water. "That's great. I love that."

Candace kept going. ". . . Victim mentality is not cool. I don't know why people like being oppressed. It is the weirdest thing I have ever heard." She began to mock her detractors in the back. "'I love oppression,'" she taunted, shrugging her shoulders and flashing the room a look of grim dismay. "'We're oppressed.'"

Her voice grew louder and more strident. "Four hundred years of slavery. Jim Crow . . . Which . . . ," she continued sharply, "by the way, none of you guys lived through. Your grandparents did and it's embarrassing that you utilize their history." She was pointing at them now, her manicured hand jabbing the air, as if this was her time, her time to unleash all her generalized pent-up rage and ire. "You utilize their history," she repeated, perhaps for emphasis. "And you come in here with more emotion than they had when they were living through it, more emotion than they had when they were living through it. It's embarrassing."

Charlie beamed at the crowd, then at Candace, assessing the situation. "Damn, you teach us girl," he boomed. "Yeah!"

It was easy to see that the twenty-eight-year-old Candace Owens harbored deep resentment toward any Black American who dared suggest that the road to equity was hard-fought and still unfinished. Her rhetoric was often crass, inflammatory, even disturbing. But when pared down to its most essential form, it wasn't idle banter. Candace believed all people, no matter their race, should be held to the same standards, so that when someone succeeds it has nothing to do with the color of their skin. These are beliefs held by a host of Black conservatives: former secretary of state Condoleezza Rice, South Carolina senator Tim Scott, and most prominently, though perhaps more radically, Supreme Court Justice Clarence Thomas. In his recent biography of the longest-serving justice, *The Enigma of Clarence Thomas*, historian Corey Robin suggests that Thomas's rulings and speeches aren't so much against racism as fatalistic about it. Whites will always be racist, even the most well-intentioned ones. The system—government or any other—is not there to help Black Americans, so why extend it, grow it, or try to improve upon it. Just let it wither away. You are the only one you can rely on. So, embrace the free market.

Candace has done her reading of the "modern" conservative canon, not to be mistaken for the cadre of more serious, densely written classics that had spewed from the pens of eighteenth-century Irish philosophers and twentieth-century Austrian economists, some of whom she has also read. But often the guides she called upon in public were the screamers. She quoted Andrew Breitbart, the self-proclaimed journalist and founder of Breitbart News, with abandon. "Politics is downstream from culture," she liked to tell anyone who would listen. Thomas Sowell, the ninety-year-old Black economist and social theorist, was another one of her idols. Sowell had been pushing out his theories at a rapid clip for fifty years, in more than thirty books, insisting, among other things, that one of the biggest problems facing Black America was Black people themselves.

Sowell's ideas are not exactly welcome in mainstream American economics. On the right, of course, this makes him a cherished voice. And Candace would soon be a cherished voice, too, on the conference circuit and the GOP gravy train, as she continued to insist to her audiences that racism was dead.

Candace hadn't always been this kind of conservative; in fact, not so long ago, she hadn't really considered herself conservative at all. She says she wasn't political until her early twenties. Before that, she didn't even vote. She considered herself vaguely liberal and was blunt in her distaste for "the totally bonkers shenanigans of the Republican Tea Party." Yet to hear her tell it now, her childhood and early twenties were a slow burn to the other side.

WHEN CANDACE WAS BORN IN APRIL 1989, IN STAMFORD, CONnecticut, a fast-growing exurb of New York City, she hardly cried, her mother, recalled. She was the third in a family of four—three girls, one boy. George H. W. Bush had just been sworn into office and a group of young Black and Latino teenagers would soon be wrongfully accused of attacking and nearly killing a jogger forty miles away, in Central Park. They would go to jail for years, before being exonerated in a case that would expose the country to the horrors of police malfeasance and the vulnerability of young men of color in the face of it.

The Black population of Stamford mostly lived downtown, a rare, inner city urban core in the white, WASPy suburbs of Fairfield County. Candace's family lived in a cramped, cockroach-infested apartment in a seventeen-story tower, one of Stamford's first low-income housing facilities. In the 1980s and 1990s, Stamford's depressed urban core began to perk up as hedge funds and financial services firms established footholds and moved downtown. But that boom bypassed Candace's neighborhood, a rundown area flanked by highways and plagued with drugs, poverty, and street crime. Candace's mother, Evelyn, worked at times as a school bus attendant. Her father, Robert Jr., was, at one point, a property manager. But money grew increasingly tight and their marriage slowly disintegrated. By the time Candace was in elementary school, her paternal grandparents converted their attic into a bedroom and insisted that the family move across town into a mostly white enclave of small bungalows and two-story shoeboxes where they lived. Yards were small but well-kept and the neighborhood children spent hours outside, climbing trees and playing pretend games. Her parents eventually split and Candace would maintain that it was her time with her grandparents that had the most indelible influence on her future self.

Candace's grandfather was stern, straitlaced, and deeply committed to his grandchildren. Born on a sharecropping farm in sleepy Fayetteville, North Carolina, Robert Sr. started working at age five, tying tobacco leaves to drying sticks to be cured before shipment. He moved north during the Great Migration and owned and operated a Stamford dry cleaners. But he never forgot where he came from. Candace remembers him telling stories of hiding under his bed when the Ku Klux Klan came around and shot at the house and how his own father shot back. Candace loves that story. "This was masculinity," she once told me. "And it wasn't toxic."

Robert and Nola Owens ran their business together and attended church and read the Bible daily. It was an ordered life, strongly rooted in faith. "If you need knowledge, read the Bible" was how Candace's sister Brittany described their ethos. Nola had a bad hip and was often bed-ridden. When she was well, she made pound cake and baked mac and cheese. When she wasn't well, Candace would spend hours with her, keeping her company.

Candace's grandfather contained her. He was strict and didn't take guff. She feared disappointing him. Once, when in the middle of the night Candace turned the house thermostat up, he said nothing. Then the next morning, he prayed out loud, as she and her sisters were having breakfast: "Lord, please help Candace to realize she should not be messing with the heat in the middle of the night." That incident made her cry.

Another time, during Candace's early years in elementary school, she and her sisters hid in the bathroom and tried to conceal the fact that one of them had fallen out of a tree while they were playing in the yard. Their grandfather said nothing about the incident but told the girls a story from his own childhood: about a girl who had been beaten with a baseball bat on the way home from school. The girl didn't tell her parents because she didn't want to get in trouble. Then, "she died in her sleep because she was bleeding on the inside."

"Brittany fell off the tree," the girls immediately blurted out.

In school, Candace was smart, an independent firecracker, who found classwork easy. A voracious reader, she plowed through books, picking up anything that was in the house. Harry Potter, biographies from the school library, anything her mother was reading. She had been in a gifted program in middle school, took AP classes in high school.

From an early age, she sought out the limelight, in fifth grade playing Daddy Warbucks's secretary Grace in her elementary school's production of *Annie*. In eighth grade she landed the star role of Sandy in the school's production of *Grease*, even though her sister Brittany, a year and a half younger, thought she would have been better suited to the role of the toughened Rizzo. Candace took the role seriously and was competitive, telling her sister: "I'm going to learn my lines in one day so I don't have to be onstage next week with a script in my hand. I'll be the only one that knows my lines."

Despite her grandparents' relative success, Candace says that many of the adults around her were in and out of jail, on public assistance, consumed by drugs and alcohol, sometimes homeless. The dysfunction around her unsettled her. When she spoke about it, she didn't sound sympathetic; she sounded angry. Through her lens, there were a lot of adults who did not fulfill their obligations. And like Cliff Maloney, she saw up close that the help they got didn't help.

She learned that lesson herself during her senior year of high school.

In February 2007, Candace received a series of disturbing and searingly racist voice mails from four anonymous young men who sat in a parked car together to prank her. They threatened to kill her, to tar and feather her, to put a bullet in her head. They listed famous Black people who had died. "Martin Luther King Jr., look at that n****r, he's dead." The "n" word peppered the calls. When she told a teacher about it the next day, she was immediately sent to the principal's office. The school called the police. It turned out one of the occupants of the car was a friend from school she had recently had a falling out with. Another was the fourteen-year-old son of Stamford's mayor, Dannel Malloy, who would eventually become Connecticut's eighty-eighth governor. Soon, the NAACP got involved, encouraging her father to sue the Stamford Board of Education. Her mother opposed the lawsuit, worrying it added a layer of family strife to an already painful situation. Candace skipped six weeks of school, while the town gossiped about the merits of the case. Was she a liar? An opportunist? A victim? Meanwhile, the NAACP staged a press conference on the steps of the school, with Candace—who grew to feel like a political prop—in tow. The story made the local papers and the news. The case eventually settled out of court; her family won $37,500. Her classmate did not return to the school.

Candace, emotionally broken and bruised, did. Her first day

back, two security guards accompanied her; one stood in the hall-way while the other attended class with her. Candace had been cast as a "victim of a hate crime" by left-wing activist groups. In time, she came to believe that the incident was overblown and that none of the young people involved—or her community—benefited from the way the incident was handled. She felt used by politi-cal activists, and the young men, she believed, were ultimately raked through the coals for bad behavior that she saw as stupid and mean-spirited, yes, but not necessarily an indication of deep-seated racism on their part. She grew depressed and developed an eating disorder that lasted years. Candace, eager to start her life anew, headed for college. She made it through to her junior year, at the University of Rhode Island, where she was studying journal-ism, borrowing money along the way. That's when she dropped out, saddled with over $100,000 in debt and lacking the means to keep going.

She headed for Manhattan. And after stints as an assistant at *Vogue* and in an entry-level job at a Wall Street private equity firm, she decided to go out on her own. First, she launched a BuzzFeed-like news website called Degree180, where one of her writers made fun of Donald Trump's penis. Positioning herself as a jaded *Cosmo* girl, she herself wrote a piece entitled "Fuck Girl Code, I Can Hook Up with Your Ex-Boyfriend If I Want To." The website didn't really gain traction, and she was soon on to the next thing.

Candace was nearing twenty-seven and decided to take charge—not just of her present, but of her past. Bullies had haunted her. She wanted to finally take them on—bully the bullies—and get on with her life. In April 2016, she launched her new project: Social Autopsy, a website that sought to out anonymous bullies who operated online. She began with a $75,000 Kickstarter cam-paign. And to spread the word, she produced a promo video called "Wave Goodbye to Cyberbullies and Trolls: SocialAutopsy.com."

The site would be a place for victims of bullies to out their predators. It would be a live database of sorts, and a way to take back control, as these bullies would now have their own personal information publicized. It was a half-baked business plan with a lot of unanswered questions—the first being how did you know that the people being inserted into the database were really bullies and not just more victims? Further, what's the definition of a bully, anyway? But those were just details, at least for now. Candace, good at getting publicity, was going after it.

When Zoe Quinn, the victim of a 2014 cyberbullying attack that later became known as Gamergate, first learned of Candace's plan via her promo video, she immediately reached out to Candace and told her about the online world she was about to walk into, according to Jesse Singal, then a writer for *New York* magazine who wrote about the incident. Quinn had recently launched an emergency hotline for victims of online abuse. And she told Candace that corners of the web were overwhelmingly male environments that could grow vindictive—and misogynistic—fast. She thought Candace's plan was the perfect tool, in fact, for an online harasser to use himself. All he had to do was claim one of his victims was a bully. She warned Candace that when cyberbullies learned about her site, they would come after her, too. And they would be brutal, seeing her as their enemy. Candace brushed off the call. She didn't see Quinn as an ally or a source of information for a field she herself knew little about; she saw her the way she was comfortable seeing a lot of people: as an opponent.

Within a few hours of releasing the promo video, as more people learned of her plan to create a database of names and contact info for alleged bullies, Candace did indeed become the target of online bullies. Both harassers and those who'd been harassed finally found something they could agree upon: their dislike of Candace and her site. They didn't want it. She was the recipient of an open letter on Medium, written by another Gamergate victim who called her a "fucking idiot" and "a goddamn train wreck." She was deluged with racist hate mail. Her project became a much-maligned topic on Reddit. Eventually, Kickstarter shut down her campaign. But out of the frustration and failure came something far more elusive: attention. People were talking about her. She was, suddenly, a presence.

Still, for Candace, the entire debacle represented something much bigger than just fame. Once again, she was facing so-called friendly liberals (Zoe Quinn and her like-minded allies were supposed to be advocates) who saw themselves as do-gooders, in the business of bettering the world. But they were actually hurting her. To her mind, like the local civil rights advocates back in Stamford, who had turned a high school fracas into a race relations reckoning that she believed ignored what was best for her, this set of internet liberals were now twisting her efforts to do good into their own self-serving opportunities for deep-seated criticism that furthered their own profiles. When Singal wrote about the debacle, he depicted Candace as a naïf, a crazy conspiracy theorist convinced that Quinn and her buddies were pretend victims—that they, themselves, had created the accounts of the harassers. Just as she would soon deny systemic racism, Candace now did not believe in this online world of male predators. The women who were claiming to be victims must be making it all up. And the media was serving as their enablers.

This episode helped tip the scales. Candace was growing increasingly disenchanted with the left—the left-wing media, left-wing girls, left-wing anything. She was crossing to the other side. At the time, Candace sometimes tells audiences, her interest in Trump and how he was being treated by the media was another red flag for her, a sign that there was something terribly wrong with the left. He was a racist, a misogynist, a hater of gay people. The media wanted her to believe all that. But it didn't ring true to

Candace, she says. Maybe the guy didn't have enough experience to be president, sure, but she was wholly unconvinced that Donald Trump had one racist bone in his body. Whether this conviction was the final impetus to switch allegiances, or just how she chooses to tell her conversion story, is something only Candace knows. And in her 2020 memoir *Blackout: How Black America Can Make Its Second Escape from the Democrat Plantation*, Candace says her grandparents were the ones who first introduced her to conservativism, long before she even realized what that was. They were Democrats, but Candace believes that if her grandfather was still alive, he would count himself a Republican. "It is necessary to know who my grandfather was in his day to understand who I am in mine," she wrote.

However Candace got there, her next venture included a new persona: that of a Black conservative.

A tireless worker, there was no stopping her and the building of her personal brand. Candace launched yet another handily named enterprise: Red Pill Black. It was a YouTube channel that featured entertaining videos about the new Candace Owens and her role as a Black woman coming out conservative. The video that catapulted her to fame was a crisp ninety-second clip in which she played a mom, dad, and daughter. It was called: "Mom, Dad, I'm a conservative!"

It was tight, succinct, and, to many, hilarious. Standing against a brick wall, Candace announces, proudly: "Mom, Dad, I'm a lesbian. I like girls."

"Oh, sweetheart," coos her champagne-swigging mother, also played by her. "We always knew . . ." Candace, as the mom, places her hands on her knees and shakes her head with glee. "Brave soul."

In the meantime, a backward-baseball-hat-wearing dad, Candace again, chimes in with a low-baritone voice: "The bottom line, we just want our children to be happy. . . ."

Now playing the daughter again, Candace offers another piece of news: ". . . Also, I think I might be a conservative."

"Ahhhhhh," Candace chokes on her champagne, clutches her chest with two hands, and shakes her head in disbelief, the mother in distress. "I don't understand," she wails. "I can't breathe."

"Hey, get that camera out of my wife's face," the father booms, while the mother, regaining her composure, offers: "We're going to get you somebody to talk to you," as if suggesting a sort of conversion therapy for the politically wayward offspring. "You're going to work through this entire mess."

The mother then grows increasingly agitated, perhaps processing the news more. She wonders what "our Spanish-speaking" friends will think about this and how the neighbors will respond knowing their daughter "is in the KKK!!!"

At the end of the video, the distressed mother begs her daughter: "Sweetie, can you please just be gay."

The video went platinum, reaching millions of viewers around the world. Some watched from France, others from as far away as Brazil, where perhaps not coincidentally the once low-key, largely underground far-right movement was erupting into the mainstream, sweeping up young and old alike. Her timing could not have been better. Coming out conservative had put Candace on the map.

CHARLIE FIRST LAID EYES ON CANDACE IN NOVEMBER 2017 AT the Breakers, the onetime Vanderbilt Mansion in Palm Beach that is now a luxury hotel. They'd each been invited to Restoration Weekend, the annual conclave meant to bring together the finest minds and wallets on the far right for a few days of sun and plotting, by the gathering's founder, David Horowitz, the far-right strategy guru.

Horowitz had once had close ties to the Black Panthers and thus could denounce left-wing radicals in a way that only someone who had once spent a lot of time with them could. He had a skill for finding young, up-and-coming political operators who could help architect the anti-immigration, anti-Muslim schemes to which he and his movement allies have dedicated their lives. When Trump senior policy advisor Stephen Miller was still in high school, he bonded with Horowitz, and Horowitz powered Miller's meteoric rise through the party's hard-right apparatus. By his thirty-second birthday, Miller would be able to claim credit for the Trump administration policy to separate immigrant parents from the children at the border. Horowitz also influenced the thinking of Steve Bannon, the MAGA world influencer. The fact that Horowitz had taken an interest in Candace was a promising sign for the twenty-eight-year-old.

Charlie first spotted Candace onstage in a carpeted ballroom, at what was a very hot discussion titled "On Second Thought: How Leftism Creates Conservatives," moderated by Dave Rubin, a onetime leftist turned conservative-leaning political commentator whose own personal journey fighting "woke-ism" was one of his favorite on-air topics. He would soon become one of Candace's fiercest allies. Joining her on the panel was James Damore, the former Google engineer, recently fired for airing his thoughts in a company memo to his officemates on why men were better suited to tech jobs than women; and Tammy Bruce, a former Democratic campaigner turned Fox News pundit. But for Charlie, Candace was the one who made the greatest impression. She was vivacious, and pristinely dressed in a navy jacket and white blouse that matched her pearl earrings. Her critique of the Democratic Party was stirring and vivid, and she did not fear overstatement. The Democrats saw Black people as "whiny people, who jump on top of cars and wanted handouts." She made it clear that no one was going to shut her up. She also knew how to make a conservative audience erupt in spontaneous cheers.

By the time the panel was over, Charlie "knew he had to have her."

"You sit down, stay here," he told Candace, rushing to text a staff member. "I am going to get you a contract."

They hit it off immediately, and that night, over dinner, they talked for hours. While Candace nibbled on a salad, Charlie wolfed down a steak and they started planning. Candace's mission was to expose the left for what it was: a bunch of power-hungry totalitarian scolds who wanted to take freedoms and reduce Black people to a state of dependence. Candace had a theory that before long, a major celebrity would break out of the "liberal matrix." She predicted it would be Kanye West.

"Is that the one married to Beyoncé?" Charlie asked, admitting later that he was "not a pop culture aficionado."

Candace had chuckled and promised to download some music for him and send it over.

That summer and the following fall, as Candace's star rose, she and Charlie became glued at the hip.

Together, they visited with donors in their sprawling homes and stopped off at various far-right conferences, where Charlie introduced her around and described her as a "Black truth-telling woman." Once, in 2019, they took a fishing trip with Foster Friess, the Wyoming investor and right-wing philanthropist. They frequented the White House, spending time with the First Family and the president, on at least one occasion watching TV with him. Candace found the president refreshingly honest, a funny guy whose humor was underappreciated by the mainstream media. Trump would soon become one of Candace's biggest fans, too, telling his Twitter followers that Candace is "so good for our country," and calling in to *Fox & Friends* to call her "the hottest thing out there right now." Together Candace and Charlie went to Jerusalem to christen the new American embassy. And they hit up the daily news shows—some mornings waking at 3:45 to make the popular AM slots.

Candace was Charlie's project, and he was showing her off. Together, they were turning heads and hoping to change minds about what it meant to be a young, modern-day conservative in Trump's America. It was a campaign still in its infancy, but Candace, an entertainer at heart, had found her calling.

CHAPTER ELEVEN

Boots on the Ground

I was in Cliff Maloney's corner office at YAL's suburban DC headquarters on a sunny afternoon in September 2018. He was all business, hovering confidently over an oversized wood desk, by a bookcase stacked with leadership guides—Jim Collins's *Good to Great*, and the self-help bible *How to Win Friends and Influence People* by Dale Carnegie. Just a few weeks earlier when hanging out at YALCON, I had still detected in Cliff little hints of the scrappy theater kid who had crawled his way out of the blue-collar 'burbs. When onstage interviewing his hero Ron Paul, Cliff gave off the golly-gee aura of a guy who still couldn't believe his good fortune. But today, Cliff looked and sounded like a hard-charging CEO, the sleeves of his white oxford rolled up, his laminated building ID attached to his belt buckle, as he talked about making "the best use of your time" and "finding out where your competitive edge is"—corporate-ese I hadn't heard from him before. On the wall next to his desk was a sign: "Do what you can, where you are, with what you have."

At the messy cubicles outside his office, though, the vibe was pretty juvenile. That's where a gaggle of twenty-somethings—mostly men dressed in faded T-shirts, baseball caps, sneakers, and wrinkled khakis—managed field staff and some students as they grew their YAL chapters and the group's profile on American campuses. Despite the casual vibe, however, the pressure to produce in Cliff's world was always intense. And when a staff member did persuade someone in the field to land a chapter, the sound of a cowbell reverberated through the office. Cliff couldn't help but boast about the incentivizing ring. "We love the cowbell," he told me. And it seemed to be working. Cliff was supersizing YAL's growth. A dozen new chapters were now popping up every month of the school year, as evidenced by the group's glossy annual report that noted how, by the end of 2017, YAL had planted its liberty flag on over 900 campuses.

CLIFF, AS ALWAYS, HAD INVITED ME TO HIS OFFICE FOR A VERY specific reason: to show me how he was putting his recruits to work for Operation Win at the Door, the initiative he had announced at YALCON. The plan was to elect 250 libertarian-leaning state legislative candidates by 2022 by deploying YAL's troops of highly trained door knockers to their districts. Cliff flipped open a folder and picked up a thick report on a twenty-seven-year-old academic advisor at a small Christian college near Niles, Michigan, who was also a city council member in the town of eleven thousand. He was running for a state house seat on a limited government platform and wanted Cliff's support.

The report was part of a complex, multistep application process Cliff's team had created to choose which candidates to endorse. It included detailed information on the candidate's political life, his fundraising achievements, and pages and pages on the crowded primary race he was in (there were five other candidates). It also included the results of a lengthy survey he had filled out—a sort of a libertarian litmus test to see if he was a "true believer." Being a no-spend libertarian meant being comfortable saying no. No to pet

projects. No to programs your well-meaning buddies in the legislature wanted. No to sentimental spending on the needy members
of your community. So, it was important to know if candidates had
the guts for that, and whether they could stand to be unpopular
and take the jeers of other moderate Republicans and Democrats
pressuring them to vote for fluff.

Cliff eyeballed the report sternly, indicating he was in a no-
nonsense mood. "Too many red flags," he quipped, tapping the
report with his index finger, as he began to read from it.

"His lack of connection to the liberty movement is concerning.
He claims to have 'flown under the radar' due to his role on the
Niles City Council." Cliff explained that this meant that the candidate was using his seat on the council—generally a nonpartisan
position—to excuse away the fact that he had not made connections with local libertarian-leaning organizations, even though the
national network was well-connected on the ground there. Michigan was home to then U.S. congressman Justin Amash, one of the
most famous libertarian-leaning Republican in DC. And the locals
hadn't heard of the guy.

"Just a good-looking kind of charismatic guy," Cliff acknowledged, peering down at a photo of the beaming candidate. "But we
could not find validation that he really stood up for our principles,"
he told me.

The candidate was one of five hundred seeking YAL's support
and one of over four hundred who would eventually be rejected.
Those who got kinder receptions included an NRA instructor
from Georgia, a gas and oil executive in Texas, a former YAL
chapter leader, a Liberty University graduate, and a volunteer with
Ron Paul's 2008 campaign. They tended to be in the liberty loop:
they knew YAL or one of YAL's alumni, worked for one of YAL's
donors, or had strong connections to the energy industry. In total,
Operation Win at the Door now had sixty-one dogs in the fight—
candidates Cliff hoped to get elected to state houses and state

assemblies. Some had been endorsed in their state's primaries; some were being endorsed in the upcoming general election. Door knockers were headed to their districts imminently. And in other cases they were already there, casing neighborhoods and brandishing flyers.

Reaching YAL's 2022 target had a lot of ramifications, Cliff told me. So it was important to pick the right candidates. It would mean that "we own 5 percent of America's legislators. And we think that's the beginning of the snowball effect. So you figure there's 5,000 state legislators . . . and so we have 250 of them . . . Remember, the whole point of this is not to win elections. The point of this is to get the ideas that we care about to become mainstream."

Cliff smiled slyly. "It's not the actual winning of the election that matters. It's that once that person is in, they now can vote for the bills and the policies that we think will be great for everybody."

These bills and policies were not in fact great for everybody. Libertarian-leaning Republicans supported cuts to programs relied on by the nation's most at-risk families: public assistance, workplace safety measures for manual labor jobs, healthcare, and public education. Still, Cliff, ever the salesman, wanted to put a kind face on a massive political endeavor that was in many ways very unkind.

Sitting back in his leather chair, Cliff told me that he and his team also had their sights on the RINOs—Republicans in Name Only—who didn't understand what small government really meant. What Cliff was talking about were moderates, and he was no fan. In his eyes, politicians who compromised were bad politicians.

"It's not just on the left. I mean, we are having a civil war on the right for the future of what it means to be a Republican.

There's like an epidemic of bad Republicans out there who run as Republicans, but then they vote to raise taxes. They vote to spend more money. They vote for more government regulation. They vote against civil liberties."

It was six weeks before the 2018 midterms, which were largely being seen as a bellwether for the Trumpification of the country. The pundits were obsessed with the federal races, making bold predictions. Rachel Maddow insisted we were headed for a blue wave. John King was expecting "hand-to-hand combat" for both House and Senate seats. The folks on *Fox & Friends* were advising candidates to sing the president's praises and not underestimate his popularity.

Cliff told me he and his team were flying under the radar. And that was fine by him. It was easier that way to catch the enemy off-guard and win more races. As for the Trump Show, Cliff knew Trump was capturing the attention of a lot of Americans. But he refused to be distracted by the dazzle. If the president supported something he liked, he often told me—say, cutting bureaucratic red tape in Washington, D.C.—he was happy to praise him. When Trump supported budget increases, he was eager to denounce him. But at the end of the day a lot of what happened in Washington was a "popularity contest." And Cliff saw himself as engaged in something a lot more serious: a game of real principles. He truly believed he could transform American politics and spread those principles from his perch in Arlington.

His short-term goal was to jettison local pols into office in order to make state legislators more friendly to the austere economics he and his associates stood for. But his long-term goal was broader and more far reaching. "We're building a bench, a farm team, the minor leagues," he added, looking wistfully out at the parking lot outside his office window. What he hoped to do was help support these state-level candidates, he told me, so they could eventually run for federal office. Maybe no one was paying attention now, but Cliff had no intention of being a bit player. He wanted to one day put a libertarian in the White House.

Cliff was excited about his plan and the thrill his liberty-loving charges were going to get out of being able to say: "I helped get that candidate elected." As he ushered me to the elevator, we passed a glass-encased conference room. Inside were half a dozen disheveled-looking young men—campaign leaders—huddled together in conversation, Styrofoam cups of now lukewarm coffee and empty soda cans scattered on the conference table in front of them. On the wall next to them was a map of the United States, with pins stuck into various locales: Texas, New Hampshire, Wisconsin, indicating where door knockers would soon be headed. "Restlessly honor the vision" was scrawled in block letters on a white board on the adjacent wall.

"That's our war room," Cliff told me.

Cliff's connection to the libertarian movement's biggest donors and their own carefully defined agenda for the country was not something he liked to talk about. And while some YAL leaders were relatively open with me about how the Koch network and YAL worked together—the Charles Koch Institute and the Charles Koch Foundation had given YAL's own foundation millions of dollars over the years and Koch network–affiliated groups like Americans for Prosperity and the Grassroots Leadership Academy worked closely with YAL on events—Cliff operated more secretively. He kept his relationship with his donors close to his chest.

By September 2018, as YAL embarked on a massive effort to plant libertarian candidates inside state houses, it seemed obvious that Cliff was increasingly being viewed as a valuable part of the larger libertarian movement donor base. Focusing on state legislators as a means of pushing forward a right-wing agenda had long been a conservative movement strategy and one that the nation's most famous libertarians—Charles and David Koch—had fully embraced. The network and its conservative Republican allies had become so good at this strategy that, between 2010 and 2014, they had gained more than nine hundred seats in state legislative bodies, filling them with pro-business candidates supportive of skeletal government. And by 2016, Republicans controlled both state legislative chambers in thirty-two of the fifty-states—ensuring more all-around conservative policies.

Primarying Republicans—or mounting aggressive challenges to party incumbents that libertarians deemed too light on the free market—was a Koch specialty. The strategy was to instill fear in more moderate Republicans who dared support measures some of their constituents might really want, like gun ownership monitoring, business licensing requirements, and local rail projects that reduced the number of gas guzzling cars on the road. In other words, if they weren't supporters of measures that libertarian CEOs viewed as good for their bottom lines, they were targets.

In addition to his passion for politics, Cliff seemed to be emulating the Koch ethos in other ways as well, exhibiting the head-to-the-grindstone, no-nonsense drive of the wildly controversial Wichita, Kansas, brothers. The two had built up the gas and oil empire they inherited from their father and founded a number of nonprofits. While the business and the nonprofits were separate entities, anyone who had read Christopher Leonard's *Kochland*, about the rise of Koch Industries and the development of its faithful and effective executives, knew the Koch way was universal. Koch employees—for both the for-profit and nonprofit outfits—were expected to be independent, driven, and ever on the lookout for expansion opportunities. In his own book, *Good Profit*, Charles Koch called the independence he gave employees "Decision Rights."

Koch executives were supposed to think like entrepreneurs,

and Cliff did. He treated YAL like a constantly growing startup, leveraging his connections to his wealthy donor base and his devotion to libertarian values to achieve political power. Seen through this light, Cliff was a model. In 2018, he was rewarded for his hard work, taking home $170,000 from YAL, nearly doubling the $86,000 that he had received a year earlier.

THREE DAYS BEFORE THE ELECTION, CLIFF HAD ARRANGED FOR ME to visit a YAL "deployment" camp—a two-story AirBnB condo perched above a winding road outside of Manchester, New Hampshire, a New England mill town dotted with Irish pubs for the old-timers and newly refurbished loft buildings for the gentrifiers. It was early morning as I sat with a dozen or so young men and one woman. They were gathering for their pregame meeting inside the condo's starkly decorated living room. Most had been there for weeks and were showing signs of campaign wear and tear: stubbly chins, soiled sneakers, and wrinkled jeans that looked like they hadn't been washed in weeks.

Despite the growing membership numbers that Cliff shared with donors in official annual reports, there weren't actually enough YAL warriors on American college campuses willing to fulfill Operation Win at the Door's urgent mission. To meet his quota—one million doors knocked—Cliff had resorted to posting ads online for "election coordinators," a fancy name for door knockers. The ads had attracted a string of sometimes down-and-out young people who often drove hours each way for the work. The street hires I met included a punk rock fan from Rhode Island who had quit a job at CVS to work for YAL and a recovering opioid addict from an old mining town in Ohio who was rebuilding his life after a stint in jail. The month-long job, with free housing and food (they were paid a flat fee of $2,300) was a boon, they both told me—never mind the ten-hour days and six-day workweeks. Newcomers like these—whom Cliff and his team maintain were carefully vetted—were often housed in small rental units with both male and female YAL college students. Later, one would complain to me that this often felt unsafe.

In keeping with Cliff's attention to detail, all his warriors had been carefully prepped, spending hours and hours learning protocol, procedure, and the language of the job. Cliff was thorough. Morton Blackwell, the conservative movement's godfather of training, had taught his protégés that to succeed you needed to pay attention to the small stuff. Cliff also knew that from his days in theater. There was no excuse for sloppiness. How you approached a front door and how loudly you knocked mattered. And there were a lot of "Don'ts": don't stand too close to a resident, it's intimidating; don't walk on lawns, it's disrespectful; don't lean on a doorbell too long, it's annoying. Your "universe" was the hundred or so houses you would be approaching on a given day. If the homeowner wasn't home, you did a "lit drop," leaving material about the candidates somewhere that was easy to find. "Walk books" were the iPhone apps you used to plug in information about the residents. And you, you were the warrior.

"Let's go!" bellowed a stocking-footed twenty-something at the morning meeting. Brandon Borke was a longtime YAL employee, shipped in from headquarters, and he was in charge of today's operation. "I know we went through a lot yesterday to get those numbers," he called out, pacing energetically back and forth on the hardwood floor. "Let's have a power clap."

The seated door knockers raised their hands robotically and clapped in slow unison. *Clap. Clap. Clap. Clap.*

"Beautiful," Borke shouted, before launching into his daily spiel. "For the next three days, we are going to be targeting districts which we have decided need our help." He scanned the room purposefully, his eyes darting from one door knocker to the next. "It's crunch time, right? Three days until election day. So at the door, you have to be bringing the point home that we're three days until election day. So, don't say: 'Can we count on your vote on November 6th?' That's not acceptable. Because that's too far off in the future. We have to be: 'Can we count on your vote this Tuesday, in three days?' So that's exactly the phraseology we should be using: 'Can we count on your vote in three days?' or 'Can we count on your vote this Tuesday?' Because it's definite, it's immediate, and you're asking them for an investment even if it's just verbal. It really means a lot."

The door knockers nodded periodically as Borke shared with them tactics culled from countless studies on personal motivation often used by both Democratic and Republican campaigns. The biggest takeaway: If you can get a person to commit to doing something—exercising, going to class, or voting—then they are a lot more likely to do it.

Though noticeably weary with dark circles under their eyes, the door knockers seemed ready for the last push. They gathered their knapsacks and headed down to the garage to pick up their Operation Win at the Door–produced campaign flyers for distribution: *Dan is willing to work with and represent everyone. Joshua is committed to defending taxpayers. Mark holds endorsements from the NRA.* Then they climbed into their cars and embarked on their mission, just as it started to rain.

I tagged along with a junior at George Washington University who was the president of his school's YAL chapter. His "universe" was a middle-class Manchester neighborhood dotted with low-hung brick and shingled homes. Because New Hampshire had a system in which voters in large districts had to nominate multiple legislators, he was door-knocking for several House candidates. They included Dan Garthwaite and Tammy Simmons, a die-hard Libertarian husband and wife team who had arrived in the Granite State in the early 2000s as part of a radical initiative called the Free

State Project, which aimed to turn New Hampshire into a libertarian mecca. Simmons's own claim to fame was building a neighborhood dog park with private dollars.

The student serving as my guide had fifty or so homes to hit that morning and another fifty or so that afternoon. He held up his phone to show me a professional-looking app that served as his campaign database. It had maps, lists, and questions to fill out each time you stopped at a house. This allowed the database to get "smarter" as it grew. The app, I later learned, was developed by i360, a for-profit analytics company that had merged with a Koch-backed non-profit to create a database of right-wing voters.

Most of the homes we hit that morning were inhabited by registered Republicans, friendly faces who needed to be lured to the polls. Easy, except that the YAL plan was to reach every household in the district as many as three times, which meant that a lot of them had been hit up a few times already. And some homeowners were simply sick of hearing about the election.

"You just kinda have to be nice and apologize if they don't want to hear from you," the George Washington University student told me.

He seemed like an ideal door knocker. Handsome, with dimpled cheeks and curly auburn locks, he was dressed casually but neatly in a kelly green thermal vest, jeans, and sneakers. He had a ready smile and an easy gait. He also knew the area well. He was from New Hampshire—a tonier coastal part, but he was still well-versed in the political scene here.

We sauntered up a driveway, slick with rain, and approached a small ranch house with brown shingles, careful not to step on the lawn. He tapped on the door and a stringy-haired young woman wearing a T-shirt, sweatpants, crocs, and socks opened the door.

"Are you voting Tuesday?" he asked.

"I certainly am," she responded. "Republican all the way."

He thanked her and offered up some "lit." She declined. And we headed off.

He did this a few more times, approaching small faux colonials and tidy brick bungalows adorned with last week's Halloween pumpkins and witchy window cutouts. At each one, he asked the homeowner scripted questions and plugged their responses into the app. It was all psychology, he told me, why people voted the way they did. It often had little to do with the actual positions a politician took. The key was not to talk policy, but to be reassuring.

"They think, Do I know them? Do I trust them? Are they going to help me?" he explained. "So you have to message in that way."

At one point, we hit a home with a weathered Clinton sign in the yard. "Oh, no!" he groaned. Seconds later, he was all smiles.

"How are you doing today, ma'am? I'm here to pass out some information on the elections. Do you know who you're going to be voting for, for state rep?"

"No, I'm just *not* going to vote Republican," said the woman at the door.

Unfazed, he kicked off his sales pitch. He didn't talk policy but instead stuck to broad topics and terms that might be friendly to a Republican opponent, as he pushed YAL's candidates.

"Okay, well I'll just give you a little info about them. They're all liberty-minded people, so they all don't like Trump. They're independent-minded. They want people to be socially free. They're more socially liberal. And they want to help small businesses. So even though you're not a Republican . . ." He paused and looked at her earnestly. "Yeah, I didn't vote for Trump either, but I hope you will consider them, like me."

"Okay, yup, yeah, that's what I was going to do this weekend." The woman had relaxed a bit; she even smiled.

He smiled back. "Well, you've still got three days. It's coming up, though. Have a good Saturday."

As he turned to leave, he said to me: "I never lie to a voter. But people are different, you've got to talk to them where they're at."

Then, he looked down at his app. "So for her, I'd put: 'neutral conversation.' You can put 'positive,' 'neutral,' or 'negative.' Didn't really get much out of her, but it wasn't entirely negative. Was it?"

ON ELECTION NIGHT, THE NATION'S EYES WERE GLUED TO THE networks' 24/7 coverage of the big races—giving constant updates on rock star candidate Beto O'Rourke and his efforts to snatch Ted Cruz's Senate seat in Texas, and Ron DeSantis, the onetime Trump darling running for the Florida governorship against rival Andrew Gillum, Tallahassee's Black mayor and a progressive favorite. All 435 of the House seats were up and there were 33 Senate races, plus two special elections. Nothing seemed certain. The 45 candidates YAL had endorsed in the general hailed from 11 different states. There were 4 from Texas, 3 from Maine, and one from Nebraska. But New Hampshire was where the most candidates, 28, were clustered and that made sense: the New Hampshire state motto, Live Free or Die, was practically a libertarian mantra. Its lax gun laws and zero sales tax had long made it a popular state for fans of free-market economics and skeletal government.

Cliff and his team had decided to make the backroom of an Irish pub in downtown Manchester their election night headquarters. He was certain it was going to be a historic night, the beginning of a powerful winning streak for him and his candidates.

Dressed for success in fancy wingtips and an expensive-looking dust-blue sports coat, Cliff positioned himself at a table near the back of the pub, where a camera and lighting crew would soon begin filming him giving an election play-by-play for Facebook Live. At a table nearby, YAL team members sat with their laptops and cell phones, keeping on top of races around the country. Calls soon came in by the minute. And by eight p.m., good news had arrived.

"Big victory alert: John Andrews in Maine," Cliff announced to his Facebook Live audience. Andrews, an avid moose hunter, was a political newbie who had only recently settled in western Maine, but had caught the state's independent spirit with promises to lighten up hunting regulations and decrease taxes in his new role as a state rep. "I think it's time to get rid of the income tax in Maine," Cliff added, chuckling.

Another highlight was the handsome Texas rancher Mayes Middleton, a thirty-six-year-old gas and oil executive who also owned a cattle ranch in Galveston. As state rep in Texas, Middleton wanted to cap property taxes and limit immigration. He'd handily beaten his opponent.

Soon word came down that a charismatic twenty-something named Jeff Shipley in southeastern Iowa had beaten a well-known incumbent in a swing seat that had been a Democratic stronghold for years. His big win had come thanks, in part, to support from a large transcendental meditation community, where members, many of them Bernie Sanders fans, were attracted to Shipley's antiwar and drug-legalization rhetoric. "That could be the win of the night," Cliff beamed. "I think this is the start of something really big."

But then things started going south. In quick succession, YAL lost several New Hampshire house seats that had looked like shoo-ins, including two that the young door knocker I trailed in Manchester had canvassed for. Then, several supposed frontrunners in Texas didn't make the cut. The final blow came in Nebraska, where YAL's prized candidate, a fifty-six-year-old incumbent and a libertarian movement die-hard who spoke often at YAL events, lost her house seat.

Cliff moaned into the crowd when he heard the news. "That's a tough loss tonight," he told Facebook.

He nursed a scotch and tried to remain optimistic. But as the night wore on, Cliff hunched lower over the table. He was slowly coming to realize, along with the rest of America, that a Blue Wave was indeed sweeping through the country's state legislative bodies—washing through Connecticut, Colorado, Maine, and Minnesota, flipping their senates from red to blue. But in New Hampshire, the blue wave was particularly strong: it would flip the senate and the house. YAL was another of the wave's casualties: of the forty-five candidates YAL eventually endorsed in the general election, less than half won.

By midnight, Cliff had switched into wound-licking mode. "We did the work. But we are looking at a lot of setbacks," he said to the camera and a half-empty room. Many of YAL's New Hampshire candidates had gone home, defeated and disillusioned.

The next morning, the *New Hampshire Union Leader* reported a record turnout: 63 percent of registered voters in Manchester had cast their ballots, higher than any midterm race in memory. The paper also reported that the national student activist group Next-Gen, funded by the liberal billionaire Tom Steyer, had also flooded the state, spending $750,000 and importing thirty-seven full-time door knockers and enlisting hundreds of volunteers to get Dems to the polls. Cliff's team knew about NextGen, that the group had its sights on 2018, and that it had dispatched door knockers to spots all over the country, including New Hampshire. But he had been confident that with hard work and enough of his own activists, his operation would be able to outperform the nascent outfit. That was before Cliff realized that NexGen's presence wasn't just a little competition, it was an onslaught. Steyer had spent more than three times what YAL did in New Hampshire. And it worked.

The last time I saw Cliff in New Hampshire, he was sitting in the lobby of his hotel, his cheeks sunken, eyes darting around the room, as he waited for his ride to the airport. He was headed back to his new condo in Florida.

"We're going to learn from this," he told me a few days later over the phone. I didn't doubt it. As far as I could tell, Cliff was now a VIP, and bouncing back from business defeats was the name of the game.

CHAPTER TWELVE

Candace Builds Her Following

By fall 2018, Candace Owens had honed her message to diamond-like precision and become a major Turning Point USA draw. She was on a mission to break the Democratic Party's hold on Black Americans and help them come out of the "sleepy coma of liberalism." She'd even come up with a brilliant media-friendly portmanteau for her campaign: BLEXIT, as in Black Exit, for which she organized a Young Black Leadership Summit and advertised via Instagram, Facebook, and her Twitter account, which had a million followers at the time.

On a blustery afternoon in late October, Candace led dozens of young Black conservatives, their crisply ironed suits and tailored dresses paired with fiery red MAGA beanies, scarves, and baseball caps, across Northwest Washington, D.C. The slow, righteous procession was headed from the leadership conference at the Liaison Hotel to the White House, where they were having a meeting with the president.

As wind swept across the boulevard, office workers peered out of second- and third-floor windows to get a glimpse of the young Black activists looking high-minded and bold, as if marching to Selma. Appropriating civil rights imagery was a trick common among modern-day conservatives. Rush Limbaugh frequently told his audiences he was more connected to Martin Luther King's vision of a color-blind America than Barack Obama had ever been. Conservatives in Florida and Wisconsin called privatizing American education "the civil rights issue of our time." Abraham Lincoln, the Republican president who freed the slaves, was frequently called upon as an example of the GOP's commitment to Black America. The same GOP seemed to conveniently forget that they had recruited millions of Southern racists to their party in the 1960s as part of a strategy that redefined what the party stood for. Candace hadn't invented this brand of amnesia, but her use of it was a sign that she was, among other things, a quick study.

For months, she and Charlie had planned the Black Leadership Summit, then brought it to the attention of the president's son-in-law Jared Kushner, who loved it. The idea was for the summit to fall under the TPUSA umbrella and be added to the annual roster of other TPUSA conferences, but Candace would spin her BLEXIT idea into a separate but related organization that would also host its own events.

At the time, Kushner had been consumed by his own efforts to lure Black voters to the polls for Trump in the upcoming 2020 race, and as part of that effort he was working on a criminal justice bill that sought some reforms inside federal prisons, including the reducing of sentences for some drug-related convictions and easier community reentry protocols for nonviolent offenders. It eventually passed, but it ended up having little impact on the vast majority of incarcerated Black Americans, who are mostly housed in state and local prisons. No matter, Kushner told people the president didn't have a race problem, he just had a messaging problem, or what Kushner termed a "knowledge gap." To fix that, Trump was increasingly playing up the nation's dipping Black unemployment rates (widely viewed as holdovers from Obama's economic recovery plan) and took full credit. He also liked to promote his 2016 voting record among Black voters (8 percent), telling audiences that he had done better than the last two Republican candidates—omitting that both Mitt Romney, who got 6 percent of the Black vote in 2012, and John McCain, who had gotten 4 percent in 2008, ran against Barack Obama. Meanwhile, Nixon, Ford, Reagan, and Dole had all outperformed Trump with Black voters.

The president also spent a lot of time lauding a bill that allotted tax breaks to wealthy investors working in areas known as "Opportunity Zones"—low-income, often predominantly Black neighborhoods—as part of his so-called urban revitalization effort. In one tweet, Trump cited the bill as a sign that "he had done more for African Americans than"—you guessed it—"any president since Abraham Lincoln." It would later be discovered that Kushner himself had owned a stake in a firm that was seeking to benefit from the breaks, before selling it in 2020.

Candace seemed to be Trump's newest surrogate, and it was not hard to see how she had become a mouthpiece for him to talk to Black Americans. And while her critics alleged that she was an opportunist willing to sell her soul to a racist president at any cost, Candace chalked these barbs up to reverse racism and fear among Democrats that she was going to lead the "ideological Black revolution" against them.

"Black lives have never, ever, ever mattered to the Democratic Party. Black votes always have," Candace roared into a megaphone in front of the White House. A coat hung from her shoulders like a cape. Before her, energized Black activists cheered her on, whistling and applauding, as she launched into her vision of history.

"They have created systems that we cannot get out of!" Candace said sharply—"They" being an amorphous group of all-powerful Democrats who, in Candace's eyes, had been conspiring for years to destroy Black America. "They removed the Black father from the home because they knew that once you break down the family, you can control. You can control the youth that are growing up." Candace paused for emphasis, then raised her hands in the air dramatically. "They gave us hip-hop," she bellowed. "They gave us the media. They didn't give us the facts."

Democrats, she continued, had "destroyed education" and were constantly going on with this narrative that Republicans were racist. "They try to scare us," she boomed. "Words like Uncle Tom, house Negroes, house slaves—those were created by leftists to make sure that we are constantly at war with one another. It is time for us to stand up against that and to stand together. This is our time."

Candace's crowd roared with enthusiasm.

Back at the hotel, Candace handed out T-shirts and baseball caps the color of blue cotton candy and melon sorbet. They were emblazoned with her BLEXIT logo—an elegant stick figure, arms rising toward the sky in a power pose. It was savvy marketing, in keeping with TPUSA's efforts to position itself as the peddler of a cool conservatism you could wear. The swag was special, she told the room, because her now-good-friend Kanye West had helped her design it. A few months earlier, West had tweeted about Candace to his 20 million followers: "I love the way Candace Owens thinks." She had struck up a rapport with the iconic artist, even visiting him in Los Angeles to discuss politics and attending an album release party in Jackson Hole, Wyoming. Now their partnership was deepening. The girl from Stamford had gone all the way to the top.

Candace's good relationship with Kanye West was thrilling for Charlie, too. During the BLEXIT conference, he took a break after a run to down a plate of steak and potatoes. Kanye West, he told me, had given him a free pair of Yeezy 700 sneakers. "Right off his feet."

CANDACE AND CHARLIE'S RELATIONSHIP WITH KANYE WEST didn't last long, however. A few days after the BLEXIT launch, the performer denounced Candace for using his name to push her personal brand. He wanted nothing to do with BLEXIT, he said. "I have been used to spread messages I don't believe in," he tweeted to his fans. West had been on and off the Trump train since the real estate mogul first announced his presidency. Pro-Trump sentiments expressed to his fans were often followed by backtracking that smelled like the work of a harried communications team doing damage control.

Devastated about West's public accusations against her, Candace crawled into bed and stayed there for days, shedding tears and mulling over her regrets. He had definitely had a say in the logo, she would later allege. But how much was unclear. In the interest of moving forward, she eventually made a rare public apology to her idol and moved on. Not surprisingly for a young woman who was practically making an art form out of the comeback, Candace was soon back in tip-top shape, getting life advice from the president, hanging out with him and Melania, and flying with Charlie across the Atlantic to address a group of aristocratic socialites and right-wing journalists at a reception for the launching of Turning Point UK, held at the fancy Royal Automobile Club, a private century-old club in Pall Mall, London. The event was attended by Lord and Lady Plunket, James Delingpole, and John and Irina Mappin—names that sounded as if they had been plucked from the pages of an Anthony Trollope novel.

Candace, looking American casual in a pair of expensive black track pants, was not intimidated. Microphone in hand, she addressed her blue-blooded crowd with her usual no-nonsense candor, schooling them on the perils of victimhood, the myth of multiculturalism, and the toxic nature of American feminism.

"We are in the midst of World War Three," she told the smartly dressed men and women, many more than twice her age. They gazed at her with fascination, swigging from their champagne flutes as they settled more comfortably into their padded chairs. "People always talk about it. When is it going to happen? When is it going to happen? It is happening right now. It is an ideological war we are fighting for Western values!" Candace continued authoritatively.

When an audience member asked her about nationalism, Candace settled in.

"I actually don't have any problems at all with the word 'nationalism,'" she pronounced, as Charlie, beside her in a charcoal gray suit, began to sway, gazing at the ground. Candace continued. "I think that it gets . . . the definition gets poisoned by elitists that actually want globalism. Globalism is what I don't want." Candace cradled her microphone with both hands. "So when you think about . . . whenever we say nationalism, the first thing people think about, at least in America, is Hitler. He was a national socialist. But if Hitler had just wanted to make Germany great and have things run well . . . Okay fine. The problem is that . . . he wanted . . . he had dreams outside . . . of Germany." Candace started making half circles with her hands to suggest the outside she was speaking of. "He wanted to globalize. He wanted everybody to be German, everybody to be speaking German. Everybody to look a different way. That's not . . . to me, that's not nationalism. In thinking about how we could go bad down the line, I don't really have an issue with nationalism. I really don't."

Seemingly unperturbed by Candace's high-five to Hitler, the audience nodded along as she detoured her way out of the pros and cons of Nazi-ism. The speech continued. Charlie relaxed. And the eventual news from London was that Candace had been a hit. One audience member, a millionaire metal trader's son named George Farmer, would even take a shine to this outspoken American freethinker. A big shine.

Back at home, at least one TPUSA employee worried about Candace's generous assessment of a psychopathic tyrant responsible for the murders of 11 million Jews, gypsies, homosexuals, and other human subsets he despised. It suggested that Candace considered mass genocide to be an "okay, fine" thing. *Just kill in your own damn backyard, please*, was how her tough-girl logic seemed to go. The employee warned that the speech should be edited before being posted online. But the speech was posted in its entirety by a British media firm. And things hummed along—until a young BuzzFeed reporter came across Candace's words. Soon, Candace was in hot water. TPUSA campus chapters were demanding her resignation. Chelsea Clinton tweeted, "There was nothing 'great,' using @RealCandaceO's own word, about the Third Reich." And Jared Kushner, whose grandparents narrowly escaped the Nazis during the Holocaust, and Ivanka, who had converted to Judaism before their marriage, were now giving Candace the cold shoulder. They had supported BLEXIT, but were now feeling less charitable toward the burgeoning celebrity.

Candace told me the video had been totally twisted out of context. Maybe she hadn't been at her most eloquent, but she understood the atrocities of the Holocaust and was in no way a defender. But in this instance, unlike with the Kanye gaffe, Candace absolutely refused to apologize. Instead, a few weeks later, she announced that she would be leaving Turning Point USA. Candace said her departure had already been in the works. And Charlie stayed relatively silent on the matter. The press, misunderstanding how things worked in the world of the far-right faux pas, speculated that conservatives had canceled Candace for her worrisome words. But no, Candace Owens had simply been redirected. She was soon hired—no doubt as a middle finger to the left—by the conservative youth movement's most famous Jew: Dennis Prager. She and Turning Point USA would maintain a tight rapport.

In March, "The Candace Owens Show" launched from a Brentwood studio, distributed by Prager's wildly popular, far-right online channel, PragerU. Her set was decked out with artsy black-and-white photos, a lacquer-topped table, and a plush dark-gray carpet. Candace's first episode would feature the Trump-supporting TV star Roseanne Barr, who herself had gotten in trouble for, among other things, posing as a mustached, swastika-armband-wearing Hitler in a satirical Jewish magazine. One million people would watch the two like-minded women opine about life in the new America, a place where such gaffes no longer destroyed your career, but actually made you even more famous.

CHAPTER THIRTEEN

Prom Night for the College Conservative

I t was late February 2019, another party night at the Conservative Political Action Conference, the largest annual gathering of conservative enthusiasts in the country. And inside the Cadillac Ranch, a Western-style restaurant/bar across the street from the convention center, TPUSA's afterhours shindig—cheekily named AmericaFest—was rocking. Hundreds of young right-wingers in MAGA baseball caps and fire engine red cocktail dresses were guzzling their cocktails.

Dan Crenshaw, a former Navy SEAL and Trump sympathizer, was mingling in his trademark eye patch; Senator Ted Cruz, looking as out of place as always in a polka-dotted tie, stopped by for a "Socialism Sucks" chant, then slipped out the double doors, presumably to bed.

Attendees swapped choice moments from the day's speeches, the words uttered by their idols, like Laura Ingraham's advice on how to deal with lefties calling you racist: "Look right back at them and say, 'You're the real racist, you're the real misogynist.'" Another notable moment was Senator Lindsey Graham's quip that before occupying the White House, Trump didn't have Graham's phone number, but now "he likes me and I like him." It was classic Trump groveling, which had practically become a CPAC art form.

Another hot topic was an exclusive invite-only party the next night, hosted by the citizen journalist James O'Keefe, a big-egoed renegade who favored leather jackets and aviators—a look that put him somewhere between the Fonz and a not-as-good-looking James Dean. Generating significantly less buzz was an upcoming luncheon hosted by Young Americans for Freedom, the storied organization increasingly overshadowed by the disruptor that was Turning Point USA.

Candace Owens, a $1,500 Yves Saint Laurent purse dangling from her shoulder, wasn't worried about the next party. She was gyrating on the dance floor with a young chapter member playfully sporting oversized sunglasses and a red, white, and blue lei. Life had certainly been going Candace's way lately. Not only was she adored by President Trump, but she'd stolen the heart of George Farmer, the Oxford-educated hedge-funder, who had "fallen in love at first sight" with Candace when he met her in London, at the event where she made her infamous Hitler gaffe.

Elsewhere in the room, steps away from the venue's mechanical bull, Charlie Kirk was chatting up a flush-faced Don Jr. By the scion's side was his new girlfriend, Kimberly Guilfoyle, a former Fox News commentator who glistened with excitement. She had left Fox in a cloud of controversy, and it would soon surface that she'd allegedly showed her former assistant naked photos of her male sexual conquests. Guilfoyle denied any workplace misconduct, and the scandal didn't seem to worry her new boyfriend nor fans of the president, whom she now championed with aggressive gusto.

While Charlie beamed and Guilfoyle looked on, Don grabbed a microphone and paid tribute to the TPUSA leader: "Thank you for making me party, man. And making people see what this party is all about!" He was feeling good—good about himself, good about Charlie, good about this party. "Honestly, the fact that you guys have the *balls* to do this makes me hopeful for the future of this movement."

CPAC, the forty-five-year-old annual gathering of conservative activists, was now run by a gregarious GOP insider named Matt Schlapp, who with his wife, Mercedes, served as socialites in Trump-era Washington, D.C. The event was known to be an apt barometer of the mood inside the Republican Party. During George W. Bush's presidency in the early 2000s, the vibe was cocktail-party WASP with a sprinkling of Texas hoopla and Christian right righteousness. In the Obama years, the tone was angrier, embodied by the shaggy-haired, hot-tempered Andrew Breitbart, founder of the eponymous Breitbart News alt-right site, who would swagger around screaming about his white nationalistic dreams. At the 2012 CPAC, Breitbart—once aptly dubbed "the Rage Machine" in the *New Yorker*—stormed out of the venue to confront Occupy Wall Street protesters. Wading into the group of peaceful chanters, he bellowed, ". . . You are freaks and animals . . . You filthy, filthy, filthy raping, murdering freaks!," looking like he was about to have the fatal heart attack he did have a few weeks later.

This year, CPAC's unofficial theme, it seemed, was how darn juvenile conservatism had become. Thanks to AmericaFest. Thanks to Charlie. Thanks to Candace. Thanks to the rowdy tween in the White House—not Barron, but The Donald, who couldn't put down his cell, and, according to several recently published tell-alls, stayed up all night watching TV, despite complaints from his housemates. And because his juvenile posturing was particularly well-received by young college conservatives who also felt disrespected and riddled with grievances, they, too, were the theme. They had arrived in droves to pay their respects. Convention organizers reported about a quarter of the estimated ten thousand attendees were, in fact, under twenty-five.

—

CPAC HAS ALWAYS HELD A SPECIAL PLACE IN ITS HEART FOR young people, ever since it was launched with four hundred fresh-faced invitees on a slushy January weekend in 1974 by the obsessively social Morton Blackwell, LI's founder, and his equally social cronies from the Goldwater campaign—along with the folks at Buckley's Young Americans for Freedom; the political operative Paul Weyrich; Richard Viguerie, the direct-mail wizard; and the American Conservative Union. The goal was to tighten the bonds between members of the burgeoning conservative movement so as to better strategize the takeover of the American political system. It was, after all, a "we" project.

Held at the exclusive Mayflower Hotel, the first gathering was hardly celebratory. Richard Nixon, the Southern Californian who had sailed into the presidency on a wave of law-and-order pledges, was about to sail out on a string of law-and-order violations. Impeachment was imminent, and the mood was bleak. According to the *New York Times*, one attendee, Kevin P. Phillips—whose prescient tome *The Emerging Republican Majority* would become an important GOP guidebook—picked up a microphone that wasn't working and quipped, "I guess that's the dead one, which might also apply to the Republican Party."

Despite the doom-and-gloom climate, or more likely because of it, CPAC's founders were forward-looking, packing their inaugural event with panels on phone-banking, door-knocking, and direct-mail fundraising—strategies that would become integral to the conservative movement's youth recruitment efforts. Soldiers were nothing if they were not trained.

In the years that followed, CPAC became more than just a training ground with a few inspiring speakers; it became a gathering of the right's political junkies, a confab of fringe activists who did what fringe activists do when they gather en masse: riled one another up and validated each other's radical ideas. From its earliest days, CPAC has not only been a good barometer of the current party mood but of what was coming down the pike. Long before the former California governor Ronald Reagan became a conservative cult figure, he was a CPAC favorite. It was in a speech at the very first one, in fact, that Reagan first co-opted the biblical image of a "city on a hill" that would become his touchstone. Two decades after that, in 1995, a bombastic Georgia congressman and newly elected speaker of the house named Newt Gingrich would start peddling his Contract with America. Back in those more dignified days, it was not yet de rigueur for arch-conservatives to belittle their political rivals. That sea change would be marked at CPAC 2007, when Fox News commentator Ann Coulter called John Edwards, then a Democratic presidential hopeful, a "f*****."

FOR THE PAST FEW YEARS, EVER SINCE THEIR DEMIGOD RON PAUL and his sprightly son Rand fell from the CPAC pedestal when the Trumpers came to town, Young Americans for Liberty had been noticeably absent at CPAC. But this year, they were back, and Cliff Maloney was ready to reassert his brand and YAL's influence. The YAL booth was a full-on celebration of their Operation Win at the Door campaign, complete with an actual door that opened and closed for passersby to pass through while taking a photo with YAL members. To visually convey what it all meant, Cliff had used another dash of theatrics: a bench. As in they were building a bench of candidates to one day fill the shoes of governors, senators, and maybe even the president.

I met with Cliff on the third day of the convention, at a French bistro inside the convention center. He was in good spirits, looking dapper in a starched oxford and a handsome gray suit jacket that fit him perfectly. He was further fine-tuning his look.

YAL, Cliff wanted to make clear, was not only back at CPAC to recruit, but also to raise money to continue building Operation Win at the Door. As usual, he told me, he would be hobnobbing with unnamed donors at receptions, dinners, and the atrium bar, which was packed from noon till closing.

Cliff had always thought of Operation Win at the Door as a "fail fast" venture, he explained, adopting an entrepreneurial philosophy that welcomes each failure as a stepping-stone to success. However, referencing the group's losses during the midterms, he said, "We didn't predict how much the national mood would flow downstream. There was too much we couldn't control."

Now, after months of assessing the 2018 election cycle and what went wrong for his candidates, Cliff had a way forward: create as many situations as possible where they *would* have control. In other words: pivot.

Leaning in conspiratorially, he told me that he and his team had started scouring the country for state races that popped up unexpectedly due to an incumbent's death or retirement. "That's low-hanging fruit," Cliff explained, "a great way to pile up wins and get to our goal." That goal, again, was 250 state legislative seats by 2022. So far, he'd clocked 36—less than he'd wanted, but still, in his eyes, an impressive start.

Cliff told me these pop-up races often got little attention, which meant his door knockers could make an impact simply by motivating a few hundred voters to get to the polls. The key was to identify small-government candidates in these races, then swoop in to support them. Already, after the November clobbering, YAL had one special election victory under its belt. Stewart Jones, a Christian, anti-abortion medical tech executive in South Carolina, had beat out a county council member with big name recognition and deep ties to the Democratic Party. Less than four thousand voters came to the polls. With the help of YAL door knockers, who made sure that the "right" voters turned out, Jones won by about six hundred votes.

Cliff was also working to fully monetize the kind of right-wing activism that he was so good at. Cliff had recently founded Mobilize the Message, a for-profit company that supplied "grassroots" activists for right-wing candidates and sundry issue campaigns. It was an Operation Win at the Door–type organization, but one that Cliff could personally profit from. As a for-profit vendor, Cliff would be charging clients, and as CEO he'd be setting his own salary. Cliff's side hustle was only a year old, but it was already taking heat from a handful of Cliff detractors, who told me privately, they saw it as a conflict of interest. One of Cliff's clients was the PAC funding his very own Win at the Door Operation, which paid Mobilize the Message $181,500 during the 2018 election cycle. Cliff brushed aside the criticism, insisting to me that he was operating at "10,000 percent compliance." He was also signing on other clients, including, eventually, a DC PAC formed to take down Congresswoman Alexandria Ocasio-Cortez. The group would pay Cliff's new company close to $32,000, according to expenditure reports published on OpenSecrets, a nonpartisan research group that tracks money in politics, to drum up ways to erode her base. It was but a sliver of what he would soon be making at his private firm. One project: distribute flyers that would bash the congresswoman for her criticism of a proposal that would give $3 billion in tax breaks to Amazon if they opened up a headquarters in the Big Apple. The behemoth had recently pulled out of the plan, amid a flurry of protests. And the DC PAC who'd hired Mobilize the Message wanted to hang the blame on AOC for the lost jobs and revenue. Cliff was all too happy to help, and to make money doing so.

On the last day of CPAC, it was finally time for the headline act: President Trump ambled onto the mammoth stage and greeted his adoring crowd. For much of the speech, Trump delivered his usual schoolyard-bully fare, ridiculing "Shifty Schiff" and of course, "Crooked Hillary." Then he switched gears. "Young Americans," he baritoned, squinting as he scanned the packed hall for young faces. "I love young Americans . . . You have the courage to speak the truth, to do what is right and to fight for what you believe and keep doing it." Then he jumped into the evergreen conservative gripe that was sure to rally the crowds: the PC campus police. "We reject oppressive speech codes, censorship, political correctness, and every other attempt by the hard left to stop people from challenging ridiculous and dangerous ideas." Trump's face now matched his crimson tie. He shook his head in dismay. ". . . We believe in free speech, including online and including on campus. And by the way, there's a young gentleman with us today. . . ."

Seizing the opportunity for a good visual, Trump warmly welcomed a buttoned-up twenty-six-year-old onto the illuminated stage. Hayden Williams was one of Morton Blackwell's "kids." A campus director for the Leadership Institute, Williams worked to bring controversial far-right speakers to campus auditoriums. He also scoured campuses for future leaders of gun-rights clubs or pro-life outfits, offering them support to launch their endeavors. Sometimes, he helped activists host attention-grabbing campus events that were like the Affirmative Action Bake Sale TPUSA had done at UNM or Free Speech Ball days, which were popular with a lot of the groups. And occasionally, he just stood on campuses helping these groups recruit new members. That's what he'd been doing on a recent afternoon at the University of California, Berkeley, a bastion of liberal thought, minding his own business, by a sign that read "This is MAGA Country," when an irate college student punched him in the face, multiple times.

"Ladies and gentlemen," Trump boomed, resting a hand on Williams's shoulder, "he took a hard punch for all of us. And we can never allow that to happen."

Trump advised Williams to sue his attacker. "But he's probably got nothing. But sue him. Sue the college, the university. And maybe sue the state."

The crowd roared with glee, then launched into the favorite chant: "U.S.A., U.S.A.!"

And then, as if he were a game-show host offering up a free trip, a big check, or a new car, the president told Hayden and his friends in the audience that he had a surprise that would right some of the wrongs that were plaguing their campuses.

"The plan," Trump began with a swoosh of his hand, was an executive order "requiring colleges and universities to support free speech." In other words, he continued, "If they want our dollars, and we give it to them by the billions, they've got to allow people like Hayden and many other great young people and old people to speak."

He continued: "And if they don't, it will be very costly. That'll be signed very soon. Every day we're restoring common sense and the timeless values that unite us all. We believe in the Constitution and the rule of law. We believe in the First Amendment right. And we believe in religious liberty."

The audience members cheered and clapped their hands. Never mind that the speech, as usual, had little to do with reality. UC Berkeley had not, in fact, endorsed the puncher. He had been arrested and charged. The executive order Trump was proposing only affirmed a protection that the university had already acknowledged and upheld: the right to free speech, guaranteed by the First Amendment.

Before the speech came to a close, Trump took further time to praise his young fans, singling out two others in particular:

"Candace is getting married," he crowed. "You've been incredible. Thank you, your whole group has been great. You're getting married. Seems like a nice guy to me. Congratulations. You've been so great. Thank you very much, Candace. Thanks."

Then he scanned the auditorium again. "And Charlie . . . Charlie, where's Charlie? Where is Charlie? Because he has done an incredible job. Thank you very much . . . Young Americans like you are leading the revival of American liberty, sovereignty, and self-determination in the face of left-wing intolerance, the anger, the unbelievable anger, I see it every day. Fortunately for you, it's mostly pointed at me."

A few hours later, nestled onstage for a fireside chat about the future before hundreds of die-hard Republicans, Ronna Romney McDaniel, the chair of the Republican National Committee, who commands a stage with the singsong voice of a kindergarten teacher, reiterated Trump's praise for the young leaders: They were "rising stars," she told the room, and they were "the future of our party."

The next day, the Daily Beast would crown Charlie and Candace "the New King and Queen of the GOP Ball."

The two had hit the big-time, and their brands, influence, and ability to shape impressionable young minds would grow exponentially from here.

PART III

CHAPTER FOURTEEN

Firebombing the Internet

On a sun-drenched day in March 2019, in a tony suburb of Phoenix, Charlie brandished a supersized pair of scissors and snipped a large red sash in two—part of a celebratory ribbon-cutting to christen his new TPUSA headquarters, situated seventeen hundred miles away from Lemont, Illinois. The slick, cavernous warehouse had a digital wing and a decked-out TV studio that streamed to Fox News. It was nestled in a small office park, across the street from a resort and spa (where donors could now stay when they came to visit) and was named after two of the org's most influential contributors: wealthy portfolio manager Bill Dunn and his wife, Rebecca, avid supporters of the kind of free-market ideas that had bolstered Bill's bottom line. Like many of his backers, the Dunns believed that in helping Charlie, they were helping to spread liberty to the next generation. So, they'd cut a check for the building.

Rebecca showed up at the Bill and Rebecca Dunn Freedom Center for the official opening in a pretty spring suit, her hair blown to perfection, along with a gaggle of other wealthy GOP luminaries to congratulate TPUSA on its growth. It now had 150 employees and had recently reported $28.6 million in its coffer.

In a guest column he wrote that summer for the Chicago-area *Daily Herald*, Charlie announced to his friends—and his enemies—that he had moved his headquarters to Arizona to avoid Illinois's "high taxes" and "excessive regulation," as well as to escape the state's political "corruption."

It probably didn't hurt that the move also put Charlie closer to many of his wealthiest supporters, who tended to favor the sunnier states, as well as the hometown of his glamorous girlfriend Erika Frantzve, a Christian influencer and a former Miss Arizona. Frantzve was also the CEO of a faith-based fashion line that sold $115 sweatshirts with Bible verses stitched on the sleeve. Charlie first met Frantzve at the new offices, then interviewed her for a job at Turning Point USA during a stopover in New York City. Over burgers, he grilled the beauty pageant winner and onetime real estate agent for hours, then told her: "I'm not going to hire you. I'm going to date you." Frantzve found Charlie's forwardness refreshing.

It made sense that Charlie's main love interest would turn out to be a woman who professed to live a "Godly life in a godless society." Charlie was now a headliner at evangelical churches around the country and counted some of the nation's most influential Christian leaders as dear friends and spiritual guides. He spent time with Jack Hibbs, an outspoken pastor from Chino Hills, California, and a promoter of "biblical citizenship"—the belief that the Constitution was divinely inspired by a God who saw the United States as a personal project he planned for his Christian children to run (sometimes referred to as Christian Nationalism). Another new friend was the decidedly intellectual Eric Metaxas, a radio host and cultural icon, who had catapulted to fame after writing a six-hundred-page biography on a Berlin-based Lutheran pastor executed for plotting to kill Hitler. But the most important new presence in Charlie's life was a longtime pastor and former mayor of Thousand Oaks, California, a city forty miles north of

Los Angeles, by the name of Rob McCoy. McCoy had a laid-back California vibe, and a down-to-Earth preaching style, calling the Ten Commandments "God's downloaded moral app" and joking that he had a "PhD in sin." McCoy also had a strong conviction he shared with his politically engaged allies on the right that "government belongs to God." Charlie would start to spend more and more time with McCoy, and eventually refer to him as his "personal pastor." McCoy would help Charlie strengthen his conviction that he wasn't just here to win a culture war, but also a religious one—and that it was his job to build the Christian army needed to fight the secularists.

Charlie's move to Arizona would also put him closer to TPUSA's new COO, who had replaced Crystal Clanton. Tyler Bowyer was a devout Mormon with a clean-cut, frat boy aesthetic and a chipper personality that belied his take-no-prisoners political drive. The thirty-three-year-old had strong ties to Trump and the Arizona GOP machine and his own fervent beliefs about the mixing of faith and politics. Born and raised not far from the new TPUSA offices, he had been the youngest leader of the Maricopa County Republican Party back in 2015. Maricopa is one of the largest counties in the country—about the size of Vermont—and encompasses more than half the state, and Bowyer's local connections made him an invaluable asset to TPUSA. But it was perhaps Bowyer's doggedness that Charlie valued the most. Back in his twenties while serving on the Arizona Board of Regents, Bowyer had led a highly controversial campaign to cut mandatory dues for the Arizona Students' Association, an advocacy group for public university students that fought tuition hikes and higher ed spending cuts. The move had earned Bowyer the moniker "schoolyard bully" in a local paper. Later, defying pushback from party officials, he'd organized one of Trump's first stump speeches in Phoenix.

Also now floating around Turning Point offices was Jake Hoffman, a local political operative and the founder of an online marketing firm that had helped get Trump elected in 2016. Hoff-man had been hired to run digital campaigns for Turning Point's new political arm, Turning Point Action.

But the most excitement at Turning Point's new headquarters was inside its growing multimedia wing, which now buzzed with activity, as analytics experts, social media specialists, and produc-ers tested the click-ability and share-ability of edited videos and brainstormed ideas for a roster of online shows to be released that winter. It was all part of a costly and pointed effort to produce conservative messaging that targeted Millennials and Gen Zs on TikTok, Instagram, Twitter, YouTube, and Facebook. The mes-saging would be a boost to Trump, indeed. But the real end goal was much more ambitious: to reach further and further into the American mainstream, influencing not just conservatives but the politically searching as well.

It made sense that Charlie and his followers were transition-ing from being boots-on-campus rabble-rousers into stewards of a multiplatform media group. When it came to pissing off liberals, luring donors, and changing hearts and minds, person-to-person interaction still had its value in 2019. But it didn't scale well. Col-lege students were online more than they were on their campus quads. Also dwindling fast was young America's appetite for tradi-tional media formats. Young conservatives, especially, were search-ing for alternatives to outdated-looking content being fed to them by buttoned-up prepsters and skimpily clad blondes on Fox News. Sure, Tucker Carlson was popular. But a lot of young web crawlers didn't have the attention span for hours of programming designed to rile them up. And why should they, when they could get riled up by a meme or twenty minutes of trash talking by a guy in a baseball cap who looked like someone they could party with?

Within months of moving into their new studio-equipped headquarters, Turning Point USA would launch an *Extra*-style entertainment show, hosted by Alex Clark, a high-energy twenty-something with a penchant for heels, halter tops, and ripped jeans. Clark had been plucked, after careful audience testing, from a morning show at a pop radio station in Indianapolis. During her three-minute, made-for-Instagram episodes, Clark sat in a white swivel chair and bashed liberal celebs like Beyoncé, Gwyneth Paltrow, and Justin Bieber. "That's freakin' weird" and "Not so fast, Wiggle Worms!" were some of her most notable catchphrases. Another rising TPUSA network star was Graham Allen, a buff and easily outraged Army veteran whose talk show catered to burly white boys pissed about all the "PC shit" in the world. There were also a myriad of shows dissecting current events through a conservative lens.

In addition to building up their own stars, TPUSA now also supported a bevy of conservative influencers in exchange for the talent's promotion of the group's right-wing content. Sara Schmachternberger, culled from an ad agency based in San Antonio, was the outfit's media director and ran TPUSA's influencer department, which gave the talent daily talking points, booked them on Fox shows (where they could promote TPUSA to older viewers), and helped them secure speaking gigs. Just as Nestlé or Adidas use different brand ambassadors to speak to different audiences, TPUSA was micro-targeting their adopted influencers to specific demographics under the right-wing umbrella. There was military veteran Rob Smith—Black, gay, and a committed liberal-hater; Anna Paulina Luna, a Mexican-American former Air Force pilot who'd chosen politics over medical school; and the Christian celebrity and author Allie Beth Stuckey, a lightning rod for young church-going women.

Another force driving TPUSA's new ubiquity on the web was Benny Johnson, the outfit's new chief creative officer, a thirty-two-year-old social media wizard and BuzzFeed alumnus, with Clark Kent–ish good looks and a cackling, near-diabolical laugh. Johnson was the left's worst nightmare—smart, savvy, super conservative, and gifted beyond comparison at "owning the libs." ("Cry More, Lib" was one of his favorite T-shirt slogans.) He was also known for his fuzzy ethics. Earlier in his career, as a BuzzFeed reporter, he'd been fired for plagiarizing lines from Wikipedia, Yahoo! Answers, and his fellow journalists for more than forty stories. Despite his lax moral code, or maybe because of it, Johnson was known to understand online natives like no one else. Fluent in social media-ese and teeny bopper TV, he once produced an explainer on the Syrian War using gifs from the reality TV show *The Hills*. To mock Obama's much-criticized response (or lack thereof) to Syrian president Bashar al-Assad's civil war atrocities, Johnson used a clip of a young woman in the show telling a friend she was annoyed: "I'm not, like, mad at you, it just, like, made me sad." It was a modern-day political cartoon, making light of a devastating war marked by torture and crimes against humanity. That was just the kind of thing Johnson found hilarious.

Now, Johnson, ever expanding his repertoire, was trying his hand at a new medium: the documentary. In 2019, to film *Everything You Think You Know About Cuba Is a Lie*, Johnson flew to Havana with a drone in his suitcase and a ragtag camera crew. It was no accident that the film he was about to make would traffic in an alarmist theme that the GOP was peddling—and would continue to peddle nearly nonstop, as the 2020 election neared—about the Democrats: that they were all socialists, if not communists, in disguise who looked at nations led by dictators and pined to bring their freedom-robbing practices to the United States. It was a message that was particularly resonant for Americans who had come from such places and still nursed scars of life under dictatorial regimes.

During the trip, Johnson and his crew waited in gas lines that snaked across crowded highways for hours, searched endlessly for bottled water, and visited a grocery store packed with little but state-issued cereal boxes and rows and rows of garbanzo beans.

"Lefties treated Cuba like a Caribbean utopia, with vintage cars, beautiful sunsets, and tasty cocktails," Johnson reported. But they needed to be outed for these deceptions. "It's all lies, all of it. It's communist propaganda."

The fourteen-minute video looked like something between a *Frontline* and a Vice Media documentary—eerie music, grainy shots, and the click-clacking of computer keys. And it could make you feel, if you didn't know better, that you were privy to truths no one else knew. Except, of course, that the entire film appeared to be based on a series of misleading assumptions: that mainstream Americans, even those who traveled to Cuba, were ignorant of the horrors Fidel Castro had inflicted on his people; that these same Americans wanted to turn the United States into Cuba; and that the Trump administration's trade restrictions on the country and crippling sanctions on Cuba's ally Venezuela had nothing to do with the food and gas shortages that Johnson and his crew were "exposing."

The video was widely shared around the internet, eventually reaching millions of viewers in swing states. Did it help Trump eventually garner a shockingly high percentage of the Latino vote in 2020—more than 30 percent, according to exit polls and surveys—winning Florida, Texas, and almost Arizona and prompting weeks of articles like one Vox headlined "Trump's Gains with Hispanic Voters Should Prompt Some Progressive Rethinking"?

"It's quite difficult to do attribution," Aaron Ginn, a Silicon Valley entrepreneur who has served as a kind of analytics guru to the conservative movement since he helped run Mitt Romney's digital team in 2012, told me. He now runs a right-wing incubator for political technology. But this type of messaging, particularly when it echoed themes already circulating around the web, no doubt helped.

In 2019, Johnson and his team would produce documentaries and short videos that fed his various far-right obsessions. An irresistible punching bag was Alexandria Ocasio-Cortez, AOC. In the summer of 2019, Johnson's fondness for mixing facts with misleading insinuations was exemplified when he and his crew approached the congresswoman's constituents, asking if they thought she deserved a raise to her $174,000 annual salary. The constituents, who were statistically unlikely to make anywhere near that much themselves, did not, and AOC was effectively scapegoated for supporting a bill that would give all members of Congress an additional $4,500 a year. Unsurprisingly, it was not noted that the bill had bipartisan support from top-ranking Republicans like Kevin McCarthy and Steve Scalise.

Another easy target for disinformation was the hodgepodge of decentralized protesters who went by the label Antifa. In TPUSA videos like "Antifa Blocks Police Car," "Antifa Harasses Family with Crying Children," and "Antifa Stomps on Blue Lives Matter Flag," Johnson's team adeptly painted this non-group as a large and extreme threat to the stability and safety of the country. Never mind that prominent watchdog groups like the Anti-Defamation League and the Southern Poverty Law Center who closely followed the activities of extremist groups had determined that Antifa was not nearly big enough or organized enough to pose a credible national threat.

Meanwhile, in September 2020, Twitter would shut down at least twenty accounts determined to be engaged in "platform manipulation" after the *Washington Post* discovered that teenagers contracted to do work for Turning Point Action, TPUSA's sister organization, were producing social media content that appeared organic, but that was actually carefully coordinated messaging designed to stoke fear about election fraud and instill mistrust in the government's handling of the COVID epidemic. One post alleged that the Democrats were trying to steal the election and thus were "thwarting the will of the American people."

The campaign, although relatively short-lived, was banking on an unsettling internet-era reality. The truthfulness of a statement did not increase its virality. Rather, it was content marked by inflammatory, us-against-them rhetoric that was proving the most spreadable. Also effective: repetition. There was no such thing, in other words, as oversaturating social media with a message. Turning Point's digital gurus knew this. So did Charlie. And his inflammatory jabs were frequently retweeted in the thousands, not only by TPUSA's corps of paid activists, but by highly influential right-wing media personalities—all the way up to President Trump, rendering him one of the highest profile social media influencers on the web. One tweet he posted in 2019—a short video of the twenty-something conservative Trump had brought up onstage at the 2018 CPAC getting punched in the face—was viewed close to 3.2 million times.

At other times, Charlie capitalized on his 1.5 million followers to amplify right-wing messaging birthed somewhere else on the web, helping to popularize catchy slogans that pushed forward Republican talking points. According to a piece in the *New York Times* that sought to unravel how these types of messages went viral, he did this in the middle of October 2018, three weeks before the midterms, when the term #JobsNotMobs began circulating online. The term was originally an allusion to the lowering unemployment rate under Trump's presidency—although unemployment had been dipping for years, well before he took office—and Black Lives Matters protesters who right-wingers liked to call mobs. Soon, it morphed into a pro-Trump anthem that went from Twitter to Reddit to Facebook and eventually to Fox News where it was used as a catch-all for Trumpism. Days before the election, the #JobsNotMobs theme was landing on voters' doorsteps as part of campaign material for GOP candidates, the *New York Times* reported. It was a classic example of the kind of cross-generational coordination that was making conservatives—young and old—so good at messaging and Charlie, as usual, was smack dab in the middle.

Lacking the paid staff, the social media infrastructure, and the ad dollars that Turning Point had, progressive activists and the youth groups they led were at a worrisome disadvantage. The Sunrise Movement, founded by a group of young environmentalists after Trump's election in 2016, for example, had a dynamic mission: to elect legislators who would help pass climate change legislation and create national urgency around environmental issues. It was also skilled at messaging. The group's catchy slogans, like "We Are Wide Awake" and "Waking Up Politicians Across the Country," were relentlessly hopeful and handily responded to the embittered "anti-woke" rhetoric coming from the right. But this type of messaging often got buried online. The Sunrise Movement simply didn't have the resources to hire a full-time team to pump out social media content at the speed of its conservative counterparts. Further, the Sunrise Movement wasn't coordinating with candidates, donors, or the DNC at the level Charlie was coordinating with leaders on the right. Charlie had his share of enemies. But when it came time to message against the real enemy, those differences were put aside. It was all hands on deck.

Adding to the problem was that Twitter, TikTok, and Instagram simply weren't ideal venues for explaining the kind of complex issues progressives cared about. Systemic racism, the intersection of women's rights and reproductive rights, how global warming stresses ecosystems, and why housing policies and educational inequality are linked simply weren't sound bite friendly.

The left hadn't always felt so clobbered by the right on social media. Progressive activists were actually way ahead of their conservative peers during Obama's 2008 and 2012 presidential campaigns. Obama loaded his staff and volunteer base with some of the nation's smartest early adopters—including Facebook co-founder Chris Hughes, Google's Dan Siroker, and teams of twenty-somethings who built enticing online communities that engaged young voters.

This online acumen was precisely what Charlie had so admired when he launched TPUSA, envisioning his group from the start as a multimedia entity that would permit young conservatives to connect over their common vision for the country and grow their ranks the way the Obama kids had.

To his great advantage, Charlie was just launching his new youth group as Obama was transitioning out of the White House and the president's revered social media team, the one that Charlie so admired, was in retreat. Key progressive players who had shined inside the administration were starting their own consulting firms, social justice nonprofits, and digital marketing agencies. What they were not doing was passing on what they'd learned to up-and-coming progressive activists over weekends inside the classrooms of a political training school like the Leadership Institute. They couldn't. The left doesn't have a leadership institute.

For all the right's complaints that the American left was filled with "collectivists," it was modern-day conservatives who were actually embracing a pass-it-down groupthink that was facilitating knowledge-sharing, mentoring, and the kind of consistent online messaging that helps win elections. On this phenomenon, Anat-Shenker Osorio, a communications consultant for progressive causes, told *Time* magazine in February 2021: "There's a lot of not-invented-here syndrome, where people won't consider a good idea if they didn't come up with it."

BY FALL 2019, THE AMERICAN PRESIDENT'S SPECIAL BRAND OF IN-cendiary rage and his willingness to do just about anything to further his power and pull seemed ever on the rise. The Democrats' move to impeach Trump for seeking foreign assistance from Ukraine to boost his 2020 reelection odds was a catch-22 by anyone's estimation. To act against the president was to risk looking like a bunch of bullies to the pool of already aggrieved Americans who supported Trump. Not to act was to say to the rest of the country: "We give in. Democracy is done." Voting thus to go ahead, the House began its public hearings that November. And TPUSA, in turn, went to town. Its chosen online stance: enraged mockery. It would treat Democrats' efforts to protect the moral and legal fiber of the American presidency as a childish game of gotcha, led by a bunch of sore losers.

Johnson took to YouTube with the relentlessly obsessive energy that had become his trademark. For one episode in his new man-on-the-street series, "Benny on the Block," he cased the Capitol Building for pro-impeachment protesters who didn't know what the impeachment hearings were about; a protester who appeared to be homeless and sounded mentally ill was meant to serve as proof that Americans were ill-qualified to determine whether impeachment was in order. In another video, he strolled along a California boardwalk and interviewed a handful of Trump supporters—deeming them living proof that Californians did not support impeachment.

But it was on a chilly afternoon in February 2020, one day before the Senate was expected to acquit the president, that TPUSA pushed the line even further. Johnson watched from his Washington, D.C., home as hundreds of legislators gathered on Capitol Hill for a very long and very winding State of the Union. Trump's campaign-style speech veered from self-congratulatory plaudits—as he praised "our roaring economy," our "completely rebuilt" military, and our "blazing, bright" future—to fear mongering about "illegal aliens" storming the country to commit heinous crimes, socialist-style healthcare systems, and the "radical left" seeking to "muzzle preachers and pastors." The rant ended with a chant of "four more years!" and a dramatic gesture on the part of Speaker Nancy Pelosi. Having sat through the eighty-minute tirade with a look of disgust on her face, the sixteen-term congresswoman rose and ripped her copy of the script in two—a powerful visual she must have assumed would play well on the internet. She was owning the moment and, it would seem, deactivating the bomb of lies that had been Trump's entire speech through the dismissive physical gesture.

Benny Johnson, the meme maestro, didn't see it that way. As far as he was concerned Nancy Pelosi had just committed an act of self-sabotage, which also happened to be a gift to him.

Not a smart thing to do, he thought to himself. *Not smart.*

Johnson was both mad at Pelosi's lack of respect for his president and excited about what he intended to do about it, in retaliation. He immediately messaged his charges. For the next fifteen minutes, he and his team tossed around ideas: What should they do with the hated Pelosi and her hateful gesture? "If you're going to give me a visual, baby," Johnson said to himself, as if speaking to Pelosi, "I'm going to use it." And he did.

The following day, Turning Point USA released a doctored version of the clip. There was Pelosi, her lips pursed with rage, ripping up the speech—not once, as the president was preparing to leave the stage, but seventeen times. When the president paid lip service to the mother of a two-year-old girl who almost died during childbirth: rip. When the president honored a military family who had lost a husband and father to a roadside bomb in Iraq: rip. When the president congratulated a one-hundred-year-old Tuskegee airman: rip. On and on . . . Rip. Rip. Rip. Pelosi was no longer a political warrior standing up for her principles, but a cold woman who prioritized partisan politics over everyday Americans. By mid-February 2020, the video had been watched more than 12 million times on Twitter, according to the Poynter Institute, and Sean Hannity and other right-wing personalities had posted it on their Facebook pages. Pelosi's people, enraged, asked Facebook and Twitter to take down the video, but the tech giants—supposed enemies of the right—refused, insisting that manipulated videos did not in fact violate their rules. Widespread coverage of the video only fueled its popularity, increasing its clickability, its relevance, and its reach.

"We won, and I loved it," Johnson told me.

Turning Point had prevailed. The group's ability to "hack the libs" had reached new heights. As for the truth, that was just an abstract concept. Reality was whatever the most cunning and creative content provider said it was. And if Washington insiders thought we had reached our low, they were wrong. These young right-wingers were just warming up.

CHAPTER FIFTEEN

The Comeback Kid

Ever since YAL's pivot after the 2018 midterms, Cliff had been laser-focused on his latest mission: harvesting "low-hanging fruit." The plan: pile up state-level legislative wins by bolstering little-known candidates in last-minute, low-turnout races. It was smart and tactical, and considering that Cliff now had 56 legislative victories under his belt, ever closer to his goal of 250, it was no doubt effective. But like any behind-the-scenes operator who truly understood how power worked, Cliff knew the way to really make a name for himself was to find a superstar.

Cliff found one in thirty-eight-year-old Nick Freitas, a libertarian-leaning, former Green Beret with JFK Jr.'s brooding good looks. Freitas was a Republican member of the Virginia House of Delegates. And in March 2018, he had raised his profile the way newbie politicians were now doing it: by going viral.

Shortly after the horrific mass shooting at Marjory Stoneman Douglas High School in Parkland, Florida, while the nation was grieving the untimely deaths of fourteen students and three adults, Freitas had stood on the House of Delegates floor to argue against gun control. In his dark suit, white oxford, and skinny tie, he looked more like a heroic defense attorney in a Hollywood thriller than a right-wing elected official protecting the needs of the NRA. And that was no doubt part of his appeal, as he calmly and authoritatively placed the blame for gun violence in America on progressive policies gone wrong. Abortion, the welfare state, and gun-free zones were, in Freitas's telling, all stepping-stones on a path that led a mentally ill young person to shoot up his classmates. Short on facts but radiating heartfelt conviction, Frietas's ability to engage a room—and horrify Democratic delegates—was conservative catnip. A video of his soliloquy to the Second Amendment went viral, reaching millions.

The married father of three was just the kind of operator Cliff could get behind. Freitas routinely voted against regulating firearms and reducing public health risks and workplace discrimination. He opposed a ban on texting while driving. Meanwhile, he supported bills that would hobble local municipalities' ability to raise the minimum wage or dismantle offensive war monuments. His big smile, cowboy boots, and inexhaustible appetite for small talk made him an ideal candidate.

I would meet Freitas on a hot day in June 2019 at a Memphis Airport Holiday Inn, where Cliff was hosting one of his weekend training sessions for officials he'd helped get elected. This was through a YAL subsidiary, then described to me as the Hazlitt Policy Center, which provided legislators with strategies to pass "liberty-friendly" bills. The center, as far as I could tell, was akin to the American Legislative Exchange Council (ALEC), the conservative bill mill co-founded in 1973 by activist Paul Weyrich that churns out policies favorable to the wishes and whims of its donors. Cliff told me that the center differed from ALEC because it was more comprehensive, a veritable soup-to-nuts operation that started not when a candidate had been elected, but even before they had thought to run for office.

At the hotel, I was immediately escorted to one of the conference rooms down a small flight of stairs, where an eccentric hodgepodge of libertarian state representatives—including a man in suspenders, a woman with a long braid running down her back, and a few lavishly bearded fellows—were listening to a workshop on the ills of "red tape" regulations. It was led by a senior research fellow from the Mercatus Center, a Koch-funded, far-right think tank that spends millions every year bolstering free-market policies.

The group chuckled as the fellow clicked through to a slide of a cartoon captioned "Day in a Regulated Life," depicting a middle-aged man eating breakfast surrounded by household items that were tagged with acronyms indicating the regulatory boards or associations that monitored them. USDA sat above the man's carton of milk, EPA next to his faucet. EPA, FDA, USDA below his banana. A grimace was plastered on the man's face, and his eyes sagged in dismay, as if deeply burdened by the consumer protection laws that kept him from ingesting toxic food and bathing in polluted water.

"If you went out and asked the average person on the street, they're not like the people in this room," the research fellow explained, matter-of-factly. "They might think, 'Oh my gosh, my toilets are not relegated by somebody. Somebody go out and pass a law to make sure that it is.' They don't want to have to worry about these things and they think that a lot of bad things will happen if someone doesn't. So the burden is on us to demonstrate . . . that the growth of regulations over time is a problem."

As the talk came to a close, I looked around and noticed a forest green booklet on some of the desks: *A Step-by-Step Guide to Using Mercatus Tools to Reduce State Regulation Levels.*

"Mercatus is here to help," the fellow promised, sounding deceptively charitable for an employee of an organization whose raison d'être was to thwart state laws designed to keep Americans safe.

When the workshop was over, Cliff, parading around the

hotel in dark jeans and trendy red sneakers, found me and ushered me to an upstairs conference room where he'd gathered
his star players. There was Savannah Maddox, a polished sixth-
generation northern Kentucky gun-owner and self-proclaimed
"strong woman," who had picked up a state house seat in 2018
and promptly sponsored a bill (and saw it through the House) that
would allow just about anyone over eighteen to carry a hidden gun
around the state without a permit. Also there was Joel Bomgar, a
thirty-nine-year-old Mississippi legislator, tech entrepreneur, and
devout Christian. He was introduced to me as the inspiration for
the Hazlitt Policy Center, given that he'd been holding informal
gatherings of libertarian-leaning legislators since before the center existed. Bomgar was a classic libertarian, geeky and off-beat; a
true believer, who liked to give local Ted Talks about the power of
individuality and the unfettered market and its ability to serve the
free-thinking industrialist.

But it was Nick Freitas, with his broad shoulders, rolled-up
sleeves, and chiseled face, who was Cliff's star pupil. The minute
Freitas opened his mouth, I knew why.

Freitas was casual but charismatic as he waxed about the
"heartbreaking" plight of American teachers subjected to union
"protections" that hampered their creativity and dulled their work
ethic. He was adamant that regulatory measures for small business
owners had been personally wounding to his single mom raising
two boys on her own and trying to launch a small real estate firm
when she wasn't on duty as a nurse. "And the moment she started
experiencing some success," he lamented, "there was the government with its hand out, taking from her." Later, he would offer
another deeply personal story to explain why he opposed abortion. His mother had dropped out of college to have him. "I don't
know what it was like for her as a woman," Freitas mused. "But I
know what it was like as her son."

So obedient was Freitas to far-right causes, he had once been featured on the American Legislative Exchange Council website as "State Legislator of the Week." He also understood the power of aligning himself with YAL, traveling often to speak at YAL conferences, mentoring new members, and hiring former ones. Cliff had already marked the telegenic delegate as a potential presidential candidate.

THAT SUMMER, FREITAS HAD A SETBACK. HIS HOUSE OF DELegates seat was up for reelection that fall. But he and his local Republican legislative committee had made an unbelievable gaffe, failing to submit his paperwork in time. Not surprisingly, Virginia's Democratic-led elections department wasn't sympathetic, which meant Freitas, who'd been projected to sweep the race, was out of the running. His Democratic opponent, Ann Ridgeway, a sixty-something political neophyte and juvenile probation officer, could hardly contain her glee. "I feel bad for the guy," she told a reporter.

Then, in September, the Illinois mega-donors Richard and Elizabeth Uihlein—who had just been dubbed "the Most Powerful Conservative Couple You've Never Heard Of" by the *New York Times*—swooped in with half a million dollars, the largest donation in the history of the Virginia House, so Freitas could run as a write-in candidate.

And wouldn't you know it, Cliff swooped in to provide the troops. During the campaign, Cliff's team of door knockers delivered yard signs, knocked on countless doors, and distributed flyers. On election day, volunteers stationed themselves outside of the district's thirty-two polling stations brandishing red and white pens with "Nick Freitas" embossed across them and a model ballot indicating exactly how to write in a candidate. Freitas won 14,694 votes, more write-ins than any candidate ever in a Virginia house of delegates race, beating his opponent with 56 percent of the vote count.

The next day, Cliff posted on Twitter: "I'm so proud that @YALiberty students were able to play a major role in @NickForVA winning his 'unwinnable' write in campaign #MakeLibertyWin."

The win secured Cliff's status as an invaluable leader of the movement. As the race toward 2020 got underway in earnest, he continued to hunt for talent, eventually boosting a former television journalist named Ron Ferguson to run for a House of Representatives seat in eastern Ohio's 96th congressional district, where opposition to fracking was souring some Dems on their party, flipping the region from blue to red. Though he'd run for the seat in 2014 and lost, Ferguson checked a sufficient number of Cliff's boxes: he had clean-cut, YouTube-friendly looks; a down-home demeanor; and ties to both the Leadership Institute and the Koch-affiliated Americans for Prosperity. In other words, he was in the "network."

Ferguson won the seat.

During the summer of 2019, Cliff moved his outfit from Alexandria to the hipper Austin. He was now working out of a glass office building with touches of cool that went well with his new look. There was exposed brick, floor-to-ceiling windows with views of the surrounding hills, and an open plan, giving the venue a trendy, natural vibe. It was all topped off by a "victory wall" of plaques commemorating YAL's dozens of wins.

Still, Cliff's considerable gift for spotting talent and his new slick digs could not inoculate him from what some women at YAL were increasingly viewing as his Achilles' heel: sexism. It was having a corrosive effect on the culture at YAL and becoming an undeniable problem for the organization.

Since 2014, according to later allegations, women had been complaining to each other of sexual harassment as committed by various men affiliated with YAL—including Cliff himself. While some who worked closely with Cliff—and Jeff Frazee, YAL's founder and board chairman—would profess to have known nothing about the alleged incidents until years later, women routinely warned one another to stay away from Cliff and others in positions of power at YAL, who were known to treat them differently than the men associated with the organization. They said women were tacitly (and not so) pressured into intimate situations with men.

In July 2017, in an incident later dubbed TacoBellGate, a former state chair, who had also worked with Cliff on the Rand Paul campaign, accused Cliff of pressuring her to "get in bed with him" after she complied with his request to deliver Taco Bell to his hotel room during a conference. According to the woman, who shared this with YAL allies and wrote about the complaint in a lengthy tweet in January 2021, Cliff spoke to her about loyalty and the fact that people who are not loyal to him "don't stick around long" in the organization. The woman says she tearfully declined and soon left the organization, but not before bringing her complaint to higher-ups.

YAL founder and board chairman Jeff Frazee says this was the first time YAL's board had heard of issues with Cliff. And after an eight-week-long investigation, Cliff was issued "a formal reprimand," and organization leaders say they instituted a series of changes, issuing an employee handbook, hiring an "independent HR professional," and setting up an employee hotline for complaints and concerns. As for Cliff, he held onto his post. "It was a hard position to be in," the woman says she was told, by way of explanation, "because [Cliff] is good at his job." Frazee says he never told the woman that, nor to his knowledge did anyone else in the organization.

In a written response, Cliff denied acting inappropriately. He claimed that there were others in the hotel room at the time of the encounter and that he had simply asked the woman "to leave the room, which offended her." He also claimed that he believed YAL's investigation "found there to be no wrongdoing."

Another woman told me that she had had a similar run-in with

Cliff during the summer of 2014, while living in a YAL house outside of DC. They were both state chairs at the time. The woman alleges Cliff cornered her in the house and pressured her to go into the bedroom with him, threatening to ruin her career if she didn't comply; she rebuked him and he backed off. The woman says she told colleagues about the incident, but did not tell YAL leadership, as she was 19, younger than most of the other state chairs, and concerned that she would not be believed in a he-said, she-said scenario. Cliff has denied that this incident occurred.

The woman says the encounter so irked her that during that same summer, she persuaded YAL leadership to let her conduct a seminar for the group's state chairs, which included advice on appropriate behavior. One slide, which she presented on official YAL National Convention stationery, was titled: "Don't be a Creepertarian! You know what is appropriate and what is not. Do not turn people away from our movement."

In the winter of 2019, Addyson Garner, another state chair, took a meeting with Cliff to report that she had been recently groped by a fellow state chair at a DC-area party. Garner would later report this incident in a string of lengthy January 2021 tweets. Garner would also tell me about this incident over the phone. Garner says she told Cliff she loved YAL, and wanted to help it grow, but her experience—eerily similar to stories she was hearing from other women within the organization—had deeply shaken her faith in the group. In order for women to feel safe, Garner says she asked Cliff to establish more comprehensive rules of conduct and institute sexual harassment training across the organization. She also requested that YAL add an in-house HR department, to replace the third-party one that currently existed to create a more professional setting. Cliff reassured her that institutional changes were underway and measures would be put in place to protect women at YAL. But Garner says significant changes did not materialize. And when she later messaged Cliff to follow up, she says he blocked her. Cliff denies Addyson's account.

As for the man whom Garner says groped her, he later ran for state office, backed by YAL's endorsement and the canvassing power of Operation Win at the Door.

Meanwhile, Cliff's own life seemed to be flourishing. He had recently married a fellow libertarian activist, and a member of YAL's 2015 intern class, in a vineyard ceremony in northern Virginia, with his old grade school buddies from Boothwyn, Pennsylvania, serving as groomsmen. He had bought a home worth close to half a million dollars in a gated community along Florida's Gulf Coast. And business at his private door-knocking firm, Mobilize the Message, was ballooning. Despite Cliff's mixed feelings about President Trump, Mobilize the Message was hired, in 2019, by the Committee to Defend the President, a PAC that would raise $17.3 million during the 2020 election cycle. Similar to the president's own scandal-ridden rise to power, Cliff's ascension spoke volumes about the Republican Party's priorities at the height of the #MeToo era. On one hand, a majority of Republicans did care about women's equality. According to a December 2017 Pew survey, 69 percent of Republican women (and 54 percent of Republican men) considered harassment and assault to be "widespread" problems in society. On the other hand, touchy-feely topics like women's rights didn't have to get in the way of political wins. And winning, of course, was everything.

CHAPTER SIXTEEN

The View from Candaceland

It was a blustery Sunday afternoon on Martin Luther King Jr. weekend in January 2020. Outside the Fillmore, a one-hundred-year-old textile mill turned music venue in Charlotte, North Carolina, hundreds of Candace Owens fans lined up on the sidewalk, soon snaking all the way around the block, to catch her on her BLEXIT—short for Black Exit—tour. It was all part of her campaign to encourage African Americans to liberate themselves from the shackles of the hateful, fear-mongering left, and presumably (though she did not explicitly endorse him on BLEXIT stages) vote for the president who had helped catapult her to fame.

Among those in line were Black college kids, white war vets, and stay-at-home moms thinking of running for office. A white woman in a navy parka told me admiringly that "Blacks are the new independents."

Most were locals of Charlotte, the New South banking capital, where jagged glass and steel towers had sprouted up over the past forty years, overshadowing a crescent-shaped swath of land inhabited by mostly Black residents who'd been largely shut out of the finance boom. Others had driven in from Greensboro and the capital, Raleigh, to buy what Candace was gamely selling: a shellacked version of the GOP as a no-nonsense party that didn't coddle the descendants of slaves, but told them to get jobs, get lives, get it together. The GOP's answer to racial strife in America: "What racial strife?"

Inside, a local group of pro-life Black Republicans were setting up their get-out-the-vote table and handing out flyers that declared "Free At Last" above a photo of a smiling, well-coiffed Black family, presumably one that didn't ask the federal government to take care of them. Candace had instructed her BLEXIT organizers to connect with local GOP groups when they planned events. A Trump victory in 2020 would come with razor-sharp margins in swing states like North Carolina, and her actions suggested that she believed bringing a sliver of unexpected Black voters to her new favorite party could well make the difference.

Besides, the president had been good to her, singing Candace's praises on *Fox & Friends* and tweeting that she was "so good for our Country!" Likewise, she had become one of his most consistent and vocal African American allies, appearing sometimes nightly on cable news shows to defend him. The more she did so, it seemed, the higher her star rose.

It had indeed been a stellar season for the thirty-year-old—personally, professionally, even spiritually. She had opened a BLEXIT headquarters in a glass and steel office tower in northwest Washington, D.C., hired a director to run the operation, and secured BLEXIT nine state chapters and 501(c)(3) status, which allowed it to take in tax-free donations.

When she wasn't touring with BLEXIT, Candace made lucrative one-off appearances in hotel ballrooms around the country for county GOP clubs, right-wing think tanks, and religious groups excited to have the conservative "it" girl in their presence. At Liberty University, she paced a stage in a pretty silk blouse and flowing black slacks, testifying about her turn to God. Her voice cracking, she told the packed room of 2,500 students: "Suddenly, after a night of drinking, I woke up in the morning and I just broke down crying. It was the most bizarre thing . . . and I said to someone close to me, 'I have this feeling . . . that God wants me to quit drinking.' Just like that, I just quit drinking because I broke down crying in a room and had a sense that God wanted me not to poison my body anymore, that he wanted to be able to open the universe up to me. . . ."

A few minutes earlier, Candace had already summarized her story well: "I believe that God picks people to have experiences in their life, the good ones and the bad ones."

Marriage was, apparently, one of those experiences. And in August of 2019, Candace and her Oxford-educated fiancé, George Farmer, married at the glitzy Trump Winery—a sprawling estate twenty-five minutes from Charlottesville, where the lethal Unite the Right rally had unfolded two Augusts before. (Candace's stance on white supremacy: it was low on her list of issues facing Black America—behind illiteracy rates, fatherless homes, and Black-on-Black crime.) Among her wedding guests were Liberty University's then president Jerry Falwell Jr., and his wife, Becki; Brexit initiator Nigel Farage, who Candace says was one of her inspirations for starting her BLEXIT group; and the Libertarian commentator Dave Rubin, escorted by his husband, David Janet. In honor of the president, who did not attend, there was a "Make Weddings Great Again" cake, and bridesmaids donning matching red baseball caps.

BACKSTAGE AT THE FILLMORE, CANDACE PREPPED TO GO ON-stage, gathering her guests together for a huddle and a prayer. She had flown to Charlotte from DC that morning. And while downing her breakfast—a bag of Doritos—she'd prepped for the day's four-hour multimedia extravaganza with a sound check, lighting test, and schedule review. Now, as audience members took their seats and the house lights flickered a five-minute warning, Candace chatted with me and her sidekick, Larry Elder, a sixty-seven-year-old Black radio personality from Beverly Hills.

"Larry's writing the intro to my book," Candace told me.

"Done," Elder corrected her. He had already written it.

Candace had once idolized the older, more experienced Elder. And she still may have. She stroked his ego, calling him a "legend," and praising his "skilled ju-jitsu" when it came to debating his critics. But it seemed undeniable that the tables were turning. In his heyday in the early 2000s, Larry had dominated the Los Angeles radio waves with his rush-hour talk show on KABC. Now, Elder worked for a Christian media network called Salem, and the vast majority of Americans had no idea who he was. In September 2021, Elder would make an unsuccessful bid for the California governorship in a recall election against Gavin Newsom, garnering some national press. As for Candace, she seemed hardly able to stay out of the press and had been the subject of pieces in *New York* magazine and the *Washington Post* magazine, and had posed in an olive-colored silk blazer and matching silk pants at the tony Mark's Club in London for the upscale British fashion magazine *Tatler.* The magazine referred to her admiringly as "Trump's spiky new darling."

Candace chugged a bottle of water and began gossiping with Larry about various pundits. There was Leo Terrell, the civil rights lawyer whom both Candace and Elder disliked. Too loud, too angry. He'd defended the reprehensible O. J. Simpson on TV during the 1995 trial, not to mention insulted Candace a few months earlier on Fox News, insisting she was nothing more than an opportunist taking her fifteen minutes of fame.

"If I could assault one person without going to prison, it would be Leo Terrell," Candace declared, pressing a manicured hand firmly to her chest. She was wearing a diamond the size of a walnut, a gift from her new husband. "Yeah," she said, noticing me noticing the stone. "We got it in Africa. So, we took out about six African tribes for it." She smiled snarkily and cackled: "I'm kidding!"

Minutes later, Candace sauntered into the spotlight, booming "Hello, Charlotte!" to cheers, applause, and blasting music.

Elder was not alone in his fervent conviction, among a widening circle of conservative gray-hairs, that Candace brought something new and exciting to the far-right table, helping to put the movement on the map. Candace didn't do politics the old and tired way, pontificating behind a stage lectern, or on a starkly lit TV set in a skimpy cocktail dress, the kind Roger Ailes had made the standard (read: required) sartorial choice for the female Fox pundit. No, Candace wore streetwear, designer track pants, or, like tonight, impossibly stylish jeans, which she paired with a leather-sleeved jacket and pointy heels. When onstage, she held her own microphone, used a video montage of her own making as multimedia eye candy, and paced back and forth, pointing authoritatively at her audience and yelling: "Guys!"

She did it with flair, arousing crowds with infectious, no-holds-barred bluster. If Laura Ingraham seemed passionate but unhinged, yelling about the left's love of "sanctuary cities" and its hatred of "American heroes" from behind her Fox News desk, Candace seemed modern and cool. She mixed loud music, flashy videos, and red-hot political commentary—a combo she had come to call "poli-tainment." And that was one reason she was there at the Fillmore, where Canadian hip-hop great Drake and the iconic seventies band Foreigner had once played.

"We are always trying to be creative and think out of the box," she told me. "It just never stops."

With larger-than-life videos of African American families in earlier, supposedly happier times flashing behind her, Candace pivoted on a sharp heel and told the room that it was an "important time in America . . . because there's something that has gone very, very wrong . . . particularly with the Black community." The enthralled crowd, many wearing T-shirts that read "Liberals Can't Bully Me," clearly wanted to hear more.

Candace took her fans down memory lane. In much the same way that white conservatives frequently harken back to a gossamer past when things were more pleasant, children more obedient, and minorities more deferential, Candace described her early years as "the golden decade." It was the 1990's, a time, she recalled, when TV was just better. She loved the Huxtables and the Jeffersons—doctors, lawyers, business owners. The left hadn't gone crazy yet. Black and white Americans seemed to be getting along. Skipping over uncomfortable racial lowlights from the decade, many of which also appeared on TV—the (Donald Trump–abetted) conviction of the innocent Central Park Five in New York City; the Los Angeles race riots sparked by the brutal police attack of Rodney King; the polarizing acquittal of O. J. Simpson in the murder of his ex-wife and her friend—Candace preferred to reminisce about the fictional nineties she'd loved on TV. "I don't know what happened," she lamented. "Some time over the next couple of decades, that kind of TV left." It was replaced with something else. "It was replaced with violence."

A few minutes later, having excoriated the media, the liberal orthodoxy, and people ignorant enough to think Black Americans were still impacted by the legacy of slavery, Candace, sweaty and out of breath, descended the stage to howls of approval.

When Larry Elder jumped on, in shiny wingtips and a crisply-pressed suit, he told the cheering crowd about how he had been taught by his mother to brush off racial slurs. "No one can make you feel inferior without your permission," she'd often told him. Once, when he recited a poem that he had learned in school about a young man whose summer was ruined when someone called him the "n" word, his mother was dismissive. "Larry, what a darn shame he let something like that spoil his vacation," she told him.

Soon, Mark Robinson, a Black gun-rights activist and pastor who was running for lieutenant governor of North Carolina, plodded onto the stage and began to vent. "I'm here today to make the left mad. And here's how you make the left mad. You make the left mad when you've got brown skin and your own mind!"

Robinson was in many ways the perfect BLEXIT candidate. Like Candace, he'd catapulted to fame on the web, after an April 2018 video of him went viral. Like Nick Freitas, the video glorified the right-wing's favorite prop: the firearm. In the clip, he urged the Greensboro City Council not to cancel a bi-annual gun show in the wake of the Parkland shooting and rising crime in the city. His Second Amendment rights were at stake, he told the council. The video garnered more than 150 million views, according to Robinson's campaign, and he got a new position as spokesman for the NRA. From there, he had grown his following through stops at hardware stores and gun shops around the state's one hundred counties, many of them rural, mostly ignoring the topic of race. ("Because that's not what he's about," his white campaign manager told me.)

This was Robinson's largest audience to date, and they loved him. After the show, attendees raced toward him. "You da bomb!" a young Black woman shouted. "I need to get a picture."

A few weeks later, the politically inexperienced Robinson would shock state GOP operatives by securing the Republican nomination. He would go on to become the state's first Black lieutenant governor.

Of course, Robinson was not the most important candidate Candace was laying her bets on. A Trump victory in 2020 would cement her status as a GOP golden girl—ensuring continued access to the White House and to the power and privilege that came along with Trump's good graces.

In 2016, Trump had done surprisingly well with Black voters in certain areas of North Carolina—including Robeson County, a large rural pocket in the southern part of the state, where 25 percent of the population is African American and 40 percent is American Indian. Despite the fact that the state's Black voters overwhelmingly voted Blue, the Robeson County results showed that Black voters were swayable, pollsters had declared in the wake of the election. This was one reason Candace was there.

Still, the biggest gift Black voters gave Trump in 2016—in North Carolina and other swing states—was staying home altogether. The 2016 election cycle represented a remarkable dip in African American turnout, meaning that even as Trump had failed to generate significant interest among Black voters (only 8 percent voted for him), his opponent Hillary Clinton's failure to convince millions of them to come out and support her had ultimately represented a significant victory for a man who wasn't averse to saying things like: "I like the Blacks." Facebook posts planted by Russian bots posing as African Americans insisting that Hillary Clinton was the recipient of Ku Klux Klan money, that "no lives matter" to her, and that "not voting is always a way to exercise our rights" is believed by many to have played a role in keeping some from making it to the polls for her as well. But so had, many suspected, an unsettling sense among some young Black voters that Clinton, and her former president husband, Bill, had been on the wrong side of one of the issues that had deeply affected the community: criminal justice. It was, after all, Bill Clinton's Crime Bill, signed into law in 1994, that had codified harsh sentencing mandates, often for petty drug dealers, and had resulted in a ballooning Black incarceration rate.

Trump was hardly a sophisticated campaigner, but he was good at sensing and then stoking the flames of bitterness. As the 2020 election neared, he began to make a ham-fisted argument, one that he would eventually tour the country with, and that he had shared with the Black conservative students who had shown up to the White House the previous October, during the second Young Black Leadership Summit Candace had hosted with TPUSA.

"Go with me, what the hell do you have to lose?" he told the crowd of three hundred. "For a hundred years, African Americans have gone with Democrats. Has it worked? Has it worked? . . . They haven't done anything for you. They haven't done anything. A hundred years—they haven't done anything."

Campaign strategists sometimes called such efforts by Republicans to leverage Black voters' disappointment with Democrats the "salt-in-the-wound strategy," because it rubbed in what they already believed to be true, without offering any real succor. It was a strategy Candace, too, liked to use. But for all her pontificating about how wrong-headed the left was, she was relatively silent on what modern-day Republicans had done for Black America.

By early spring 2020, as the first cases of COVID ravished the country, Candace was pregnant and settling into life with her new financier husband in a townhouse near Georgetown. Back in DC full time, the couple occasionally attended Vice President Mike Pence's DC area church and had begun hosting Sunday-night dinners with Farmer's British expat friends, Candace told me. She flew to Los Angeles every few months to interview Christian-right activists, conservative comedians, and at least one alt-right blogger and conspiracy spreader for her new eponymous PragerU talk show. Her set, which initially looked like a budget bachelorette pad, now featured blue velvet chairs, dark wood paneling, and Chinese vases—projecting the Old World affluence of a British manor house.

On social media, Candace was now practically inescapable, posting at a near frenetic rate on everything from her and George's run-in with a police officer during a trip to their local Whole Foods over mask-wearing, to Prince Harry's marriage to the "D-list actress" Meghan Markle—which would surely lead to Harry "losing his soul." Despite her 2-million-plus followers and daily tweets numbering in the dozens, her packed social calendar and regular Fox News appearances, Candace, along with other right-wing media stars, continued to cry foul over what she deemed social media suppression at the hands of America's tech giants. Candace was unapologetically dismissive when others claimed Black victimhood in the hands of the nation's jails, schools, courts, and corporate suites where systemic racism had long been documented. Yet she was eager—adamant, in fact—that others sympathize with her own victim status at the hands of an internet culture that had catapulted her to fame. Claiming victimhood, while denying it to those who history suggested might actually have legitimate complaints, was a right-wing trope that Candace had fully embraced. It seemed to be working. The more she railed about being muzzled by Twitter and Facebook, the more her audiences in those very spaces grew.

But not everyone was so easily swayed. Candace's husband, George Farmer, by then the new CEO of Parler, a social media platform favored by "canceled" right-wingers, reiterated Candace's claim that she and others were being bowdlerized by mainstream social media platforms on an episode of *Sway*, Kara Swisher's *New York Times* podcast. Swisher, famed for her candor and no-holes-barred skepticism, wasn't buying it: "I feel like your wife has plenty to say and gets to say it everywhere," Swisher told Farmer in January 2022. She added a few seconds later: "I seem to know what she's thinking in every moment of the day."

CHAPTER SEVENTEEN

Sowing Seeds

On the morning of March 13, 2020, a scandal broke out of Miami, via Twitter. Andrew Gillum, a married African American darling of the Democratic Party who had made a heavily funded, but ultimately unsuccessful bid for the Florida governorship in 2018, was discovered passed out and partially naked on the floor of a South Beach hotel room, surrounded by clear plastic bags filled with what looked like crystal meth. With him was a male sex worker. It was the kind of grimly tragic story that tabloid journalists live to break. In this case, the person who'd scooped them all was one Candace Owens, who had somehow obtained a copy of the police report and shared it online. "BREAKING: Democrat Andrew Gillum was involved in a crystal meth overdose incident last night in a Miami hotel. Orgy suspected, but unconfirmed," Candace called out to her 2-million-plus Twitter followers.

If the line between professional and amateur journalism was already blurring beyond recognition, the fact that Candace had just broken one of the biggest political scandals in recent Florida history seemed like a sign that it had now been all but erased.

Dutifully embracing her new role as news gatherer, Candace

updated the story multiple times that morning, with more information from her sources. Disturbing photos eventually surfaced. There were soiled hotel sheets, an empty beer bottle, and pills strewn on the carpet. Meanwhile, Candace became the subject of stories about the story. Who had tipped her off? The police? Hotel staff? Private investigators? Like Woodward and Bernstein, Candace refused to reveal her Deep Throat. Meanwhile, reporters from at least one Florida news outlet credited her as their original source. "I can't say I didn't enjoy that," she told me later.

Candace's foray into tabloid journalism didn't stop with the Gillum story. Two months later, when George Floyd was murdered by a Minneapolis police officer who leaned his knee on Floyd's neck for more than nine minutes, the nation was ablaze with rage, swept up in an outpouring of emotion that would drive millions into the streets and online to grieve and demand justice. But it was Candace's eighteen-minute video on Floyd's death that commanded one of the largest spotlights. A few days after it was released, it was the day's most popular post on Facebook, outperforming Mark Zuckerberg's own post proclaiming his support for the Black Lives Matter movement, according to Kevin Roose at the *New York Times*.

In the video, Candace expressed disdain for Floyd and anyone who saw him as a victim. Floyd was no hero, she proclaimed. He was a "horrible human being," who was "up to no good," and it was wrong-headed to turn him into "a martyr." Candace had become a megaphone for far-right views that even members of Trump's inner circle did not dare utter. Ivanka Trump, hardly a bastion of sympathy for America's needy, tweeted that her heart went out to "George Floyd's family and all Americans who are hurting."

Candace was just getting started, settling more deeply into her role as a modern woman of letters and a go-to advisor on Black conservatism. Her book *Blackout: How Black America Can Make Its Second Escape from the Democrat Plantation* would soon arrive on store shelves and rise to the top of the *NYT* bestseller list, just below Bob Woodward's *Rage*. It was a publishing coup that tickled the newbie author.

MEANWHILE, AS THE DEADLY CORONAVIRUS CONTINUED TO SPREAD through the country, killing Black Americans at a disproportionate rate, Candace donned yet another hat: that of science reporter, offering up her expertise and analysis of the pandemic, often with an eye on race.

"Remember the 40 year Tuskegee Experiment when our government pretended to give Black people a 'vaccine'—but actually gave them syphilis?" Candace asked her Twitter followers in June, tagging an article about concern among researchers that African Americans were underrepresented in clinical trials—and that could mean the vaccine, once produced, risked being less effective for them. (Genetics, socioeconomics, and environmental conditions all play a role in how people react to drugs.) Some researchers believed the Tuskegee tragedy, in which federal health investigators denied hundreds of Black men treatment for syphilis, had left many Black Americans with little to no trust in medical trials. They were scrambling for ways to increase participation, but Candace wasn't there to help.

Some Twitter followers offered Candace a correction. As shameful as the Tuskegee Study was, it did not in fact include a vaccine, they pointed out. You could almost see the eye rolls.

"They didn't give them syphilis you dodo bird!" one Tweeter noted, adding, "Just as horrific, but get your facts straight!"

Others pushed back on Candace's efforts to spread fear.

"Remember the billions of vaccines that have been safely administered ending many debilitating and life-threatening diseases?" one poster noted, hopefully.

But others accepted Candace's words at face value, seemingly appreciative of the reminder that so-called experts were not to be trusted.

". . . Humans are not Guinee pigs," one poster exclaimed.

"I'm not taking a vaccine. It's rushed. Its clumsy. And most importantly its unnecessary," came another disgruntled voice from the world wide web.

"Anti-Vaxer, as well . . ."

"Never trust the government."

The conversation kept going. But Candace was on to her next tweet.

On Fox News, during interviews with Laura Ingraham and Tucker Carlson, Candace chastised liberals for "racializing" medicine. The reason Black Americans were getting infected at higher rates than white Americans, she insisted, was because "leftists" made it hard for Black people to get jobs, creating economic disparities that rendered African Americans more susceptible to the virus.

Candace had plenty of company on her COVID soapbox. Science was now the new "it" beat in the far-right media ecosphere. In this world, an expert was anyone who wanted to be one. And the truth was anything they said. Charlie served as a clearinghouse for misinformative tidbits, tweeting to his 1.7 million followers Trump's assertion that hydroxychloroquine, a malaria drug that the FDA would soon advise those infected with COVID to *not* use, was a viable antidote. Will Witt at PragerU found a Beverly Hills primary care doctor to interview for a video titled "Don't let Covid-19 Fear Replace Your Freedom." The doctor, looking officious in a lab coat by a wall of his diplomas, chastised Americans for trying to avoid death. Once upon a time, death was "a chronic companion," he told Witt, who looked back at him, appearing earnest and intrigued. "People died all the time. People had ten children because only two would survive." James O'Keefe, the right-wing journalist-provocateur known for his undercover stings aimed at progressive institutions, produced a nine-and-a-half-minute video in which he informed viewers what some dudes he'd met on the street thought. "I'm speaking with these Army guys. I mean, they're basically just telling me it's just the bad flu. That's all they're saying. It's not as bad as the media is saying and everything."

NOT COINCIDENTALLY, AS THE CORONAVIRUS RAN RAMPANT through the world, and misinformation about it followed suit, the far-right conspiracy theory QAnon, Q for short, was also gathering steam, going from a cultish belief system championed in the far-right fringes of the internet to a mainstream phenomenon. By September 2020, a Pew Research Center study had found that roughly half of all Americans had heard of QAnon, two times the number of a year earlier. A few months later, 17 percent of respondents would tell pollsters for NPR and IPSOS, a market research firm, that they believed in the central lie that had launched the online community: that a global cabal of "Satan-worshipping elites who run a child sex ring are trying to control our politics and media."

Teasing out where QAnon's followers were coming from and how they were spreading became a new obsession of academics and online watchdog groups who soon discovered that the lies were generally filtering out from a small group of imageboard websites like 4chan and 8chan, which were popular among members of the alt-right. They migrated to REDDIT and eventually into the mainstream via right-wing media celebrities with large social media followings, like actress Roseanne Barr, and the radio commentator and conspiracy theorist Alex Jones, who had helped spread lies about the tragic Sandy Hook shooting. There were so many interconnected threads to the QAnon lie machine, all interlaced with hints of apocalyptic panache, dashes of Christian iconography, and whiffs of New Age spirituality, it was hard to keep track of them all. There were rumblings about white people being immune to COVID-19 and Asian people being more likely to contract it. Rumor spread that a vitamin supplement deemed dangerous by the FDA, Miracle Mineral Supplement, was a good preventive tool. Even relative moderates like the comedian Joe Rogan were now introducing unfounded health claims and discussions of "the deep State" to their mainstream audiences via guests who came on to talk about them.

These conversations grew the looming fears that QAnon adherents lived with on a daily basis: that evil bureaucrats were poised to take over the country. As the phenomenon spread, virus-like, trust in the knowledge of verifiable experts—with hard-won degrees and practical experience—was dissipating even more. What you saw or read was authoritative simply because you were seeing it or reading it. No gatekeepers. No institutions. The facts weren't just submerged—they were irrelevant. It was creative, it was free-form. And for many, it was a new lease on life.

QAnon's alleged founders were middle-aged—one was married with kids—and there is no evidence that their theories were particularly appealing to young conservatives. But they softened the ground for more untruths. And over the next few months, as the country's appetite for these untruths rose, young conservative influencers were more than happy to feed the beast, increasingly relating these conspiracies to one Trump was hoping to plant deep into the American psyche: that the American electoral process was reaped in corruption—and if he lost in 2020, it was because the election had been stolen.

Soon, on her PragerU show, Candace was ranting that the pandemic was the "greatest rigging of an American election that has ever taken place." As for Charlie, he now had a daily podcast show. And he, too, used his pulpit to stoke fear about the grave concerns he had about 2020 pro-Trump ballots suddenly disappearing.

As the 2020 election neared, Students for Trump—a new

TPUSA arm—was being empowered to help corral more young people to the polls for the president and help him to spread the stolen election myth. Charlie had acquired the name and the assets from Campbell University graduate Ryan Fournier, who had founded the first Students for Trump in 2015. In June of 2020, inside a North Phoenix mega church, Students for Trump would invite hundreds to risk infection in exchange for a chance to hear the president share his conspiracies. The church holding this indoor Trump rally was in a county that was losing an estimated fifteen people per day to COVID. It was appropriately named Dream City, had seven locations in the Southwest, and was founded as a Pentecostal tent revival in 1923. A few days before the event, as newscasters and anxious Phoenix residents got wind that a "superspreader" was hitting their town, the church's leaders announced a miracle, in a video posted on the church's website. A filtration system had just been installed inside the church, designed by one of the congregants no less. And it "kills 99.9 percent of Covid within ten minutes."

"So when you come into our auditorium, 99 percent of Covid is gone, killed, if it was there in the first place," the pastor, Luke Barnett, assured potential attendees in the video. "You can know when you come here, you'll be safe and protected. Thank God for great technology and thank God for being proactive."

The video was eventually taken off the web, amidst a flurry of bad press over the unsubstantiated claims.

The next day, close to three thousand people stormed through the church doors, maskless and free, in flip-flops and jean shorts, sleeveless tops and cargos, presumably convinced they were safe. They settled shoulder to shoulder in comfy movie theater–style seats and listened as the president, largely ignoring the health crisis gripping the nation, instead gave a winding speech about "the radical left" and its "mob violence." He spoke of the building of his border wall, and his dream that the United States would be the first to plant a flag on Mars. Then, he unfurled his own conspiratorial yarn on the topic that now obsessed him: voter fraud.

"Will they be stolen? . . ." Trump asked of the mail-in ballots that would make it easier and safer to vote during the pandemic, but that he now feared, perhaps above all else. ". . . Taken from the mailmen and the mailwomen. Will they be forged? Who is signing them? Who's signing them? What, are they signed on . . . the kitchen table and sent in? Will they be counterfeited by groups inside our Nation? Will they be counterfeited, maybe by the millions, by foreign powers who don't want to see Trump win because nobody has been tougher on trade or making our country great again? Nobody. No, mail-in ballots is a disaster for our country . . ."

Trump continued his apocalyptic tale while thousands of his supporters listened with alarm. He was planting his "stolen election" seeds, one speech at a time, surely confident that the poisonous kernels would flourish under the care and feeding of high-profile disciples like Candace, Charlie, and Benny at TPUSA. And he was right. Trump loyalists came in all shapes and sizes, but they all shared one common trait: their willingness to tell his stories, no matter how unbelievable they were.

CHAPTER EIGHTEEN

Spreading the Steal Story

S tanding behind a podium in a near-empty room, flanked by ten large American flags, Charlie focused his gaze on the camera in front of him and declared President Donald Trump "the bodyguard of Western civilization," a man elected in 2016 to "protect our families from the vengeful mob that seeks to destroy our way of life, our neighborhoods, schools, churches, and values."

It was August 2020 and Charlie was taping his speech for the Republican National Convention, usually a high-spirited party-palooza of an event—but this year, thanks to COVID, more or less a staid, mostly prerecorded affair. The convention production team had given Charlie five minutes, then requested that he dwindle his speech down a bit. He was accommodating, made the appropriate edits, and was told he might make the first day.

Charlie ended up opening the entire four-day affair, setting the tone—as Charlie was prone to do—for that night and the entire convention. Trump, buckling under the pressure of a killer virus he couldn't manage, was going to save the nation from the real devil—which in GOP World meant the mail-in ballot. It was the conservative movement's latest punching bag in their effort to win in November.

A few days later, *Esquire* magazine astutely noted: "The theme of the RNC is already clear: Any election where Trump doesn't win is illegitimate."

Besides Charlie's opportunity to shine, the 2020 Republican National Convention was largely a dud. Pesky COVID had made sure of that. The procedural to-do list—the delegate roll call, the formal re-nomination of Trump, and the party platform discussions—took place in a largely shut down Charlotte. To keep crowds to a minimum, only 336 delegates—a seventh of the usual number—were permitted to show. And the typical frolicky parties, oozing with booze, had been clamped down. Plans for a Toby Keith concert, a prayer breakfast at the Billy Graham Library, and a "Southern Comfort" bash with bluegrass, beach music, and all varieties of Carolina barbecue had been canceled.

Tyler Bowyer, the TPUSA COO and politically engaged careerist, who was simultaneously building the youth outfit and his own power inside the Arizona GOP, did fly in from Phoenix, but only because he was now an RNC national committee member. Bowyer was increasingly convinced that not only were Democrats guilty of trying to rob Americans of their president, but so, too, were the hated RINOs. Some in Arizona would eventually reject his delusional beliefs about who had won the election.

But that was later. Now, Bowyer was focusing on a different enemy: county election workers, the kind of people small-government conservatives tend to see as incompetent tools of a bloated bureaucracy. Yet in the face of the voter fraud fantasies being whipped up by the GOP, these workers were now uber competent professionals, able to orchestrate wide-spread voter suppression schemes. "The fraud is real!" was a favorite Bowyer talking point.

As for Charlie, he hoped that his successful showing at the convention, rather than the canceled live events, signaled the real future for his president and the larger GOP. Personally, for the young activist, though, it had been a tough summer. In July, not long after TPUSA posted a meme of a young, relaxed Nicolas Cage with a snarky caption that read: "Me, Not Wearing A Mask"—a sort of middle finger to uptight mask-obsessed Americans— Charlie's onetime wingman and TPUSA co-founder Bill Montgomery, eighty, had died of COVID-related complications. Charlie trekked back to Lemont, Illinois, to give a speech, extolling Bill, the Fox News watching gadgeteer, a man who was "relentlessly positive" and "perpetually optimistic."

"I miss him, I really do. Terribly," Charlie mourned.

Still, it was not a great look when your business partner dies of a virus whose Center for Disease Control–approved preventive measures you have been publicly refusing to follow.

That August, just as the convention was getting going, news had also broken that Jerry Falwell Jr., Charlie's friend, Liberty University president, and co-creator of the Falkirk Center, a Christian think tank the two had founded in 2019, was embroiled in a sex scandal. A Miami pool attendant had alleged that, for years, he had been having sex with Falwell's wife, Becki, while Jerry sometimes watched. In a statement, Jerry told reporters that Becki had had "an inappropriate personal relationship" with the young man, but insisted that he "was not involved." Soon after, he resigned from his Liberty post. And in March 2021, the university would announce it wasn't interested in renewing Charlie's contract. The think tank would get a new name and a new focus.

Now, as election day approached and mail-in voting commenced, Charlie threw himself into further promoting the GOP's sad sack story: that Democrats were plotting to steal the election. The stories already circling the web were Hollywood-esque in their complexity. Bags filled with ballots were going missing, suitcases with ballots in them were suddenly appearing. And zombies were preparing to rise from the dead and head to the polls.

In October, Charlie, misquoting an article from the Pulitzer Prize–winning investigative news site ProPublica, tweeted to his fans: "Pennsylvania has just rejected 372,000 mail-in ballots. One voter was said to have submitted 11 duplicate ballots. Pennsylvania might be the key to winning the election—what's going on?" he asked his followers.

What the article had actually said was that the state had rejected 372,000 general election ballot applications. And in more than 90 percent of the cases that was because the requesters were already getting mail-in ballots. Charlie eventually deleted the tweet.

Even Candace was in on the game, fully committed to a host of her own misleading claims that depicted Democrats as ruthless manipulators. One claim was that former New York mayor Michael Bloomberg was "paying off the debts of 31,000 Floridians to get them to vote for Joe Biden." She called for imprisonment, ignoring the fact that Bloomberg was, himself, responding to widespread voter suppression efforts at the hands of Florida Republicans.

Despite the fraud claims, the real worry Charlie and his Republican allies had with the upcoming election was not that there were stolen ballots, or a massive number of illegally filled out ballots, as they alleged. Rather, it was a central head-scratching dilemma that the American GOP had to regularly grapple with: their fear that more donkeys were roaming the country than elephants. The more Americans who voted, went the conventional wisdom, the more likely the Republicans were to lose. And Trump's numbers, despite a small bump after the convention, were already in the toilet. Everyone seemed to know they had an uphill battle ahead of them. And keeping Democrats from the polls was the best tactic they had.

Like most of the plots to preserve power in the nation's conservative circles, the campaign to curb voting wasn't original. In 1980, Paul Weyrich, the cunning conservative movement mind and founder of the American Legislative Exchange Council, told a

Dallas gathering of right-wing Christians: "I don't want everybody to vote . . . As a matter of fact, our leverage in the elections quite candidly goes up as the voting populace goes down."

Twenty years later, in 2000, after a nail-biting recount in Florida that left many wondering if he'd really won fair and square, newly elected president George W. Bush, under the tutelage of his senior advisor Karl Rove, launched his own campaign to fight back on a make-believe enemy: voter fraud. So pernicious was the effort, the *Atlantic* published a piece called "Karl Rove's Voter Fraud Fetish." And after five years of intense scrutiny, all that could be found, the article noted, were a few cases of "confused felons and immigrants."

No matter: in the coming years, extensive efforts were made by the GOP to rectify a problem it couldn't prove existed. In 2011 alone, early-voting periods were restricted in six states, two states did away with same-day registration, and three states enacted voter ID laws.

In 2013, when the Supreme Court struck down key portions of the 1965 Voting Rights Act, insisting that such protections, originally designed to franchise more Black voters, were no longer necessary, giddy Republicans went to town. The ruling paved the way for nine states to rewrite election laws without federal oversight. Ohio, in 2016, slashed a whole early-voting week. And Nebraska cut its early-voting period from thirty-five days to no more than thirty days.

Since then the dark art of voter suppression had become a favorite pastime of the politically engaged Republican activist. So, it should not have been a surprise that a few months before the election, Charlie would laud diminished voting to his fellow right-wing activists who had gathered for a closed-door meeting of the Council for National Policy, another group that Weyrich had founded years earlier, when he, too, was seeking to garner more gains for the right. In a video obtained by the *Washington Post*, Charlie was heard telling a room of cheering conservatives that

COVID-related campus closures meant that at least some students were likely to refrain from voting. "So, please keep the campuses closed . . . Like, it's a great thing."

For all his proclaimed efforts to engage college kids in politics, when push came to shove, Charlie wasn't actually very excited about young people expressing their views at the polls.

BY MID-SUMMER, TRUMP'S NUMBERS WERE SO LOW THAT CHARlie believed the left was "betting on a conservative surrender." But he wasn't giving his enemies that satisfaction. Mostly maskless, he launched his final push. He hopscotched from one state to the next, sometimes flying commercial, other times flying with donors on their planes. Charlie told me he wasn't sleeping much, subsisting on Perfect Bars and iced coffees from Starbucks. With his hair unusually long and disheveled, he was looking more and more like a modern-day Che Guevara—except instead of fighting for the people, in the name of Marx, he was fighting for a millionaire real estate mogul in the name of Christianity. "God will win," he had tweeted that spring. And on his podcast, he sometimes dedicated hours to his erudite thoughts on various Bible passages and their connection to science and the Constitution, a holy document, Charlie often reminded his listeners.

Charlie now traveled with an entourage, a rotation that included his girlfriend, Erika Frantzve, and his personal pastor Rob McCoy. McCoy believed that what went on inside Charlie's brain was near magical. He regularly wrote down words Charlie said and looked them up. Choosing McCoy as a traveling companion was not random—McCoy, a pastor at Godspeak Calvary Chapel near Los Angeles, was part of a powerful consortium of pastor politicians who rejected the Christian right's decision in the late nineties to retreat from the culture wars and turn inward.

Charlie and McCoy's increasingly close relationship aligned

with their shared belief in the Seven Mountain Mandate—or 7M to insiders—a kind of biblical manifesto that sees the world as cloaked in evil and calls on Christians to take charge of every sphere of American life: including education, media, arts and entertainment, finance, family, politics, and of course religion. Charlie had spoken openly about this in a CPAC speech in 2018. Trump, he said during the speech, was the first president who really understood the "seven mountains of cultural influence." McCoy had put the project to work in his own life in 2015, when he was elected to the Thousand Oaks City Council. He then served as mayor, a post he resigned from in protest of California's COVID-mandated church closures, which his church proudly defied. Now, he and Charlie were working together to try and get Trump re-elected. For many on the left, the 2020 race was about truth and lies, science and conspiracy. For Charlie and this new band of religious zealots, the 2020 election was a "cataclysmic collision" between worldviews. And God was working through them.

THAT FALL IN A MIAMI BALLROOM, AFTER A PRO-TRUMP MARIACHI band played outside, Charlie told the crowd that if the president didn't win it would "become nearly impossible for decent and normal people ever to have a voice again."

He talked to lobstermen in Maine and farmers in Iowa. In October, he made a stop in Omaha, a swing region of Nebraska, looking to help Trump snag all of Nebraska's five electoral college votes (Nebraska is one of two states, along with Maine, that divides up its votes). In a wedding hall across from a wheat field, Charlie listened attentively while a rambling Don Jr. told stories about his father, including one in which he caught Junior coming late to the office, again, after a night of partying. Soon after, Don's girlfriend Kimberly Guilfoyle, the former Fox News commentator turned Trump advisor, offered the audience a reason to vote for Trump. He works so hard, she told the crowd of supporters—many of them Students for Trump members who had driven miles to get there.

"You're really getting a bang for your buck," Don added.

After the dynamic duo had slipped off for their next event, Charlie stood on the stage solo and begged those in attendance to spend the next few weekends knocking on doors, planting signs, and making calls.

"All of you," he bellowed out into the darkened hall. "If you feel like you're losing your country, if you feel like this is our last chance, guess what? You're living in a place that could determine the future of the republic. Where it could be the tie breaker . . . Could you imagine if Joe Biden gets elected president and this district turns on its values? And I'm not trying to scare you," he added, as he tried to scare them.

With a burst of energy, Charlie finally let out: "Everybody elevate the level of activism . . . My goodness, vote correctly and vote your values."

Charlie continued to make his anxiety over voter fraud a keystone issue as he traveled around the country. In Flagstaff, Arizona, he stood on a makeshift stage in a small airport hangar, facing a crowd of unmasked red-T-shirt-wearing fans who were ready to fight the good fight by knocking on doors nearby. As was often the case now, the elder McCoy was there by Charlie's side as he spoke about the need to win Arizona.

"If we rise up, we win. This is a battleground state. I know that's a wake-up call for a lot of you. It is not a comfortably Republican state. It's not. Get that out of your mind—you now basically live in the Southwestern equivalent of Ohio."

After Charlie finished rallying the troops, I regrouped with him in a back room at a conference table strewn with empty water bottles. Ruth Bader Ginsburg had died just ten days earlier and Amy Coney Barrett, a law professor from Notre Dame and powerhouse in Christian conservative legal circles, was about to be announced as Trump's choice to replace Ginsburg on the Supreme Court. Coney Barrett was an outspoken opponent of *Roe v. Wade*, and the Dems were distressed as they waited for the confirmation hearings and her inevitable appointment to the bench. Meanwhile, TPUSA staff, always ready for a graphic design challenge, was pumped. Black T-shirts with Coney Barrett's face and "ACB" scrawled across them were soon released, a not-so-original effort to suggest she would become a youthful icon for the right the way Ginsburg had been for the left.

Asked about Coney Barrett, Charlie said it was payback for what they did to Kavanaugh. "Gloves are off."

I had been covering Charlie for close to three years at this point. And over the course of my reporting on him, he had changed, going from an awkward conservative kid who had gotten a lot of his info from YouTube videos to a power player who called multimillionaires his friends and saw himself as a messenger from God, committed to telling young people how to live their lives. And as each month passed, he was more and more reluctant to talk to me, often pawning me off on others in his circle instead. Even my requests to hear about what I called his "faith journey" were rebuked.

Charlie's critics delighted in depicting him as a buffoon, a silly man with low intelligence who was always steps away from his comeuppance. But like many of the people who inhabited the far-right religious bubble he now lived in, Charlie was smart—astute about politics, about Trump's popularity, about what the Dems didn't get. He was also alarmingly comfortable mixing fact and fiction. Whether he was denying that he had made a statement that reporters had on video, telling pumped up Trump supporters that ballots were "coming out of nowhere," or warning his young, devoted fan base that "some doctors think masks actually make you sicker," his grasp of reality seemed shaky at best. And he seemed not only okay with that, but liberated by it.

My approach as a journalist was to remain honest but not contentious. If Charlie said something I knew to be untrue, I kept my mouth shut. I didn't need to argue; I needed to listen.

I was trying to convince him to give me access to the rest of his campaign stops. But he was deeply resistant.

"I don't trust journalists," he told me matter-of-factly.

I didn't doubt it. And he didn't seem persuadable, on this or any other front. One didn't need to be a reporter to deduce the unshakability of Charlie's conviction that no matter what he did or said, it was the right thing, because God was on *his* side.

JUST BEFORE MIDNIGHT ON THE EVE OF THE ELECTION, TRUMP landed in an airfield in Grand Rapids, Michigan—a superstitious scheduling move, as it had been the locale of his last rally in 2016, before he ramrodded to victory, shocking the nation and himself. It was bitter cold, 31 degrees, with blustery winds. Trump's kids and their significant others were there. And Charlie was headed there, too. As he drove along the highway, the crowded lane next to him was packed with one car after another, headed for the parking lot where buses would take the locals to see their president. It went on like that for miles. At the rally, Trump's fans chanted, "Four More Years! Four More Years!" beneath a large blue sign that read *The Best Is Yet to Come*. Michigan guitarist Ted Nugent performed the national anthem. And Charlie, who had been worrying about Trump's chances for months, tweeted to his fans: "Don't believe the polls. Enthusiasm is surging like never before."

It was entirely unclear to me whether he really believed this.

ON THE EVENING OF NOVEMBER 3, AS THE LAST OF THE POLLS were closing around the country, a video of a near-hysterical woman outside a Phoenix-area polling station, reportedly recorded around eight p.m. that night, began circulating the web. She told a story about polling officials who were handing out Sharpies to Republican voters, so their votes for the president would go uncounted. The Sharpies, she was certain, were rendering them illegible and dooming them to be rejected by voting machines.

"They had a bowl of pens behind them that they were not giving to people and only giving Sharpies out," the voter claimed.

#SharpieGate was born. The conspiracy theory, tailor-made to erode confidence in the electoral process, would spread rapid-fire throughout Arizona and beyond. Within twenty-four hours, it was one of a series of storylines stoking fear among millions of Americans that their president was being robbed of a second term in the White House.

TPUSA staff, including Tyler Bowyer, were some of the first to pass on the video. "If this happened," tweeted Bowyer, late in the morning on November 4, "the entire AZ election is in question."

Charlie spent election day doing Fox interviews and his own show and tweeting out his own fraud claims: "The question isn't whether or not Donald Trump can beat Joe Biden—we know the answer to that. The question today is whether he can beat voter fraud and Democrat lawsuits to steal the election."

The Students for Trump team at the Arizona headquarters huddled in front of laptops, chugging sodas and eating from pizza boxes. It appeared it could go either way. And no one seemed certain of anything, which may have been why, in recent months, Charlie had been making his own plans—ones not dependent on a Trump victory. He was migrating his increasingly popular independent podcast to the Christian conservative radio outfit Salem Media, the old haunt of recently deceased Rush Limbaugh. As for TPUSA, it was adding stars to its YouTube lineup and committing to a live three-hour Facebook show that would air every Monday through Friday with a whopping twelve contributors. They included a buff, blond-haired sportscaster; a former contestant on *The Apprentice*; and a polished-looking activist who founded a group called Young Americans Against Socialism and sold vintage American flags online. It was a Dream Team that would appear together in promo videos all dressed up and looking cheerful and relatable, as if they were a morning news lineup on a mainstream network.

That night, as Charlie watched the numbers come in on the various networks, he grew increasingly agitated. There was something very suspicious about the lag time, he felt. Florida polls closed at seven p.m. And Trump won by a decisive 370,000 votes. So why did the Associated Press wait until well past midnight to call the state?

On the other hand, Charlie noted, newscasters at Fox News and the Associated Press were strangely quick to call Arizona for Biden. The AP called it shortly before three a.m. Washington D.C. time. But there were still hundreds of thousands of ballots out, and Charlie was already fantasizing about the hated liberal networks—and the apostate Fox—being forced to retract the Arizona call. Other early battleground wins for Biden included New Hampshire and Minnesota, while Trump took Ohio and Iowa.

At four a.m. Charlie went to bed, unsettled.

BY NOVEMBER 4, 2020, AS THE VOTE TALLYING CONTINUED, THE odds were not looking good for Trump. "We are up BIG," Trump shot out to his 88 million Twitter followers, shortly before sunup. "But they are trying to STEAL the Election. We will never let them do it."

Charlie was also sure something was terribly off. "It looks increasingly clear that there was a plan," he shouted out to his own conservative radio audience—whipping himself up into a frenzy as he echoed the cries coming that morning from across the far-right web.

"Welcome to the third world," Charlie wailed.

His listeners were getting riled up, too.

"Civil War," typed someone on his online chat stream.

"We want Civil War," wrote another.

A multipronged post-election misinformation campaign that had begun months before with Trump's insistence that his loss would mean a stolen election was soon in full swing. And Charlie, Candace, and the TPUSA gang were soon smack dab in the middle of it, driving traffic like few others.

As for Tyler Bowyer, he was on #Sharpiegate duty, collecting fishy stories about tampered ballots, with or without Sharpies. "Please DM me your detailed statement and contact information," he tweeted out helpfully, now assuming the role of evidence gatherer.

Later that morning, Charlie endorsed an online announcement for a rally that Friday outside the Maricopa County tabulation center in Phoenix, where ballot counting was still underway. It was one of a series of protests that took place over the following few days, there and in other spots around the country. Many fell under the loose #StoptheSteal umbrella launched by far-right renegade and convicted felon Ali Alexander. A prolific conspiracy-theorist, Alexander had experience recruiting for unfounded election-fraud movements. During the 2018 midterms, he had paired up with Trump advisor and ruthless Republican operative Roger Stone—also a convicted felon, but one whose sentence Trump eventually commuted—during a #StoptheSteal campaign for a close Florida senate race where ballot counting went well beyond election day. The Republican candidate eventually won, which apparently meant there had been no steal. They dropped the campaign.

On the night of November 4, Mike Cernovich, the far-right provocateur and #Pizzagate conspiracy booster, showed up in Arizona after a seven-hour road trip from California to join his comrades outside the state capitol.

But for days, it was the Phoenix tabulation center that became the real hub for hundreds of impassioned protesters. Many were armed, some with AR-15 rifles. Others were wrapped in flags, their faces painted red, white, and blue. They clutched *Stop the Cheat* signs donated by FreedomWorks, a training center for right-wing protesters that had supported Tea Party activists and COVID lock-down protests. It was now assisting the efforts of the #StoptheSteal movement. There were tambourines. There was crying. There were men, women, and children lying on the pavement, praying. There were people dancing, playing guitars, and swirling glowsticks. There were grizzled Trump supporters insisting they were done being nice. There was Charlie telling attendees that Democrats had launched "a governmental coup."

And there was Alex Jones, the right-wing radio host who for years tormented the families of children murdered in the Sandy Hook shooting by denying the massacre had happened. Blasting hoarsely into a megaphone, Jones told protesters, many of whom had been lured there by Charlie and Turning Point Action, that Democrats were calling for "mass murder," that Antifa and BLM would be "launching their attacks this weekend," that "people needed to go to DC and surround the White House."

It was only a harbinger of things to come.

CHAPTER NINETEEN

The Insurrectionists

As the weeks passed, a string of legal attempts to further discredit the election were struck down in the courts, and ballot recounts affirmed Biden's wins. But the TPUSA gang and its friends—most notably Candace, Benny Johnson, and now Jake Hoffman, the Rally Forge social media executive who had just won an Arizona House seat (somehow untouched by the rampant "fraud" that had befallen Trump), continued to press the Stop the Steal narrative, relentlessly saturating social media with erroneous "evidence" that the Republican incumbent had been robbed of a rightful second term in the White House. The theories TPUSA promoted were, as always, confidently and confusingly presented. And their particulars said a lot about the personalities of the people pushing them.

True to form, Johnson posed as a wound-up voice of inexhaustible paranoia, there to shock the bejesus out of his devoted followers.

"You have every right to be suspicious about an election that was suspicious as hell," he ranted to his peanut gallery on a late November episode of *The Benny Report*, his Newsmax show.

A frenzied Johnson went on to tell his audience members that there was "a trillion-dollar corporate media industry" gaslighting them, brushing aside their legitimate questions about Biden's victory and trying to convince them that they were "nuts."

Johnson hyped a new Trump lawsuit in Nevada that claimed dead voters had cast ballots and tens of thousands of Nevada residents had voted twice. (The suit would be dismissed by a district court judge in Nevada's Clark County and the appeal would be thrown out on December 4, as well as by the state supreme court.)

Gaining steam, he repeated the conspiracy theory that Dominion Voting Systems equipment, used to process votes in twenty-eight states, was rigged against Trump. The equipment was "about as trustworthy as Ilhan Omar's marriage certificates," he quipped. Soon trying for another crowd-pleasing dig against a favorite target, he told his audience that the company "employs Trump-hating Antifa members as security engineers" and "their votes are counted off of American soil."

(All claims against Dominion would be debunked by election technology experts and voting industry officials, and the company would file a $1.6 billion suit against Newsmax, among other conservative news outlets, claiming that the channel "created an entire brand out of defaming" the company.)

Meanwhile, Candace was developing her own post-election voter fraud style: keeping the tweets flowing and her tone teen-magazine sassy. "People that are pretending that @JoeBiden & the Democrats didn't rig this election despite the overwhelming evidence are the same kind of folks who claimed O.J. Simpson didn't do it," she tweeted. After she unloaded a litany of conspiracy theories that included "faked plumbing leaks" and "overnight ballot dumps," she ended with another sprinkle of zippy teenage-like flare. "Haha NO. #BidenCheated."

Charlie's Twitter feed was also a tsunami of conspiracies. But the self-proclaimed movie buff tended to favor ones that came with enticing plots, stories with suspense that could get the imagination going. "BREAKING: Corroborated, eyewitness testimony alleges that up to 280,000 completed ballots were shipped from New York to Lancaster, Pennsylvania," he told his followers, as if conveying Act One of a movie script. Act Two: "The ballots AND the trailer then disappeared."

Anyone with the analytical ability and intellectual confidence to say "Wait, these stories don't add up" was branded a deep state sympathizer. No matter how far-fetched an election fraud claim might be, no matter how many times it was discredited in the courts or by ballot recounts, TPUSA's golden-tongued talking heads and their followers insisted that it was the left that was gaslighting the public, not the right.

IN EARLY DECEMBER, FLEETS OF RED BUSES EMBLAZONED WITH Donald Trump's likeness—paid for in part by Mike Lindell, the My Pillow founder and TPUSA honorary board member—traversed the United States to encourage protesters to attend a January 6, 2021, "March for Trump" rally in DC.

At the same time, Charlie and the team at Turning Point Action, TPUSA's political action arm, also began promoting the March to Save America. "Join us in DC!" beckoned an online flyer for the event. "Ride a bus & receive priority entry; Stay in a complimentary hotel; Meet us there."

At least three other protests were also being organized to coincide with the day Congress would certify the election and officially declare Joe Biden the next United States president, with armed members of far-right groups, including the Proud Boys, pledging to attend. Numerous news organizations reported a significant increase in insurrectionist online chatter in the days leading up to the protests. On the fringe message board 8kun, previously known as 8chan, members debated just how violent their rebellion should be. As reported by NBC News, one 8kun user posted before the siege: "We will storm the government buildings, kill cops, kill security guards, kill federal employees and agents, and demand a recount." While some on the board balked at violence, analysts at the Network Contagion Research Institute, a nonprofit that monitors disinformation on the web, were among many experts to deem the upcoming event "a plausible threat."

On January 5, seven Turning Point Action buses, carrying a total of 350 passengers, departed from cities across the country. Charlie had originally tweeted that the group would be sending more than eighty buses. Later, that tweet would disappear from his feed, and a public relations representative for Turning Point Action and TPUSA would offer a revised, smaller number.

The original plan was to drive all night, arrive in time for Trump's morning speech, hit the rally, and stay the night in a hotel. But one rider told me that upon boarding the bus in North Carolina, he was informed that they would not be staying in hotels after all; following the speech, they were to get right back on the buses and return home.

The young man said that several students wanted to know why the march was no longer part of the schedule. "And a lot of the times that we asked, they didn't answer," he told me. "But some of the answers we did get were things along the lines of: 'Well, this is a risky endeavor.'" The young man was told there was concern that some of the high school students on board might get lost. "It was going to be very easy for us to lose each other. And we just didn't want to have any mistakes like that come up," he says he was told.

Even with the decision to pull back, Turning Point Action appears to have transported at least one violent protester, a fifty-five-year-old retired Pennsylvania firefighter by the name of Robert Sanford. In a court filing, Sanford claimed he boarded a bus he thought was organized by Turning Point USA to Washington, D.C. When he got to DC, he attended Trump's "Save America

Rally," then heeded the president's calls to head for the Capitol. Once there, according to a criminal complaint, he climbed over a short wall and then hurled a fire extinguisher into a group of police officers, hitting three of them in the head. He was charged with multiple federal crimes and, as of this writing, has reached a plea agreement with the government. Turning Point Action told *Business Insider* that it had "no record" of the man boarding one of their buses.

Trump's raging, mournful speech in a park near the White House lasted more than an hour. "Our country has had enough," he bellowed. "We will not take it anymore. And that is what this is about. And to use a term that all of you people really came up with, we will 'stop the steal.'" Trump rambled on: "Big tech is now coming into their own . . . And by the way, does anybody believe that Joe had 80 million votes?" As Trump approached the end of his speech, he offered up fighting words, literally: "And we fight. We fight like hell, and if you don't fight like hell, you're not going to have a country anymore."

Most attendees who had come via Turning Point Action headed for the buses. But many other attendees did not. They headed for the Capitol, where Congress was counting the electoral votes. The group progressed slowly, and then more quickly, soon joined by more and more protesters. They had dressed up for the event. Some in superhero costumes, others draped in faux animal skins, American flags, and spandex. They accessorized with ballistic helmets and military-style backpacks. They clutched knives, axes, police batons, hockey sticks, baseball bats, pepper spray, electric shock devices, and flags they would eventually weaponize and brandish as clubs. Some carried 9 mm Glocks.

Once at the Capitol, they stormed the grassy lawn, many of them in a heightened state of hysteria. They chanted: "America! Let's Go! Let's Do This Thing! U.S.A.! U.S.A.!" At one point, there were chants to kill the vice president. A group of rioters who had arrived about twenty minutes before Trump's speech ended were the first to push past a series of preliminary barriers on the west side of the Capitol, sparring with Capitol Police, knocking them over and punching them. The group breached three more barriers, forcing officers up to the Capitol steps, and stormed inside, as rioters on the east side of the building were also approaching. Some breached the west wall and struggled with more officers. Others pushed their way in via a west side tunnel, eventually trampling a thirty-four-year-old woman to death. The antigovernment group known as the Oath Keepers, made up of former law enforcement officers and military veterans, pushed their way through the Rotunda door, holding on to each other and pelting objects at officers and spraying them with pepper spray. Once inside, members flooded through the building, waving their flags, clambering up stairwells. They broke glass, sometimes with their bare fists, wounding officers and each other, as more protesters streamed in from the east side of the building.

At home, millions watched in disbelief. But Charlie, recording his live podcast, the *Charlie Kirk Show*, from Phoenix, appeared little surprised as the Capitol walls were first breached and the violence began to escalate.

Between reporting on a bomb threat and the evacuation of Vice President Pence, Charlie bantered with his podcast team—correspondents in the studio, and a reporter on the ground—about Hillary Clinton, Michael Flynn, TPUSA T-shirts, and human nature.

The messaging was clear. Charlie repeated multiple times that he did not support the insurrectionists. But he also wanted his listeners to know he had warned against this. He oscillated between denouncing the unfolding violence—calling it "reprehensible" and urging perpetrators to "stop it"—to suggesting that the protesters were in fact members of ANTIFA, or perhaps a group of "leftwing agitators" posing as MAGA supporters.

But most notable was Charlie's assertion that if indeed the protesters were Trump supporters, their rage was understandable. "Look, you can only insult and poke people in the eye for so long until they're going to burst."

Over the next few hours, police officers would be attacked, protesters would be injured, and property would be destroyed, while Charlie remained matter-of-fact, a sportscaster narrating a series of impressive touchdown drives. He and his in-studio team watched clips of the insurrection, pulling them up for audience members to see, chatted with Madison Cawthorn, the young, scandal-ridden North Carolina Congressman, and took note of what one protester was wearing: a lot of black.

When Charlie watched the bloody body of Ashli Babbitt, the Trump supporter and Air Force vet shot and killed by a police officer, being removed from the Capitol on a stretcher, Charlie offered up one of the first signs that he truly understood the gravity of the situation. "Yes, it looks like people are getting very, very hurt, covered in blood and in bad shape . . . ," he said. "Wow."

TWO DAYS AFTER THE JANUARY 6 CAPITOL RIOTS, ADDYSON GARner, the Liberty University graduate who had tried unsuccessfully to implement more comprehensive sexual harassment training across YAL, decided it was time to start an uprising of her own. Though she had since stepped back from YAL and had recently finished up a legislative correspondent position in the U.S. House of Representatives, Garner remained troubled by what was happening to women inside YAL. It was wrong, and she wanted to stop it.

Garner, the daughter of a social worker and a pizza shop owner, had grown up in Peoria, Illinois, in a tight-knit Baptist community where girls were expected to dress modestly and conform to traditional gender roles. Most of the young people she went to her small Christian high school with went on to small, faith-based colleges like Bob Jones University or Pensacola Christian College. Going to the large, evangelical Liberty University marked her as a rebel. (At Liberty, women wore pants, men could have ponytails, and couples could hold hands in public.) Soon after Addyson arrived on the Lynchburg, Virginia, campus, she emerged as a rebel there, too, self-identifying as a feminist. She even opposed Candace Owens's visit to the school in September 2018. To counter Candace's MeToo-bashing statements she'd made online and during campus tours, Addyson had requested that the administration set up a table to distribute Title IX information. When the school denied her request, Garner and her allies stood on one of the school lawns, brandishing signs that read *We support victims of sexual assault, MeToo,* and *Time's Up.*

Joining the YAL chapter at Liberty had been an act of rebellion, as well. Although members of the young Christian right formed an important subset of YAL's membership, the group was still viewed as somewhat risqué. Libertarians, after all, believed in the legalization of drugs, and had members with varying views on gay marriage—issues it tended to downplay because politically libertarians garnered a fair amount of their power by allying with the evangelical community. But rules were rules. And at a school that shunned all alcohol and drugs, YAL's support for legalizing marijuana pitted it against administrators.

"I raised a lot of hell with YAL," Garner told me.

Garner had first come to libertarianism through its emphasis on economic freedom. Her father, a small-business owner, distressed by pesky regulations, including one that curtailed the number of hours she could work at his pizza restaurant when she was a teenager, had first introduced her to some of the free-market ideas libertarians championed. Soon, it was the idea that a person ought to be entitled to do whatever they wanted—unconstrained by overly restrictive laws as long as they were not doing harm to others—that lured her in more deeply. Libertarianism spoke to her own free spirit. In her worldview, to be a libertarian was to fight for a person's right to self-actualize, to be whatever they wanted to be, no matter their gender or race.

Garner was devoted to God. She was pro-life and fiscally conservative. But she supported gay marriage. And the closed nature of the Christian community of her childhood—where young people were taught to distrust outsiders—had stifled her. Hence her disappointment when she became increasingly involved with YAL and discovered the culture there to be similarly insular. As she described it to me, if you cared about the liberty cause, then letting anyone outside the organization know about the sexual harassment that happened behind closed doors meant going against the cause. Further, among libertarians, sexual harassment was sometimes viewed as something a woman ought to deal with herself. Everyone was free and responsible for protecting their own rights, after all. And societal protections were generally viewed as contrary to the ethos of the movement. Things worked themselves out, just as the free market did.

But staying quiet, Garner had come to realize, had not protected the women at YAL. Quite the contrary, it had protected and perpetuated the bro culture that had victimized them. And so, on January 8, Garner posted a damningly eloquent document on Facebook and Twitter, and #YALtoo was born:

"Let's talk about sexual abuse and lack of consequences in certain corners of the liberty movement," wrote Garner in a long letter posted as multiple images (there was no containing her chronicle of grievances to a mere 280 characters): "We can start with one of the more vocal groups, Young Americans for Liberty, headed up by Cliff Maloney Jr. Ah, Cliff Maloney Jr. He fancies himself the godfather of the liberty movement, but instead of sending people to kneecap the goons who assaulted your daughter, he'll promote the goons—and maybe help them run for office. Consent is supposed to be a cornerstone of libertarianism, but consent has been violated by staff members of Young Americans for Liberty for years with little or no repercussion."

Garner proceeded to describe a string of disturbing incidents that she and other women in the organization had allegedly experienced—from harassment and groping by a YAL coworker, to Cliff trying to pressure a female employee to get in bed with him in the infamous TacoBellGate episode, to myriad accounts of YAL women being demeaned and harassed by high-ranking males in the organization—with sometimes little to no consequences whatsoever to the perpetrators. Within hours of Garner's tweet, dozens of YAL women began to post their own stories on the platform.

One woman reported in a series of texts she sent Garner (who then tweeted out the texts) that while phone-banking before the Ohio caucuses in 2016, during Cliff's time running the youth operation for Rand Paul's presidential campaign, Cliff told her she needed to smile more, so as to keep "moral up for all the guys." She says she was also asked to "cook and clean" for the men in the house and "be the house mom." Cliff insists this never happened.

Another young woman claimed that at that same 2018 YAL conference I had attended, a YAL employee plied her with drinks—she was still a minor—and then "harassed and stalked me for the remainder of the conference."

And a former intern with the Twitter handle @anarchakelly accused YAL male staffers and young men associated with partner organizations of plying women with alcohol at a party in 2014, in order to get them "blackout drunk." Once, she said, she'd felt it necessary to watch over an inebriated colleague in the house she shared with other YAL interns "to the point where I was confident she would wake up in the morning. Still I didn't trust the men in the house and ended up spending the night sleeping on the floor in front of her door to insure that no one entered her room."

Yet another alleged victim, a former YAL regional director,

tweeted that when YAL's leadership took the rare step of firing an offender, she was then subsequently shunned by coworkers. The employee, posting on Twitter, recounted: "Since his termination I have experienced social isolation and targeted harassment from members all the way up to staff. The past six months have been extremely lonely for me."

Frazee says he was not aware of any of the above incidents—save for the July 2017 TacoBellGate incident, which resulted in an investigation—and learned about them via social media, during the January 2021 online outpouring.

But women inside the libertarian movement said they were not, in fact, surprised to learn that so many of their peers felt un-protected. Some went so far as to assert that Cliff Maloney's YAL was infusing conservativism as a whole with sexism and misogyny. In the words of a former state chair going by @Grace4Liberty: "It's really unfortunate that YAL gave many of us a start in this movement. Many of whom have now gone on to other places with the same mindset and culture that was fostered there. The sexism, abuse, & entitlement to others' bodies . . . It's now sprinkled across the movement."

It was hard to argue that Cliff wasn't a boon for the overall Lib-ertarian cause, even if many women at YAL had grown to see him as an impediment to their own growth. Galvanized by his candi-dates' disappointing performance in the 2018 midterms, Cliff had doubled down on his efforts to propel gun-obsessed, tax-hating liberty-lovers into state office, through his tireless work at Young Americans for Liberty. Thanks to that work, 123 libertarian-leaning candidates had secured legislative seats in the 2020 elec-tions. Coupled with the 2018 wins and the one-offs throughout the last few years, there were now a total of 179 YAL-backed politi-cians sitting inside state legislatures, ready to do the larger liber-tarian movement's bidding. Cliff's own private company, Mobilize the Message, had also helped secure slots in the U.S. House for

Citadel graduate and Obamacare-hating Nancy Masse, known in political circles for her love-him/hate-him flip-flops on Trump. He'd also helped elect the conspiracy theory-spreading Marjorie Taylor Greene, from Georgia, earning Mobilize the Message nearly $2.4 million during the 2020 election cycle.

But now, with the public spectacle of #YALtoo threatening to undermine YAL's image, both Cliff and his boss, Frazee, were in a very hot spotlight. Some Libertarians, like Michigan congressman Justin Amash, began to demand action:

"At a minimum, any investigation should be conducted by persons independent of YAL, and anyone accused of misconduct should be placed on administrative leave pending completion," wrote Amash. "It will be difficult to rebuild trust, but it will be impossible without a full and fair examination."

On January 11, 2021, three days after Garner's first public complaint, Frazee posted a public letter saying that Cliff—who called the allegations "100 percent false"—would be placed on administrative leave, pending investigation, and YAL would begin "the process of healing and rebuilding a culture of trust, safety and accountability." Liberty lovers weren't satisfied, however, and pressure mounted for Cliff to finally face the consequences of his actions.

Two days later, Cliff Maloney was sacked. "Losing the confidence of the board, YAL staff, and key stakeholders makes the ability to lead impossible and this action necessary," the YAL board wrote in its statement announcing the termination.

The statement also said that YAL was "continuing its full, independent investigation into all allegations." Frazee declined to disclose the findings of that investigation to me, saying they were confidential. After the investigation, YAL's board did vote to adopt a series of new policies and procedures, he told me, including: expanding and clarifying the organization's alcohol policy, signing on a leadership and culture coach, and adopting new safety and oversight measures.

That spring, YAL would get a new leader, its first female CEO—a 30-something movement insider and Libertarian Party fundraiser. Lauren Daugherty was a Leadership Institute alum, had degrees from Emory, Johns Hopkins, and the Institute of World Politics in DC. She had managed the 2016 Libertarian Party convention and had run for Justice of the Peace on the Libertarian ticket in 2018 in Waco, Texas.

In one of her first official correspondences with her new charges, she wrote: "The 'human side' of free markets is so important."

THROUGHOUT THE EARLY MONTHS OF 2021, AS CLIFF LICKED HIS wounds and entrenched himself behind the scenes at Mobilize the Message—where he remains the CEO today—a larger cloud hung over the nation, still in a state of collective shock over the events of January 6. Trump's refusal to promptly instruct the protesters to leave and to call in the National Guard had been troubling even to many of his supporters. Yet on February 26, fifty-one days after the insurrection, the mood within the Republican Party began to shift. As it had every year since 1974, the Conservative Political Action Conference was rolling out the red carpet for right-wing movers and shakers from across the country. This year, due to COVID restrictions, the event was being held at the Hyatt Regency hotel in Orlando instead of the usual Maryland venue. Florida was notoriously lenient in the COVID department, thanks to Governor Ron DeSantis, who welcomed CPAC with open arms.

It was business as usual and denial over the magnitude of the chaos and destruction at the hands of Trump supporters on January 6 was in vogue. Any discussion of how some of the conservative movement's most cherished representatives, its media outlets, and the former president had egged on a deadly insurrection was not. Texas senator Ted Cruz downplayed the January 6 insurrection and threats by violent activists to murder lawmakers. Instead, during his speech, he took great issue with the fortified barricades now surrounding the Capitol, telling audiences that the left was trying to turn the Capitol into a "military outpost in Baghdad." Others, like political commentator and Fox News contributor Deroy Murdock, blamed judges who dismissed Trump's election fraud lawsuits, telling a room that he believed they "bear a lot of responsibility for the chaos that ensued."

As I wandered among the well-heeled crowd, I overheard not one mention of the number of officers who had died in the uprising, nor talk of how the party could discourage such violent activities in the future. Onstage, speakers bent over backwards to sing Trump's praises. In private conversations, attendees seemed mostly preoccupied with Trump and Trump alone. The question of the hour was not: What happened? What did we do? What do we do now? The question was: Is Trump still leading the party? Or not? As one attendee told me, matter-of-factly, "No one knows what to do, it's all wait and see."

As to be expected, CPAC, started by movement newbies forty-seven years earlier, still relished its rising stars. This year, attention was being heaped on Madison Cawthorn, the twenty-five-year-old newly seated North Carolina congressman who had been accused by multiple college classmates of sexual harassment, sometimes from his wheelchair. In spring 2022, Cawthorn, enmeshed in a growing number of scandals, would lose his popularity, his GOP primary, and his shot at a second consecutive term. But at this CPAC, he spent a lot of time signing autographs. Ditto the swashbuckling Florida congressman Matt Gaetz, who would soon find himself under investigation for allegedly having sex with a teenage girl and violating sex trafficking laws by inducing her to travel over state lines. (As of now, neither has been charged and both have denied any wrongdoing.) In the pool area, the New York Young Republicans, who had rented two large cabanas close to the bar, were blasting music and downing frothy beach drinks. "This is where it's all happening," Vish Burra, the group's then vice president, told me in his bathing suit. "We're the real CPAC."

Meanwhile, inside the conference hall, speakers droned on. Florida governor Ron DeSantis dissed pandemic lockdowns and bragged about defying the CDC's safety measures, calling his state an "oasis of freedom in a nation that is suffering in many parts of the county under the yoke of oppressive lock downs."

But he was just a placeholder until everyone could figure out the pesky Trump question. Round and round they debated privately to each other. Was he in? Was he out?

On the second day, I headed to the main hall, where Charlie was slated to speak after Matt Gaetz. The MC joked that backstage, Charlie and Gaetz were betting on who would get more press for their speech. When it was Gaetz's turn, the thirty-something party-boy politician motored through a script propped up on the podium, his eyes glancing down as he turned the pages. When it was Charlie's turn, he spoke as if off the cuff. "You might be saying what on earth is Charlie wearing?" he opened, gesturing at his multicolored tie. "This is a 1990 Rush Limbaugh tie, and I thought, 'What better place to honor one of the greatest Americans ever to live, than at CPAC?'" The tribute just a few weeks after Limbaugh's death, although gracious, also seemed cleverly designed for Charlie to declare his spot as a potential successor to the legendary talk-radio star. He was, after all, now airing *The Charlie Kirk Show* on Limbaugh's former radio station and had taken his midday slot. Charlie went on to exalt free speech, Ron DeSantis, and limited government—and to bash big tech for muzzling conservatives. He definitely won the bet.

Afterward, I waited outside the main auditorium to talk to

Charlie. But his PR representative brushed me off. "CK," I was told, was too busy. He was having a steak house lunch, then heading out soon, inundated with interviews. Too much press. No time. When Charlie finished his obligatory Fox interview, he slipped off his stool and unclipped his microphone as fans gathered around him. A group of middle-aged women wanted autographs. A young man in an ill-fitting suit, looking like a Charlie wannabe, held up a piece of paper for Charlie to sign. But Charlie, accompanied by his fiancé, Erika Frantzve, in a pair of $1,400 Valentino combat boots and a flowing pink skirt, was ensconced within the protective circle of his entourage. He hardly saw the boy. He began to walk toward the exit, and the boy followed, persistent, just as Charlie had been years earlier at the 2012 Republican National Convention, when he boldly stopped the multimillionaire Foster Friess to tell him about his plans. Friess had listened graciously, and soon sent Charlie the first of many, many checks.

Just a few months after CPAC, Charlie would sob at a memorial service for Friess, who would die of myelodysplastic syndrome, a blood cell and bone marrow disorder, at the age of eighty-one. Charlie would call him "a giant of man" who "had transformed" his life forever—a man who talked to everyone, who taught him to be kind. That's how Charlie would spin it, anyway, to a room full of millionaires in mourning.

But now, as the young fan pushed closer, determined to get that autograph, Charlie was too busy for niceties. Frantzve gave the boy a look of disdain. "Can you not?" she snapped, and he slowly retreated, blank paper in hand.

They left him standing there. And the Charlie Kirk show sped forward.

CHAPTER TWENTY

Armed for the Future

As the nation plowed through 2021, the intensifying gulf between left and right did the seemingly impossible: it widened. The left, spurred by the racial justice movement of summer 2020, overwhelmingly called for a more egalitarian and multiracial democracy. Meanwhile, the right was convinced that the country had gone way too far in the "woke" direction. It continued to demand stronger borders, smaller government, a return to the country's founding Christian values, and eventually early elementary school classrooms in which discussion of sexual orientation was prohibited. The two sides viciously faced off in Congress, online, and sometimes in the streets over issue after issue—from the government's role in combating the ongoing COVID-19 pandemic, to what version of the nation's founding history American kids should learn in school.

While division within the country was nothing new, what was new was the sense from both sides that the opposing party wasn't just the enemy, but pure evil. And from their various posts, and in their own trademark ways, Charlie, Candace, and Cliff continued doing their part to stoke the division.

When not promoting her new clothing line (a collection of

hoodies, joggers, beanies, and totes with "Yes, We Candace" scrawled across them, a grandiose nod to Obama's 2008 campaign slogan), Candace devoted much of 2021 to tweeting out denunciations of the COVID-19 vaccine, extolling the right to bear arms, and denying America's racism problem. On *Tucker Carlson Tonight*, she complained that "the left can pull a racist narrative from thin air where it doesn't exist."

In spring 2021, Candace and her husband relocated from DC to Nashville, Tennessee, with their newborn son. She had recently moved "The Candace Owens Show"—now just called "The Candace Show"—to Ben Shapiro's platform, the Daily Wire. It, too, had found a new home in the Red State. Candace was given a grand welcome when the Tennessee General Assembly issued a proclamation, lauding her for "her perceptive criticism of creeping socialism and leftist political tyranny." And a billboard featuring Candace looking Southern chic, in a black sequined top and flowing skirt, stared down at the country music capital. It declared her "Uncancelable Since 1989."

Cliff Maloney, who after his initial online denial was choosing to publicly ignore the allegations made against him by the women of YAL, was also busy. And not surprisingly, theater was serving as both hobby and balm. That fall, on a small stage in the Florida Panhandle, Cliff belted out the lyrics to the ballad "Beauty School Drop Out," from the 1971 musical *Grease*, in a community theater production near his home. Cliff was playing the Teen Angel—the role played by Frankie Avalon in the 1978 film. In the snapshot he sent me of the production, Cliff, in a white tuxedo and matching white wingtips, posed with the cast. He was surrounded by doting women and beaming.

When Cliff wasn't onstage, he was building up his for-profit firm Mobilize the Message. And like Charlie and Candace, he was also stoking division around COVID-19. The threat, and the government's response to it, he frequently claimed, were overblown.

"Normal people are afraid because if you don't get in line they will come after you. They will destroy you." Presumably "they" meant the government.

Never straying far from his ultimate mission, Cliff said the best way to push back against government overreach was to run for local office, just like the candidates he was helping through Mobilize the Message. "Get involved at the local level and the state level where you can have an influence," he told conservative interviewer Mike Crispi.

Cliff, who was still fighting tirelessly to keep government at bay, would ultimately find himself ensnared more deeply within its grasp, when in winter 2021, a former college classmate contacted the University of Pittsburgh at Johnstown police about an incident she alleges happened in 2013. The woman told police that while in college, Cliff, a resident director at the time, drugged her champagne and then raped her in his dorm room after she passed out. Cliff was charged and arraigned in April 2022 on two counts of rape and two counts of aggravated indecent assault. Asked about the charges, Cliff responded through his lawyer via email. "Mr. Maloney denies these historical allegations. They are false. Of course under our justice system he is presumed innocent. We look forward to establishing a vigorous defense before a jury of his peers."

Meanwhile, across the country local fights over classroom curriculum were proving particularly incendiary. School boards were now undergoing intense scrutiny, as progressives pushed schools to rethink how history and literature were being taught, sometimes to the exclusion of everything else. And conservatives maligned these efforts by labeling them critical race theory, or CRT for short, a forty-year-old academic theory that racism was not just perpetuated by biased individuals, but by legal systems, policies, and institutions.

So incendiary was the topic that the book *Beloved*, by Toni

Morrison, was featured in an ad in the Virginia governor's race, an example of the threatening material progressives wanted to thrust on white students. It helped to swing the race in favor of the Republican candidate, Glenn Youngkin, who sailed to an unexpected victory over the Democratic incumbent, Terry McAuliffe. Youngkin had made school curriculum, and more specifically critical race theory, one of his rallying cries. Right-wing activists and Fox News anchors argued, with fantastic success, that CRT labeled whites as racist oppressors and made kids feel bad about their heritage.

That fall of 2021, as school board meetings around the country erupted into shouting matches and sometimes even violence, thirty-six states took legislative action to regulate how educators could discuss racism, sexism, and systemic inequality in the classroom. In rural Eatonville, Washington, the CRT backlash helped a member of the far-right, militia-loving Three Percenters movement win a school board seat, the second of five seats to now be held by a member of the movement. And back in Arlington, the Leadership Institute had added a new workshop: School Board Campaign Training.

As for Charlie Kirk, he undoubtedly applauded the infiltration of hard-right groups into local school boards. Both CRT and gun restrictions were issues that fired him, and his followers, up. And in his mind, these evils were best fought with God's help. So Charlie actively sought to get more of his allies in the Christian right into local public office. Earlier that year, in the spring of 2021, he launched TP Faith, a new 501(c)(3), with thirty-two employees charged with planting chapters inside evangelical churches, where members could learn how to get "civically engaged" and bring their Christian values into the public square. In case it wasn't clear who the enemy was and what they were doing, he also launched a School Board Watchlist, much like the Professor Watchlist that had done so much harm on college campuses. School board members, he told his podcast listeners, were "parasites." He also announced the forthcoming launch of Turning Point Academy, an "America-first" K-12 academic curriculum, which the group touted as "America's best hope to inspire countless young people to love America Again." (As of February 2022, the curriculum had yet to materialize.)

While education may have been a politically expedient passion, Charlie had long extolled the right to bear arms, once describing guns strapped to parishioners in an Oklahoma church he visited as "an extension of who you are," saying they were necessary to "defend you against evil." Now Charlie and his group were stepping up their pro-gun rhetoric. Since the Black Lives Matter protests of 2020, TPUSA had been churning out videos celebrating the militia mindset. One featured the infamous St. Louis couple who'd aimed firearms at Black Lives Matter protesters marching past their home in 2020. Another depicted as heroes a band of armed white, male Philadelphia residents taking back their city from protesting looters in the wake of the George Floyd murder.

Charlie was also a staunch supporter of Kyle Rittenhouse, the seventeen-year-old high school dropout who shot and killed two protesters and injured one at an August 2020 protest against racially motivated police violence in Kenosha, Wisconsin. Charlie deified Rittenhouse on his podcast and Twitter feed, saying the teenager had acted in "self-defense," and reverentially interviewed the far-right's new golden boy on his show. Rittenhouse had been acquitted on charges of murder and reckless endangerment, and for many Americans, his story was a tragic cautionary tale of how right-wing rhetoric could spur violence. Charlie, of course, saw it differently. Rittenhouse's use of his gun was to be heralded. He'd defended himself against the enemy: the left.

It was only a matter of time before Charlie's followers took the issue of gun use to the next level. For much of 2021, Charlie had traveled the country for his Exposing Critical Racism speaking tour, explaining to young audiences that critical race theory was "an existential threat to the American way of life" that would make America "a more dangerous and less pleasant place to live." So it could hardly have surprised him when, on an October evening at Boise State University in Idaho, he got a question about guns. That night, Charlie had spoken for an hour or so about how it was up to his audience to speak out and get politically engaged. "No more spectator conservatism," he'd intoned. Now, a young man in a black button-down shirt, with a touch of a beard, squinted up at the stage.

"At this point, we're living under corporate and medical fascism," the man noted, parroting some of Charlie's earlier talking points.

"This is tyranny," he continued. "When do we get to use the guns?"

The question was an indicator of the increasing comfort many Americans now felt, in the wake of the January 6 insurrection, with the idea of brute force as a political tool. An alarmingly large number of Americans on the right now believed that violence was justified to preserve their way of life. A November 2021 survey by the nonpartisan Public Religion Research Institute found that 30 percent of Republicans (and 11 percent of Democrats) agreed with the statement: "Because things have gotten so far off track, true American patriots may have to resort to violence in order to save our country."

After a moment's pause from Charlie, the Boise State audience member continued his line of questioning: "No, and I'm not— that's not a joke. I'm not saying it like that. I mean, literally, where's the line? How many elections are they going to steal before we kill these people?"

Charlie, looking distinguished in a dark blue suit, raised a finger authoritatively and immediately denounced the question. "You're playing into all their plans," he said, "and they're trying to make you do this." The left had pushed this man to the edge, was the message. They wanted this young patriot to get violent "to justify a takeover" of his "freedoms and liberties." But Charlie told him getting violent would be "a mistake." His enemy was a "teetering regime" that played at "psychological warfare." "Self-control and discipline," he noted sternly, was important.

"We must exhaust every single peaceful means possible," he told the man, ticking off a series of measures that the man ought to encourage right-wing politicians in his state to initiate. Idaho, Charlie suggested, should kick federal agencies out of the state, and refuse to enforce unwanted federal laws that did not conform to the state's own constitution. The ideas were radical, arguably revolutionary.

But the man wasn't satisfied. He wanted an answer to his specific question. "I just want to know, where's the line?"

That evening, Charlie never told his clearly volatile acolyte that there was no line, that violence was never acceptable. With his omnipresence on the web, his millions of podcast listeners, and his frequent speaking tours, he was now the conservative voice of his generation, a potential future president and one of the most powerful figures inside the GOP. So, like any ambitious conservative today, he had to walk a fine line himself. Without pointedly condoning violence, Charlie needed to make it clear that indeed, there was a point in which the right would, as the audience member had put it, *get to use the guns*.

"The line," he answered, "is when we exhaust every single one of our state ability to push back against what's happening."

Charlie believes that his fight is a holy fight—that he has been chosen to wage the battle for the soul of the nation. Democracy is a bit player in this power game.

Many—on both sides of the political spectrum—now believe that Charlie may well represent the future, and if they are correct, his vision of a Godly nation may well be the one that we will live in because he is hardly alone.

Charlie is a general in a much larger war that's being waged here and in other parts of the world. It's a war to preserve tribalistic values and an old-world structure that reserves power for a small few. Of course, the young right's increasing zeal for amassing victories in the name of Christianity may feel genuine to some of them. Others may understand that faith is, foremost, a fine tool for what Sun Tzu in *The Art of War* calls "maneuvering the army."

Fifty years ago, a generation of young conservatives, intent on defining the future, began their journey. They were purposeful and driven. They raised up a generation. And they raised them right. Now, that generation has come of age. The new ultra-conservatives are reaping what their predecessors sowed.

That foreboding October night on the Boise State stage, as Charlie addressed his far-right warriors-in-waiting, he repeated an idea he often utters, a sign to America that at twenty-eight years old, he's just getting warmed up.

Charlie told the crowd, "We haven't even started."

EPILOGUE

In November 2021, I sat in a room in downtown Brooklyn, filled with progressive activists and donors who were frustrated by the state of democracy. Despite the right's relentless campaign to discount the election results, Biden was now safely in the White House, but with an ambitious political agenda that he did not have the votes in Congress to push forward. The Democrats had won 221 seats in the House, and 50 in the Senate, but that was not enough of a majority to overcome resistance from a few lone detractors—namely Arizona senator Krysten Sinema and West Virginia senator Joe Manchin, a longtime coal industry ally.

The event I was at had been spearheaded by a grassroots organizing group formed in 2017, after Trump's flabbergasting victory, to help activate frustrated citizens. Swing Left had since become an influential player in Trump-era Democratic circles, raising millions of dollars an election cycle—and activating thousands of volunteers. It was one of a host of groups that had sprung up in recent years with the goal of trying to figure out how to respond to the right's assault on democracy.

A few years in, Swing Left had come to the conclusion, one I'd come to as well, that one of the Democrats' biggest problems was their weak network building. Donors thought election cycle to election cycle and tended to give directly to candidates—and not always as strategically as they should. They were also under-playing and underappreciating the work of grassroots activists on the ground, many of them youth groups who worked during election cycles, but also in between them, to build ties with communities that mattered when it came time to hit the polls. As a result, whatever inroads, institutional knowledge, or voter lists that were gathered during a candidate's election cycle were lost if the candidate didn't win. Further, donor money went only so far when it targeted one candidate—a shame when multiple Democrats were on a ticket, and all needed pushes to get folks to the polls for them.

To help rectify that, Swing Left had formulated a new subsidiary, Blueprint, whose goal was to get donors to think more about the ecosystem. Benefactors were invited to create a portfolio that contributed dollars to specific candidates—who were chosen for their winnability and cash needs—but also to groups inside the ecosystem whose ground games could often make a difference between a win or a loss. Start early and think long term was the message.

I'd been invited to the Brooklyn gathering to help bring that message home. By this point, I had spent years watching how the right deftly supported, funded, trained, and organized its youth groups. And I had seen the sway these groups' leaders pulled within their party.

"I was invited here to scare the hell out of you," I told the activists. "And I will do that."

There to help bring home the point were two representatives from a grassroots activist group called LUCHA, which was founded in 2009 by impassioned young Latinx high school and college students as a response to Arizona's Republican-driven assault on undocumented residents (led by Sheriff Joe Arpaio, who bragged that he was "America's toughest sheriff"). LUCHA—an

acronym for Living United for Change in Arizona—was in many
ways a local counter to Turning Point USA and was headquartered
in a modest office space with a low-hanging roof and cement sid-
ing, just a few minutes away from TPUSA's plush Phoenix digs.

LUCHA had a powerful ground game, well-trained activists,
and deep ties to the neighborhoods where it door knocked. But
perhaps most importantly, it was hooked into a powerful network
of local grassroots groups who worked together. Members included a handful of youth groups along with Planned Parenthood
Advocates of Arizona, Black Phoenix Votes, and Progress Arizona.
These groups shared lists, resources, messaging, sophisticated
polling data, and training techniques. They avoided redundancies
by communicating early and often.

And it was working. While Arizona Democrats narrowly lost
the 2016 presidential, they held their blue seats in Congress. And
in the 2018 midterms they flipped a house seat and elected Democratic senator Kyrsten Sinema, a former Arizona Green Party
member who was at the time a progressive stalwart with a strong
record of supporting the LGBTQ community. The coalition also
helped bring about the elections of a secretary of state and a new
schools superintendent, posts that hadn't gone blue in years, and
ushered in Mark Kelly to the Senate, in a special election. In 2020,
despite the Democrats' hemorrhaging of Hispanic voters, the activists helped secure a crucial Arizona win for Biden by in part
appealing to many of the state's 1.2 million Latino voters, whom a
lot of LUCHA door knockers knew by name. A group of Arizona
Republicans responded to this victory with a dishonest and un-
seemly effort to delegitimize the results, with the cooperation of
Turning Point USA's leader Tyler Bowyer. I had spent hours with
Bowyer and knew how very deep his political aspirations were. But
this surprised even me. A recount conducted by Cyber Ninjas, a
Florida-based group that has since shuttered as a result of crush-
ing debt and legal challenges, eventually reaffirmed Biden's win,

even giving him 360 more votes. It seemed to be a sign of how utterly dirty segments of the Arizona GOP were willing to play—but also how scared they were.

For those paying attention, the Arizona network was an incredible example of what could happen when fired-up young people got together, with the support of an infrastructure, a vow to stay united, and the discipline to unify their messaging. But it was also an example of how they and other such vital networks were limited by their resources.

Among other things, what LUCHA and its sister groups didn't have money to do was create a strong online game; even though they were deeply hooked into how young voters thought and understood intuitively something the Democratic Party seemed to sorely misunderstand: how diverse the Hispanic community in Arizona was, and how different members of that diverse community needed to be spoken to in different ways.

They also hadn't had materials to combat the #stopthesteal rallies around Phoenix, where some protesters clutched signs courtesy of FreedomWorks, the heavily endowed advocacy group bankrolled by billionaires and multimillionaires.

In Brooklyn, Alejandra Gomez, LUCHA's co-executive director, told the room that there was a hesitation among donors in big cities to invest in what looked to them like a scrappy group. "We're not taken seriously," she told the room. "We're Brown kids from trailer parks. When we go into conference rooms, they're looking at us like, that's a cute anecdote."

I knew about this funding disparity and the relative lack of support coming from the Democratic donor base because I'd been to Arizona as activist groups were gearing up for 2020. On one side of Phoenix was Turning Point USA's sister organization, Students for Trump, which started fifteen months before the election to raise its $15 million to help elect Trump and other Republicans. Students for Trump offices were starting to buzz with activity.

When I visited Arizona Wins, a progressive activist group, however, the headquarters looked like an empty insurance office. One
new hire was there, trying to plug in a ratty laptop. This was the
case all over the country, as underfunded liberal grassroots groups
bit their nails and waited for the checks.

But there was another problem. Young activists on the ground
weren't being listened to. In 2016, when young galvanized volunteers in Pennsylvania asked Hillary Clinton for more yard signs,
they were told there were none left. (Clinton lost Pennsylvania.) In
Wisconsin (which Clinton also lost), Democratic activists warned
about a pro-Trump mood on the ground that wasn't tracking with
the polls. Their demands for an influx of campaign literature were
ignored. When young Bernie Sanders organizers in Michigan offered to support the Clinton campaign once she had won the nomination, they were told to buzz off. (Clinton lost Michigan.)

Tensions between young progressives and the establishment
base are not new. And in some cases, they are unavoidable. Young
activists by nature are forward thinking and derive their energy
and verve from the confidence that today's impossible may well be
a reality tomorrow. They're pushy. But we as a nation have benefited greatly from their foresight. Young progressive activists are
the ones who have most aggressively pushed for—and continue
to push for—women's rights, civil rights, environmental justice,
and gun reform. The supposedly radical ideas they had twenty,
thirty, and forty years ago are no-brainers now. Keeping them at
arm's lengths, underfunding them, and dismissing their visions
and know-how—as the Democratic establishment is prone to do—
undoubtedly creates mistrust and tension. It precludes mutually
beneficial cooperation and hampers their ability to help the party
get the seats in Congress it needs to get the impossible stuff done.

In 2018, the Democratic National Committee, aware that they
were neglecting their young, launched a national training program for the midterms—an initiative they talked up to the press.

A good start, but their follow-through was lacking. They were forced to turn down countless requests for training because they hadn't sufficiently funded the program.

During my four years of reporting for this book, I was often struck—and enervated—by the wildly off-base impressions young conservatives had of Democrats. They were lazy, looking for handouts. They were Venezuela-loving socialists. They were unpatriotic, ignorant of the Constitution, anti-family, intolerant of the religious, and above all else: the Dems were collectivists.

None of these stereotypes held true, but one should have. When Democrats are at their best, they indeed act like collectivists: thinking about the well-being of all, even sometimes at the expense of the individual; striving for greater equity and gains for the most vulnerable; listening.

What my years of reporting taught me was that socialist-fearing right-wingers are doing a better job of acting like "collectivists" than their counterparts on the left.

If Democrats want to grow their infrastructure and change the country—if they want to win—they must first find their "collectivist" nature. They must unite, collaborate, cooperate, and take care of their greater network. This means giving *real* support to young activists on the ground: looping them into a national network that shares data, proven techniques, and messaging tools; investing in a nationwide, scalable training academy to teach young activists strategy but also the inner workings of the DC political structure; and connecting them to legislators, free internships, campaigns, and jobs. And perhaps most of all, Democrats have to hear the fears and frustrations of young Americans, who see the challenges ahead more clearly than any of us. After all, it's their future we're fighting for.

ACKNOWLEDGMENTS

I could not have written this book without the wisdom and hard work of the gifted journalists who have dedicated much of their professional lives to understanding and keeping a watch on the American right. I am grateful for their commitment to a transparent democracy.

Jane Mayer's dogged reporting at the *New Yorker* and in her masterpiece *Dark Money* has been invaluable to many journalists, myself included. I relied on her careful reporting on Turning Point USA, its leadership, and its related organizations, as well as her reporting on the larger right-wing movement. I am grateful for it. I am also thankful for Anne Nelson, whose deep dive in *Shadow Network* gave me a better understanding of what exactly I was seeing. Rick Perlstein's *Nixonland* and *Reaganland* offered valuable background and Michelle Goldberg's *Kingdom Coming* and Frances Fitzgerald's *The Evangelicals* helped me understand Christian Nationalism and the people pushing it. Christopher Leonard's fair and absorbing book *Kochland* was an eye-opening and engaging account of ambition and business acumen. Tim Alberta's absorbing page-turner *American Carnage* and his incredible pieces in *Politico* and now the *Atlantic* continue to inspire and educate. A quick thank you to Corey Robin, whose *The Reactionary Mind* explained a lot, as did his gem of a book *The Enigma of Clarence Thomas.*

I am also grateful for all the incredible investigative sites working tirelessly to keep an eye on the money, including ProPublica's Nonprofit Explorer and OpenSecrets. A thanks also, to *Mother Jones,* the Center for Media and Democracy, and UnKoch My Campus.

At the virtual desk every day, there was one person who became a constant companion to me and I am ever grateful. Christen Gall, you are a supremely gifted researcher, fact checker, citation expert, investigative reporter, and workaholic. Your sweat, blood, and tears are on every single page of this book. And I could never have written it without you. Thank you for your dedication and your commitment to getting this out and getting it right.

Will Dana and Genevieve Field, I have no words for my appreciation that you shared your storytelling gifts with me. Will, I am particularly grateful for all your background knowledge and your help understanding the pull of power in politics. Genevieve, I will never forget those deadlines and how willing you were to go the whole way with me. Thank you. Thanks also goes out to the fabulous fact-checking work of Matt Mahoney.

I have much gratitude for my agents Larry Weissman and Sascha Alper for being amazingly attentive advocates. You make this writing business human.

I am indebted to the team at Harper Collins/Ecco—first to Denise Oswald and the publishing giant Daniel Halpern for welcoming my project so warmly into the Ecco fold—and then to my ace editor Sarah Murphy, who is the best orphan mom a writer could get. She has been a total joy to work with. Also a huge, huge thanks to the legal team, in particular Andrew Jacobs—legal mind, fact checker, sentence whiz—whose patience and sage advice kept us on track. And thank you, Norma Barksdale, for finding no question too ridiculous; and Meghan Deans and Caitlin Mulrooney-Lyski for believing so fervently in this book.

Thank you Beowulf Sheehan for reminding me that since I'd taken four years to write the book I could take a few hours to get a good photo.

I am grateful to *Politico*, the *New York Times*, and the *Hechinger Report*—and all the wonderful editors I have worked with at those publications, who sent me off to visit colleges around the country, giving me my first glimpses of the modern American campus, and spurred on the idea for this book.

The Spencer Foundation afforded me much needed time, resources to do the enormous amount of travel this book took, and the wisdom of experts at the Columbia Journalism School. Lyn-Nell Hancock offered steady guidance. I would also like to express my gratitude toward Nicholas Lemann, who introduced me to the work of Theda Skocpol and a new way of thinking about politics and special interest groups.

Also thanks to the Young Guns for your work with me, especially for being my eyes and ears at The Republican National Convention in 2020: Kyle Igraham, Anwar Boutayba, Greta Travaglia, Elizabeth Sills, Emma Cunningham-Bradshaw, Daniel Myrick, and Eve Neumann.

I am grateful to my many sources willing to take the hours and hours they did to enhance this book. A special thanks to fellow journalist Alex Linzmeier.

To some of my favorite Brooklyn sounding boards: Anne and Thanassis, Julie, and a special thanks to some newbies: Deborah Copaken and Stacy Kramer. Stacy, you are a powerhouse and you give me hope. I am so grateful to be spreading the word with you.

I will always be grateful for the support of the gifted—and inspiring executive coach—Alicia Bassuk, whose COVID-era guidance came at a crucial time in this project.

To my speed-dial gang: Carolina Hall, because you are my

forever friend . . . Lisa Angel . . . who exemplifies all that is good and right about a purple state, Monique El-Faizy because, you get it . . . Mark, I'll always be grateful for your sobering advice. You know you are family.

To Severn Taylor and the Ladies—I love you all so much for being so enthusiastic and supportive during the writing and reporting of this.

To my soul sister Georgia. I wouldn't want to be seeking serenity with anyone else.

And to Lara, who I love, love, love . . . and who deserves so much credit for putting up with my frequent departures into writerland.

I am eternally indebted to my father, George Spencer, who is always a source of inspiration, but was particularly enthusiastic about this book and reminded me often why it mattered. I will never forget Barcelona August 2015, when you called it: We were going to get what we deserved: a Trump presidency.

To my father-in-law, Terry, and my mother-in-law, Sandi, for cracking me up on my writing breaks. Lady, you really are getting funnier over time. And to Jason, Pam, Kathy, and a special thanks to Flint for my first *Raising Them Right* swag.

I am blessed to have the best brothers in the whole world— George, you bleed blue in the best way possible, and Mike, you are my favorite red-stater, a fabulous conversationalist, a source of joy and pride in my life, you know how much I love and admire you. And to my sister Liz, please more lunches!

Thanks to my daughter Logan, a gifted researcher in her own right, for being relentlessly forgiving about my long work hours . . . and my all-nighters. And to my son Spencer, who was kind when I complained, but also understanding, saying once: "But . . . you actually . . . really love doing this, don't you?" I am so proud of both of you.

I have a lot of faith in God. And I'm not afraid to say it. I thank

Liora Yalof for helping me in my darkest hours see what a loving and compassionate higher power guides us—particularly important during a reporting process where I spent a lot of time with people whose idea of God was upsetting, sad, and extraordinarily self-serving.

Finally, thanks to Seth, my husband, best friend, cheerleader, and sage. I will never be able to thank you enough for your love and support during the reporting and writing of this book. Your relentless insistence on truth above all else, has been my guiding light, a reminder that there is so much goodness in this world and many Americans who wholeheartedly embrace the imperfect beauty that is this country.

This book is really dedicated to them, all the truly patriotic flag-loving Americans I know who are not afraid of truth, of forgiveness, of science and compassion, of mourning, of apologizing, and of this growing, improving, increasingly inclusive nation, where tolerance and faith, knowledge and care for our land, our skies, and our seas can co-exist. We are a collective, at least for now. And I am honored to be on this journey with you.

NOTES

For this book, I conducted formal and informal interviews with more than 200 people from May 2018 through May 2022. In the name of brevity, I have omitted citations for any information garnered from my own real-time conversations.

I conducted hours of interviews with Cliff Maloney at YAL, Tyler Bowyer, and to a lesser extent Charlie Kirk at TPUSA. Candace Owens also provided me several hours of her time. Countless other young conservatives and people who know or knew them did, too. Many of my sources asked to remain anonymous. I honored that.

After the insurrection, my contact with TPUSA was largely ruptured. Requests for a last interview with Charlie and/or answers to questions to fill in certain gaps and to get responses to comments about him or the organization were repeatedly denied.

INTRODUCTION

x As the music came: "CAMPUS CLASH IS LIVE! Watch Charlie Kirk and Candace Owens Live at Cleveland State University," *Candace Owens*, November 9, 2018, https://www.facebook.com/watch/live/?ref=watch _permalink&v=195918724696555.

x Charlie, who toured: Joseph Guinto, "Trump's Man on Campus,"

Politico Magazine, April 6, 2018, https://www.politico.com/magazine /story/2018/04/06/trump-young-conservatives-college-charlie-kirk -turning-point-usa-217829/.

xi A white kid from: Charlie Kirk, *The MAGA Doctrine: The Only Ideas That Will Win the Future* (HarperCollins, 2020), 119.

xi Kanye West had: Kanye West @kanyewest, "I love the way Candace Owens thinks," Twitter, April 21, 2018, https://twitter.com/kanyewest /status/987696355341553665.

xiii Trump may have: Kim Parker and Ruth Igielnik, "On the Cusp of Adulthood and Facing an Uncertain Future: What We Know About Gen Z So Far," *Pew Research Center*, May 14, 2020, https://www.pewresearch.org /social-trends/2020/05/14/on-the-cusp-of-adulthood-and-facing-an -uncertain-future-what-we-know-about-gen-z-so-far-2/; https://www.pew research.org/social-trends/2019/01/17/generation-z-looks-a-lot-like -millennials-on-key-social-and-political-issues/.

xiv Back in my: "About Gun Owners of America," Gun Owners of America, accessed April 19, 2022, https://www.gunowners.org/about-goa//.

xiv NRA U, I soon: "NRA University," NRA-IL, accessed April 19, 2022, https://www.nraila.org/campaigns/grassroots/nra-university/.

xiv The NRA even: NRA Collegiate Coalition, NRA-IL,accessed April 19, 2022, https://www.nraila.org/campaigns/grassroots/nra-collegiate -coalition/.

xiv The Intercollegiate Studies Institute (ISI) didn't: "Fill the Void in Your Education," ISI, accessed April 19, 2022, https://isi.org.

xiv But missing was: "In Memoriam: Richard Devos (1926–2018), ISI, September 6, 2018, https://isi.org/intercollegiate-review/in-memoriam-richard -devos-1926–2018/.

xv The website for: "Set Your Path, Change The World," FEE, accessed April 19, 2022, https://fee.org.

xvii There was the Lynde: Stephanie Saul and Danny Hakim, "The Most Powerful Conservative Couple You've Never Heard Of," *New York Times*, June 7, 2018, https://www.nytimes.com/2018/06/07/us/politics /liz-dick-uihlein-republican-donors.html.

xvii To that end: Generation Progress, "Building Tomorrow: The Need for Sustained Investment in America's Progressive Youth," April 5, 2017, http://youngpeoplefor.org/building-tomorrow-the-need-for-sustained -investment-in-americas-progressive-youth/; David Armiak, "Donors-Trust and Donors Capital Pumped at Least $90 Million into Rightwing Causes in 2019," December 3, 2020, https://www.exposedbycmd .org/2020/12/03/donorstrust-and-donors-capital-pumped-at-least-90

-million-into-right-wing-causes-in-2019/; UnKoch My Campus, "Increased Funding, Increased Influence: Koch University Funding Update," May 2021, http://www.unkochmycampus.org/funding-report.

xviii As Charles Koch opined: Jane Mayer, "The Secrets of Charles Koch's Political Ascent," *Politico*, January 18, 2016, https://www.politico.com/magazine/story/2016/01/charles-koch-political-ascent-jane-mayer-21 3541/.

xix While Alinsky's thirteen: Saul David Alinsky, *Rules for Radicals: A Practical Primer for Realistic Radicals* (Vintage, 1989), 126, 130.

xix In 1979, the John M. Olin Foundation: Jane Mayer, *Dark Money: The Hidden History of the Billionaires Behind the Rise of the Radical Right* (Doubleday, 2017), 103; John J. Miller, *A Gift of Freedom: How the John M. Olin Foundation Changed America* (Encounter Books, 2006), 73.

xx In Charlie's case: Charlie Kirk, "This historic event will likely be one of the largest and most consequential in American history. The team at @ TrumpStudents & Turning Point Action are honored to help make this happen, sending 80+ buses full of patriots to DC to fight for this president," Twitter, January 4, 2021, https://web.archive.org/web/20210105234031 /https://twitter.com/charliekirk11.

xx One of the apparent: Sarah Al-Arshani, "A Former Firefighter Charged in the Capitol Riot Took a Bus Organized by Turning Point USA to DC, Filing Says," *Business Insider*, March 3, 2021.

xxi For Charlie: "CHAOS AT THE CAPITOL—Joint Session of Congress Interrupted in Washington DC," *Turning Point USA*, *YouTube*, January 6, 2021, https://www.youtube.com/watch?v=X8a9rvwJUCw.

xxi A review of three: Jean M. Twenge, Nathan Honeycutt, Radmila Prislin, "Young Americans Are Actually Not Becoming More Progressive," *Time*, August 22, 2017, https://time.com/4909722/trump-millen nials-igen-republicans-voters/; Jean M. Twenge, "More Polarized but More Independent: Political Party Identification and Ideological Self-Categorization Among U.S. Adults, College Students, Late Adolescents, 1970–2015," Personality and Psychosociology Bulletin, September 7, 2016, https://journals.sagepub.com/doi/suppl/10.1177/014616721666 0058.

xxi These young voters are: Vianney Gómez and Andrew Daniller, "Younger U.S. Adults Less Likely to See Big Differences between the Parties or to Feel Well Represented by Them," *Pew Research Center*, December 7, 2021, https://www.pewresearch.org/fact-tank/2021/12/07/younger-u-s -adults-less-likely-to-see-big-differences-between-the-parties-or-to-feel -well-represented-by-them/.

CHAPTER ONE: THE RISE OF A WHITE, MALE OBAMA-HATER

Much of the information in this chapter about Charlie's early Chicago-area years comes from "Turning Points Into Action w/ Charlie Kirk, Founder of Turning Point USA" on the podcast *Ditch Digger CEO* with Gary Rabine.

3 "If you were not wholeheartedly worshipping": "#13 Turning Points Into Action w/ Charlie Kirk, Founder of Turning Point USA," *Ditch Digger CEO*, February 1, 2019, https://open.spotify.com/episode/3hq9Jc5jh9jwv K51VXxFjG.

3 Sometimes referred to as: Julie Deardorff, "'Drain' Fix at Wheeling High School," *Chicago Tribune*, May 9, 1997, https://www.chicagotribune.com /news/ct-xpm-1997–05–09–9705090281-story.html.

4 The change—by 2010, minorities: William Frey, "Melting Pot Cities and Suburbs: Racial and Ethnic Change in Metro America in the 2000s," Brookings, accessed February 15, 2022, https://www.brookings.edu/wp -content/uploads/2016/06/0504_census_ethnicity_frey.pdf.

4 By the early 2000s: David Ibata, "New Majorities Emerge," *Chicago Tribune*, April 1, 2001, https://www.chicagotribune.com/news/ct-xpm-2001 –04–01–0104060022-story.html.

5 After years of demographic change: Illinois School Report Card, 2008, Wheeling High School Township, HSD 124, Wheeling Illinois, accessed February 18, 2022, http://webprod.isbe.net/ereportcard/publicsite/get Report.aspx?year=2008&code=1401621400006_e.pdf.

6 "I knew people that were": Stephanie Hamill, "Charlie Kirk Opens Up About His Upbringing, TPUSA, Trump and More," *Daily Caller*, August 3, 2019, https://dailycaller.com/2019/08/03/charlie-kirk-talks -childhood-tpusa/.

7 In his book: Charlie Kirk, *The MAGA Doctrine: The Only Ideas That Will Win the Future* (HarperCollins, 2020), 1.

7 Architectural work was contracted: Otto Friedrich, "Flashy Symbol of an Acquisitive Age: DONALD TRUMP," *Time*, January 16, 1989, http:// content.time.com/time/subscriber/article/0,33009,956733–5,00.html.

7 Charlie describes his father's interaction: Kirk, *The MAGA Doctrine*, 119.

7 Documents show Trump: Casetext Search + Citator, "Office of Cantor v. Swanke Hayden Connell, 186 A.D.2d 71," accessed February 15, 2022, https://casetext.com/case/office-of-cantor-v-swanke-hayden-connell.

7 Her relatives on her mother's side: John S. Dankowsky, United States Federal Census, 1930, accessed April 19, 2022, Ancestry.com.

7 Kathy grew up: Amita Health, "Kathryn Kirk," accessed February 15, 2022, https://www.amitahealth.org/welcome/associate-stories/kathryn -kirk.

7 After college: Ibid.

7 Charlie credits her: Charlie Kirk and Brent Hamachek, *Time for a Turning Point: Setting a Course Toward Free Markets and Limited Government for Future Generations* (Simon and Schuster, 2016), 4.

8 Kathy and Robert: Ibid.

8 They were supportive: Kerry Lester, "Perfect Storm Launches 19-Year-Old Wheeling Native into Political Punditry," *Daily Herald*, April 29, 2013, https://www.dailyherald.com/article/20130429/news/704299942/.

8 But they were not news: Kirk and Hamachek, *Time for a Turning Point*, 4.

8 Charlie was the family anomaly: Lester, "Perfect Storm Launches 19-Year-Old Wheeling Native into Political Punditry."

8 In high school: Facebook, "Mary Tish," accessed February 15, 2022, https://www.facebook.com/mary.tish.3154.

8 She spent a year: LinkedIn, "Mary Kirk," accessed February 15, 2022, https://www.linkedin.com/in/mary-kirk-4139a6118/?locale=fr_FR.

8 She supported Bernie Sanders: Mary Tish, "I was the bird," Facebook, May 28, 2016, https://www.facebook.com/photo.php?fbid=1132964996754662&set=pb.100001235180712.-2207520000.&type=3.

8 Charlie was an antsy: "#13 Turning Points Into Action w/ Charlie Kirk, Founder of Turning Point USA."

8 But Charlie says: Ibid.

9 After a teacher trash-talked: Charlie Kirk, "Liberal Bias Starts in High School Economics Books," *Breitbart*, April 26, 2012, https://www.breitbart.com/politics/2012/04/26/liberal-bias-starts-in-high-school-economics/.

9 His family felt: Hamill, "Charlie Kirk Opens Up."

10 In front of audiences: "#13 Turning Points Into Action w/ Charlie Kirk, Founder of Turning Point USA."

11 "It drove them nuts": "Millennial Conservative on Trump, Social Issues, & Religion," *Rubin Report*, January 19, 2018, https://www.youtube.com/watch?v=dZ8Cy4wULxg.

11 One time, when: Ibid.

11 District officials had just announced: Michelle Stoffel, "Student Facebook Group Takes Stand Against Hike in School's Cookie Price," *Chicago Tribune*, September 21, 2011, https://www.chicagotribune.com/news/ct-xpm-2011-09-21-ct-talk-cookie-protest-0921-20110921-story.html.

12 "How many of you": "Santelli's Tea Party Rant, February 19, 2009," *CNBC*, February 6, 2015, https://www.cnbc.com/video/2015/02/06/santellis-tea-party-rant-february-19-2009.html.

13 The spring of his senior year: "SOS Liberty High Schoolers: 'We Are

Tomorrow,'" *Illinois Review*, accessed February 15, 2022, https://web
.archive.org/web/20201028025446/https://www.illinoisreview.com/il
linoisreview/2012/04/sos-liberty-we-are-tomorrow.html.

14 "High schoolers all over Illinois": Ibid.

15 On top of that: Kirk, "Liberal Bias Starts in High School."

15 Diamond and Krutikova had passed: "SOS Liberty on Fox News 5–21
–12," *Fox News*, May 22, 2012, https://www.youtube.com/watch?v=L
22CrKVi_Dw.

16 A few years later: "Charlie Kirk ~ The Conservative Forum ~ 9–8–
2015," *Liberty Forum*, September 9, 2015, https://www.youtube.com
/watch?v=ihaMOHCVYsQ.

16 "I kind of got": Ibid.

16 later insisting: Jane Mayer, "A Conservative Nonprofit That Seeks to
Transform College Campuses Faces Allegations of Racial Bias and Illegal Campaign Activity," *New Yorker*, December 21, 2017, https://www
.newyorker.com/news/news-desk/a-conservative-nonprofit-that-seeks
-to-transform-college-campuses-faces-allegations-of-racial-bias-and
-illegal-campaign-activity.

16 dismissing it as: Joe DePaolo, "Charlie Kirk Shouts 'Fake News' At A
Town Hall Questioner . . . ," *MEDIAite*, November 5, 2019, https://
www.mediaite.com/tv/charlie-kirk-shouts-fake-news-at-a-town-hall
-questioner-for-asking-about-something-he-actually-said/.

17 One afternoon, shortly before: Rebecca Nelson and National Journal, "The 21-Year-Old Becoming a Major Player in Conservative Politics," *The Atlantic*, March 25, 2015, https://www.theatlantic.com
/politics/archive/2015/03/the-21-year-old-becoming-a-major-player-in
-conservative-politics/451110/.

17 "Washington is spending": "The Speech That Launched Turning Point
USA," *Turning Point USA*, July 27, 2017, https://www.youtube.com
/watch?v=Tnrn9OKZLoY.

17 He'd owned a Cajun: Kirk and Hamachek, *Time for a Turning Point*, 5.

18 Montgomery would later tell: Julie Bykowicz, "This Boy Wonder Is
Building the Conservative MoveOn.org in an Illinois Garage," *Bloomberg*, May 7, 2015, https://www.bloomberg.com/news/articles/2015–05
–07/conservative-boy-wonder.

18 friends were skeptical: Hamill, "Charlie Kirk Opens Up."

19 Furthermore, Charlie was paying: Ibid.

20 They spent weeks zigzagging: "Memorial Service Honoring Bill Montgomery," *Turning Point USA*, August 21, 2020, https://www.youtube
.com/watch?v=tNzx8K7ylak.

CHAPTER TWO: BIRTH OF A LIBERTARIAN MESSENGER

21 It was summer 2011: Daniel Lippman, "BIRTHDAY OF THE DAY: Cliff Maloney, President of Young Americans for Liberty," *Politico*, May 3, 2018, https://www.politico.com/story/2018/05/03/playbook-birthday-cliff-maloney-566037.

21 "If we think that": American Presidency Project, "Republican Presidential Candidates Debate in Myrtle Beach, South Carolina," accessed February 15, 2022, https://www.presidency.ucsb.edu/documents/republican-presidential-candidates-debate-myrtle-beach-south-carolina.

30 He kept close tabs: John Richard, "Only 28 Will Win Seats," *The Advocate*, April 10, 2013, https://upj-advocate.com/news/2013/04/10/only-28-will-win-seats/.

31 He promised to bring: Brandon Zeris, "Wi-Fi Expands," *The Advocate*, November 14, 2012, https://upj-advocate.com/news/2012/11/14/wi-fi-expands/.

31 At the end of his first: Cliff Maloney Jr., "Letter—Senate Progress," *The Advocate*, January 31, 2012, https://upj-advocate.com/opinions/2012/01/31/letter-senate-progress/.

32 By the time Cliff graduated: Andy Hsiao, "Campus' Wi-Fi Completion Set for 7 Buildings," *The Advocate*, September 25, 2013, https://upj-advocate.com/news/2013/09/25/campus-wi-fi-completion-set-for-7-buildings/.

32 As a fundraising tool: Elizabeth Williamson, "Fed Critic Boasts the Gold Standard of Political Cookbooks," *The Wall Street Journal*, June 5, 2012, https://www.wsj.com/articles/fed-critic-ron-paul-opens-door-to-food-critics-in-political-cookbook-11591379071; Dan Amira, "An Exclusive Look Inside the Ron Paul Cookbook," *New York*, November 30, 2011, https://nymag.com/intelligencer/2011/11/exclusive-look-inside-the-ron-paul-cookbook.html.

35 Their leader was: Lawrence W. Reed, "An Interview with Jeff Frazee," *Foundation for Economic Education*, July 23, 2014, https://fee.org/articles/an-interview-with-jeff-frazee/.

35 A true believer: Nick Corasaniti and Alan Rappeport, "At CPAC, Pushing Republican Hopefuls to Dive into Policy Specifics," *New York Times*, February 26, 2015, https://www.nytimes.com/2015/02/27/us/politics/cpac-republicans.html.

35 Then he convinced: Reed, "An Interview with Jeff Frazee."

36 Another time, his group: Brandon Zeris, "Students Protest Syrian Involvement," *The Advocate*, September 11, 2013, https://upj-advocate.com/news/2013/09/11/students-protest-syrian-involvement/.

36 Cliff, wearing a: Young Americans for Liberty at Pitt-Johnston, Image of student protesters, Facebook, September 3, 2013, https://www.facebook.com/UPJYoungAmericansForLiberty/photos/a.38417053 8379017/384170551712349.

37 The candidate was: "Igor Birman—Former Guest Speaker," Leadership Institute, accessed February 15, 2022, https://www.leadershipinstitute.org/training/contact.cfm?FacultyID=9729.

37 He'd gotten a: Emily Cahn, "Ron Paul Endorses in Competitive California House Race," *Roll Call*, March 21, 2014, https://rollcall.com/2014/03/21/ron-paul-endorses-in-competitive-california-house-race/.

Some of the information from this chapter comes from the video "Memorial Service Honoring Bill Montgomery" by Turning Point USA. https://www.youtube.com/watch?v=tNzx8K7y1ak.

Some of the information for this chapter comes from two podcast episodes conducted by Charlie's friend and advisory board member Gary Rabine on his *Ditch Digger CEO* with Gary Rabine. They are here: https://open.spotify.com/episode/3hq9Jc5jh9jwvK51VXxFjG.

https://open.spotify.com/episode/3UwMp7UbVmxp6JOnyzAXOt.

CHAPTER THREE: THE NEW SON

39 Walsh, a former social worker: Don Terry, "Illinois Lawmaker Proves a Tough Target for G.O.P.," *New York Times*, October 24, 1996, https://www.nytimes.com/1996/10/24/us/illinois-lawmaker-proves-a-tough-target-for-gop.html.

40 Joe Walsh and his wife: Representative Biography, "Illinois General Assembly," accessed February 15, 2022, https://www.ilga.gov/house/Rep.asp?GA=100&MemberID=2515.

40 Fundraisers for these groups: Young People For, "Building Tomorrow: Generation Progress Report," accessed February 16, 2022, http://youngpeoplefor.org/wp-content/uploads/2017/04/Youth-Infrastructure-Paper-FINAL-1.pdf

40 The two biggest events: Horowitz Freedom Center, "Restoration Weekend," accessed February 16, 2022, https://www.horowitzfreedomcenter.tv/video-category/restoration-weekend/.

41 Wyoming was hopping: Wyoming Hunt Planner, "Wyoming Game and Fish Department," accessed February 15, 2022, https://wgfd.wyo.gov/Hunting/Hunt-Planner/Elk-Hunting/Elk-Map.

42 In August 2012: Adam Liptak, "Supreme Court Upholds Health Care Law, 5–4, in Victory for Obama," *New York Times*, June 28, 2012.

42 Charlie boarded: Kirk and Hamachek, *Time for a Turning Point*.

42 On board, while: "Memorial Service Honoring Bill Montgomery," *Turning Point USA*, August 21, 2020, https://www.youtube.com/watch ?v=tNzx8K7ylak.

42 Once in Florida: Ibid.

43 Charlie thought: Ibid.

43 Charlie, who has multiple: Kirk and Hamachek, *Time for a Turning Point*, 268.

43 In another telling: "Memorial Service Honoring Bill Montgomery," *Turning Point USA*.

43 The last day: Ibid.

43 Charlie told Friess: Kirk and Hamachek, *Time for a Turning Point*, 268.

43 Friess was a politically: Lucy Madison, "Foster Friess: In My Day, Women 'Used Bayer Aspirin for Contraceptives,'" *CBS News*, February 17, 2012, https://www.cbsnews.com/news/foster-friess-in-my-day -women-used-bayer-aspirin-for-contraceptives/.

43 He was a big spender: Ben Gose, "Wyoming Philanthropist Foster Friess: Hates Taxes, Opens Wallet Wide to Those in Need," WyoFile, January 17, 2012, https://wyofile.com/foster-friess/.

44 "It matters where": "Condoleezza Rice's R.N.C. Speech," *New York Times*, August 30, 2012, https://www.nytimes.com/video/us/politics /100000001749910/condoleezza-rices-rnc-speech.html.

44 The speech had: Tim Murphy, "GOP Megadonor Foster Friess on RNC: 'This Is a Nightmare For Me,'" *Mother Jones*, August 30, 2012, https://www.motherjones.com/politics/2012/08/foster-friess-rnc -tampa/.

44 And he was constantly: Neil Genzlinger, "Foster Friess, Big Donor to Republicans, Dies at 81," *New York Times*, May 29, 2021, https://www.ny times.com/2021/05/28/us/politics/foster-friess-dead.html.

44 A few weeks later: Guinto, "Trump's Man on Campus."

44 Charlie, in return: "Only in America," *Turning Point USA*, accessed February 15, 2022, https://www.tpusa.com/onlyinamerica.

44 Another time, Charlie: "#13 Turning Points Into Action w/ Charlie Kirk, Founder of Turning Point USA," *Ditch Digger CEO*, February 1, 2019, https://open.spotify.com/episode/3hq9Jc5jh9jwvK51VXxFjG.

44 "I gave him": Ibid.

45 "It doesn't matter": Ibid.

45 "The really cool": "Charlie Kirk—Western Conservative Summit 2016," *Centennial Institute*, July 25, 2016, https://www.youtube.com/watch ?v=HZWJYN4D2Go.

46 Caleb Hull, a conservative: Caleb Hull @CalebJHull, "Cherish the people

you love. They could be gone tomorrow," Twitter, July 28, 2020, https://twitter.com/CalebJHull/status/1288139809974824960.

46 got in trouble: Jared Holt, "Popular Pro-Trump Digital Strategist Made Racist Comments on a Secret Twitter Account," *Right Wing Watch*, July 1, 2020, https://www.rightwingwatch.org/post/%E2%80%8Bpop ular-pro-trump-%E2%80%8Bdigital-strategist-made-racist-comments -on-a-secret-twitter-account/.

46 "Whoever has the": "Illinois Congresswoman Mary Miller Tells Crowd Hitler 'Was Right on One Thing'," *Mahomet Daily*, January 6, 2021, https://mahometdaily.com/illinois-congresswoman-mary-miller-tells -crowd-hitler-was-right-on-one-thing.

46 Mike liked Charlie: Kirk and Hamachek, *Time for a Turning Point*, 11.

46 Things really began to go Charlie's way: Cal Skinner, "Bill Prim Rakes in Over $50,000 for Sheriff's Race, Newt Gingrich Outlines Optimis-tic Future for USA," *McHenry County Blog*, February 19, 2013, https://mchenrycountyblog.com/2013/02/18/bill-prim-rakes-in-over-50000 -for-sheriffs-race-newt-gingrich-outlines-optimistic-future-for-usa/.

46 In a twenty-minute speech: Sarah Sutscheck, "Gingrich Returns to County for Sheriff Candidate's Fundraiser," *Shaw Local News*, Febru-ary 19, 2013, https://www.shawlocal.com/2013/02/18/gingrich-returns -to-county-for-sheriff-candidates-fundraiser/az1eyf6/.

47 But he still had a vivid memory: "#1 The Story of the Ditch Digger CEO Interview w/ Gary Rabine, Host," *Ditch Digger CEO*, https://open .spotify.com/episode/3UwMp7UbVmxp6JOnyzAXOt

47 But instead of learning: Ibid; Kirk and Rabine, "#13 Turning Points Into Action w/ Charlie Kirk."

48 And he was sometimes: Gary Rabine @Gary Rabine, "It's an honor to be described as the Elon Musk of Road Paving," Twitter, May 27, 2018, https://twitter.com/GaryRabine/status/1000813955282079744.

48 As of 2018: Crain's Chicago Business, "The Book 2021: The Ultimate Guide to Everything and Everyone in Chicago Business," accessed April 23, 2022, https://s3-prod.chicagobusiness.com/s3fs-public/2020–12/The Book2021.pdf.

48 His biggest national: Rabine, "# 1 The Story of the Ditch Digger CEO."

49 "Thanks for nothing": Shane Goldmacher, "A Times Square Billboard Hits Ocasio-Cortez on Amazon. She Hits Back," *New York Times*, Feb-ruary 21, 2019, https://www.nytimes.com/2019/02/21/nyregion/aoc -billboard-amazon.html.

49 An ad the Network: Job Creators Network, "New Ad: Dr. Fauci, We'd

Like a Second Opinion," May 20, 2020, https://www.jobcreatorsnetwork
.com/new-ad-dr-fauci-wed-like-a-second-opinion/.

49 Other splashy national: Job Creators Network, "Fight For Higher
Skills, Not Job Killing Mandates," December 9, 2016, https://www.job
creatorsnetwork.com/fight-for-higher-skills-not-job-killing-mandates/.

49 "Send the kid": Kirk and Rabine, "#13 Turning Points Into Action w/
Charlie Kirk."

49 It was at this: Kirk and Hamachek, *Time for a Turning Point*, 12.

49 The Hanleys weren't: "A Multi-Millionaire Gives Business Tips and
Talks About Serving Others," *AM/PM Podcast*, November 19, 2020,
https://www.ampmpodcast.com/retail-expert-tips-on-ecommerce-2/.

49 Lee, the heir to: Yale University Class of 1964, "In Memoriam: William Lee Hanley, Jr.," accessed February 15, 2022, https://yale64.org
/remembrances/hanley.htm.

50 In November 2013: Kirk and Hamachek, *Time for a Turning Point*, 12.

50 At that point, it was being held: The Breakers, "About Our Luxury Palm
Beach Resort," accessed February 15, 2022, https://www.thebreakers
.com/about-breakers/.

50 Meanwhile, Allie Hanley: Kirk and Hamachek, *Time for a Turning
Point*, 12.

51 In 1979, she: Georgia Dullea, "Harrumph: Social Abandon in Greenwich," *New York Times*, May 30, 1987.

51 As charming as he was: Evan Osnos, "How Greenwich Republicans
Learned to Love Trump," *New Yorker*, April 30, 2020, https://www
.newyorker.com/magazine/2020/05/11/how-greenwich-republicans
-learned-to-love-trump.

51 He was hanging: Foster Friess, "#TBT Lynn and I enjoyed fishing with
@donaldjtrumpjr @realcandaceowens @charliekirk1776 and other committed patriots working . . . ," Instagram, August 19, 2019, https://www
.instagram.com/p/B06u_PcFu-l/.

51 In November 2014: "Annie Taylor Awards," The David Horowitz Freedom Center Restoration Weekend, November, 15–18, 2018, https://vimeo
.com/303070100?embedded=true&source=vimeo_logo&owner=153
33690.

51 A year earlier: Steve Bannon and Patrick Caddell, "Trump: The President at War," David Horowitz's Restoration Weekend, Vimeo, November 16–19 2017, https://vimeo.com/303070100?embedded=true&source=
vimeo_logo&owner=15333690.

52 Lee Hanley was circulating: Vicky Ward, "The Blow-It-All-Up Billion

aires," Highline/Huffington Post, March 17, 2017, https://vickyward
.com/article/the-blow-it-all-up-billionaires/.

52 Charlie sat comfortably: Kirk, "Annie Taylor Awards."

CHAPTER FOUR: FROM THE GROUND UP

55 By late fall 2012: "Representative Robert J. Dold," Congress.gov, accessed
February 16, 2022, https://www.congress.gov/member/robert-dold/D0
00613.

56 Among them were: "Our Mission & Goals," TPUSA, December 10,
2010, http://stratml.hyperbase.com/TPUSA/TPUSA.html.

56 Conservative youth groups: "The Heathen College Boys," *New York
Times*, May 1, 1982, https://timesmachine.nytimes.com/timesmachine
/1892/05/01/104127457.pdf

56 Young Americans for Freedom: Young America's Foundation, "History," July 10, 2015, https://www.yaf.org/about/history/.

57 Charlie, with the help: "TPUSA," December 10, 2010, http://stratml
.hyperbase.com/TPUSA/TPUSA.html.

57 Eventually, the leaders: YAF Memo to Program Team, May 25, 2018,
https://www.yaf.org/wp-content/uploads/2018/06/052518TPUSA
Memo.pdf.

58 In 1964, the historian: Richard Hofstadter, "The Paranoid Style in American Politics," *Harper's* magazine, November, 1964, https://harpers.org
/archive/1964/11/the-paranoid-style-in-american-politics/.

58 "We must reframe": Katherine Yurica, "Paul Weyrich's Training
Manual," September 14, 2004, http://www.theocracywatch.org/yurica
_weyrich_manual.htm.

59 Just about anyone could start: Turning Point USA, "Chapter Directory,"
June 24, 2013, https://web.archive.org/web/20130924035646/http:/www
.turningpointusa.net/chapters/chapter-directory/.

59 In addition to: Turning Point USA, "Staff," September 23, 2013, https://
web.archive.org/web/20130923015934/http://www.turningpointusa.net
/staff/.

59 A standout volunteer: Turning Point USA, "Staff Directory," May 16,
2014, https://web.archive.org/web/20140516043958/http:/www.turning
pointusa.net/staffdirectory/.

59 Raised by her: Carolyn Waller, "Warren Township High School Students Make Second Semester Honor Roll—Gurnee News, Photos and
Events—TribLocal.Com," *TribLocal*, June 23, 2010, http://www.trib
local.com/gurnee/community/stories/2010/06/warren-township-high
-school-students-make-second-semester-honor-roll/index.html.

59 and being crowned: Gurnee Community Pageant, "Gurnee Queens," accessed February 16, 2022, http://www.gurneecommunitypageant.com /gurnee-queens.html.

60 "I had no shortage": Crystal Clanton, "How to Debate Your Teacher (and Win!)," *Turning Point USA*, accessed February 16, 2022, http://victory sitespolitical.org/turningpoint/wp-content/uploads/2015/04/HowTo DebateYourTeacher.pdf.

60 In a September 2019: Jackson Faulkner, "College Democrats Requires Support of DNC to Succeed," *Tulane Hullabaloo*, September 12, 2019, https://tulanehullabaloo.com/48593/views/dnc-college-democrats -support/.

63 In summer 2014: "The Power of Grassroots Campus Organizing—Big Government Sucks! 2014," Turning Point USA, December 22, 2014, https://www.youtube.com/watch?v=gOLALi6–690.

63 When he shared: Turning Point USA, "Advisory Council," accessed February 16, 2022, https://web.archive.org/web/20140905095628/http:/ www.turningpointusa.net/advisory-council/.

63 Clanton and her team: Turning Point USA, "Big Government Sucks," accessed February 16, 2022, https://web.archive.org/web/20140703122 652/http:/www.turningpointusa.net/biggovernmentsucks/.

64 The campaign, he told: "Big Government Sucks! Project on Fox News," *Fox News*, August 26, 2014, https://www.youtube.com/watch?v=zH -6Z3GXv0M.

64 It was "edgy": Dan Joseph, "'Big Government Sucks!': Conservative Group Takes Message to 700 College Campuses Nationwide," *CNSNews*, August 25, 2014, https://www.cnsnews.com/mrctv-blog/dan-joseph /big-government-sucks-conservative-group-takes-message-700-college -campuses.

64 According to a 2013: David Corn, "Inside the New Strategy Group Where Right-Wing Activists and Journalists Coordinate Messaging," *Mother Jones*, July 25, 2013, https://www.motherjones.com/politics/2013/07 /groundswell-rightwing-group-ginni-thomas/.

65 By the end of 2014: Turning Point USA, Wayback Machine, accessed February 16, 2022, https://web.archive.org/web/20151014181127/http:// www.turningpointusa.net/wp-content/uploads/2014/01/2014Year InReview.pdf.

65 But no matter, TPUSA marked: Charlie Kirk, "Squad," Facebook, February 26, 2015, https://www.facebook.com/photo/?fbid=80910173 5812045&set=pb.100001366790052.-2207520000; Robert Costa, "Hillary Clinton Takes Center Stage at CPAC 2015," *Washington Post*,

February 27, 2015, https://www.washingtonpost.com/news/post-poli tics/wp/2015/02/26/hillary-clinton-takes-center-stage-at-cpac-2015/.

65 It was the ultimate confab: Turning Point USA @TPUSA, "#TBT to our huge #BigGovSucks wall at #CPAC2015," Twitter, August 20, 2015, https://twitter.com/TPUSA/status/634485070359736320.

65 Their camp spanned: CNN Politics, Image of Turning Point banners and students at CPAC, Facebook, February 26, 2015, https://www.face book.com/cnnpolitics/photos/pcb.868446663197168/868446216530546.

67 Like his father: David Rogers, "Rand Paul Unveils $500B in Cuts," *Politico*, January 25, 2011, https://www.politico.com/story/2011/01/rand -paul-unveils-500b-in-cuts-048178.

67 "We must believe": "Senator Rand Paul Remarks at CPAC," *C-SPAN*, February 27, 2015, https://www.c-span.org/video/?324558–12/senator -rand-paul-r-ky-remarks-cpac-2015.

67 They were mostly: Alexandra Jaffe, "Rand Paul Wins 2015 CPAC Straw Poll," *CNN*, February 28, 2015, https://www.cnn.com/2015/02/28 /politics/cpac-2015-straw-poll-results-rand-paul/index.html.

68 That spring and summer: "Senator Rand Paul Campaign Rally in Des Moines, Iowa," *C-SPAN*, January 29, 2016, https://www.c-span.org /video/?403796–1/senator-rand-paul-campaign-rally-des-moines-iowa.

68 By the end of: American Presidency Project, "Press Release—400 Students For Rand Chapters Established Throughout the Country," February 19, 2015, https://www.presidency.ucsb.edu/documents/press-release -400-students-for-rand-chapters-established-throughout-the-country.

68 By spring: "YAL Transition Webinar," Young Americans for Liberty, June 3, 2018, https://www.facebook.com/watch/?v=1015373815970019.

69 To emphasize this: James Hohmann and Michelle Ye Hee Lee, "How the Koch Network Learned to Thrive in the Trump Era," *Washington Post*, January 28, 2018, https://www.washingtonpost.com/politics/how -the-koch-network-learned-to-thrive-in-the-trump-era/2018/01/28 /f71979d0–0448–11e8-b48c-b07fea957bd5_story.html.

70 He directed student activists: "Young Americans for Liberty Protest War on Drugs," *Daily Illini*, April 18, 2013, https://dailyillini.com /uncategorized/2013/04/18/young-americans-for-liberty-protest-war -on-drugs/.

72 "I'm all for": Eliza Gray, "How Trumpian Is the GOP's next Generation? I Talked to 52 Young Conservatives to Find Out," *Washington Post*, June 16, 2016, https://www.washingtonpost.com/news/style/wp/2018/07/16 /feature/the-next-generation-of-republicans-do-they-stand-with -trump/.

CHAPTER FIVE: THE KID IS GONE

Some of the information from this chapter comes from "Turning Points into Action w/ Charlie Kirk, Founder of Turning Point USA" on the podcast *Ditch Digger CEO* with Gary Rabine, https://open.spotify.com /episode/3hq9Jc5jh9jwvK51VXxFjG.

73 The esteemed political: Robert O'Harrow Jr. and Shawn Boburg, "How a 'Shadow' Universe of Charities Joined with Political Warriors to Fuel Trump's Rise," *Washington Post*, June 3, 2017, https://www.washing tonpost.com/investigations/how-a-shadow-universe-of-charities -joined-with-political-warriors-to-fuel-trumps-rise/2017/06/03 /ff5626ac-3a77-11e7-a058-ddbb23c75d82_story.html; Ward, "The Blow-It-All-Up-Billionaires"; Jane Mayer, "The Reclusive Hedge Fund Tycoon Behind the Trump Presidency," *New Yorker*, March 27, 2017, https:// www.newyorker.com/magazine/2017/03/27/the-reclusive-hedge-fund -tycoon-behind-the-trump-presidency.

73 In 2014, they convinced: Ibid.

73 Expert, if not intimidating: Ibid.

73 Charlie would eventually: Charlie Kirk @charliekirk1776, "God Bless Ted Cruz and his family," Instagram, May 3, 2016, https://www.insta gram.com/p/BE90hOVKPoQ/.

74 He even featured Cruz: Charlie Kirk, "Ted with TPUSA. #BigGovSucks," Facebook, February 26, 2015, https://www.facebook.com/photo.php?f bid=809332915788927&set=pb.100001366790052.-2207520000.&type=3.

74 Payden Hall, who was: Mayer, "A Conservative Nonprofit That Seeks to Transform College Campuses."

74 For their organizations to maintain nonprofit: Internal Revenue Service, "Exemption Requirements—501(c)(3) Organizations," accessed Febru-ary 16, 2022, https://www.irs.gov/charities-non-profits/charitable-organi zations/exemption-requirements-501c3-organizations.

75 In July 2014: Mark Weyermuller, "Where's Weyermuller? With Bruce Rauner at the Turning Point USA Event," *Illinois Review*, July 14, 2014, https://illinoisreview.typepad.com/illinoisreview/2014/07/wheres -weyermuller-with-bruce-rauner-at-the-turning-point-usa-event.html.

75 Charlie would later: Kirk and Hamachek, *Time for a Turning Point*.

75 A year later: John Keilman, "Before Trump and Kanye Became Fans, Charlie Kirk Battled 'Marxist' High School Teachers in Chicago's Sub-urbs," *Chicago Tribune*, October 22, 2018, https://www.chicagotribune .com/news/ct-met-charlie-kirk-turning-point-campus-conservatives -profile-20181019-story.html.

76 As for Charlie: Charlie Kirk @charliekirk11, "Cruz didn't send that photo

for the last time. Trump is a pure demagogue," Twitter, March 30, 2016, https://web.archive.org/web/20160330163037if_/https:/twitter.com /charliekirk11.

76 In fact, in March 2016: Pam Vogel, "Meet Charlie Kirk, The 'Boy Wonder' Trump Ally Behind A Poorly Sourced McCarthy-Like Watchlist Of Professors," Media Matters, December 2, 2016, https://www .mediamatters.org/charlie-kirk/meet-charlie-kirk-boy-wonder-trump -ally-behind-poorly-sourced-mccarthy-watchlist.

76 Trump promised that: Michelle Boorstein and Julie Zauzmer, "Thrilling Christian Conservative Audience, Trump Vows to Lift Ban on Politicking, Appoint Antiabortion Judges," *Washington Post*, June 22, 2016, https://www.washingtonpost.com/news/acts-of-faith/wp/2016/06/20 /how-can-trump-win-the-many-undecided-evangelicals-we-asked -them/.

77 One of the eleven: Donald J Trump for President, "Trump Campaign Announces Evangelical Executive Board," June 21, 2016, https://web .archive.org/web/20160622080352/https://www.donaldjtrump.com /press-releases/trump-campaign-announces-evangelical-executive -advisory-board.

77 MacDonald would eventually: Patrick M. O'Connell and Morgan Greene," Harvest Bible Chapel Pastor James MacDonald Fired: 'A Hard but Necessary Day for Our Church,'" *Chicago Tribune*, February 13, 2019, https://www.chicagotribune.com/news/ct-met-harvest-bible-chapel -james-macdonald-turmoil-20190211-story.html.

77 He did not: "Republican National Convention, Day 1 Afternoon Session," *C-SPAN*, July 18, 2016, https://www.c-span.org/video/?412399–1/day -republican-national-convention-afternoon-session.

77 Further, he admitted: Issie Lapowsky, "At the Republican Convention, Millennials Search for Signs of the Future." *Wired*, July 20, 2016, https:// www.wired.com/2016/07/republican-convention-millennials-search -signs-future/.

77 And it was at: Mayer, "A Conservative Nonprofit That Seeks to Transform College Campuses."

77 "We don't know": Osita Nwanevu, "How Young Conservative Activists Party at CPAC," *New Yorker*, March 4, 2019, https://www.newyorker .com/news/news-desk/how-young-conservative-activists-party-at-cpac.

77 By the end of: Charlie Kirk, "60 Days with Don Trump Jr.–HYPE LINE," Hypeline, November 16, 2016, https://web.archive.org/web /20161116170313/http://hypeline.org/on-working-with-donald-trump-jr/.

78 Don, UPenn classmates: Sandra Sobierai Westfall and Tierney McAfee,

"'Stay Away from Donnie Trump': Inside Don Jr.'s Drinking, Womanizing and Frat Guy Antics." *People*, July 19, 2017, https://people .com/politics/donald-trump-jr-college-partying-womanizing/; Nikki Schwab, "'Diaper Don's' Hard-Partying College Days Detailed in New Book," *New York Post*, June 18, 2018, https://nypost.com/2018/06/18/bio graphy-details-trump-jr-s-hard-partying-college-days/.

78 Hicks pled no: Jake Pearson, "Want to Meet with the Trump Administration? Donald Trump Jr.'s Hunting Buddy Can Help," *ProPublica*, July 22, 2019, https://www.propublica.org/article/trump-inc-podcast -tommy-hicks-jr-donald-trump-jr-hunting-buddy.

78 and Beach had seen: Sue Ambrose and Miles Moffeit, "The Art of the Schmooze: Trump Pal from Dallas Enjoys Special Access to White House," *Dallas Morning News*, May 22, 2017, https://www.dallasnews .com/news/politics/2017/05/22/the-art-of-the-schmooze-trump-pal -from-dallas-enjoys-special-access-to-white-house/.

78 Now the trio: Laura M. Holson, "Donald Trump Jr. Is His Own Kind of Trump," *New York Times*, March 18, 2017, https://www.nytimes .com/2017/03/18/style/donald-trump-jr-business-politics-hunting -twitter-vanessa-haydon.html.

78 Once, while driving: Kirk and Rabine, "#13 Turning Points into Action w/ Charlie Kirk."

78 A few weeks before: Donald Trump Jr., *Triggered: How the Left Thrives on Hate and Wants to Silence Us* (Center Street, 2019), 140.

79 They made a: Ibid.

79 On the eve of: Charlie Kirk, "The past 60 days I had a once in a lifetime chance to travel, learn from, and work w/ @DonaldJTrumpJr," November 16, 2016, Instagram, https://www.instagram.com/p/BM4DJwA jVXN/.

CHAPTER SIX: "COMING OUT CONSERVATIVE"

83 The young man, later identified as: Celia Raney, "Affirmative Action Bake Sale Charges Customers Based on Race," *Daily Lobo*, September 22, 2017, https://www.dailylobo.com/article/2017/09/umm-group -protest-affirmative-action.

84 "Coming Out Conservative": Mackenzie Eldred, "Turning Point USA Holds 'Conservative Coming Out Party' at UNC • UNC Mirror," *UNC Mirror*, October 12, 2017, http://www.uncmirror.com/news/2017/10/12 /turning-point-usa-holds-conservative-coming-party-unc/.

85 The fact that UNM didn't use: Jessica Dyer, "Bake Sale with Prices Based on Race Was Not Sanctioned, UNM Says," *Albuquerque Journal*,

September 22, 2017, https://www.abqjournal.com/1067251/bake-sale-with-prices-based-on-race-was-not-sanctioned-unm-says.html.

85 To test this: John M. Carey, Katherine Clayton, and Yusaku Horiuchi, "It's College Admissions Season, and Students Are Looking for Diverse Campuses," *Washington Post*, April 14, 2020, https://www.washingtonpost.com/politics/2020/04/14/its-college-admissions-season-students-are-looking-diverse-campuses/.

88 In November 2017: Vimal Patel, "After Campus Protests Against a Local Bakery, Here's Why a Jury Said Oberlin Must Pay $44 Million," *Chronicle of Higher Education*, June 14, 2019, https://www.chronicle.com/article/after-campus-protests-against-a-local-bakery-heres-why-a-jury-said-oberlin-must-pay-44-million/?cid2=gen_login_refresh&cid=gen_sign_in; Mark Gillispie, "$25 Million Judge Against Oberlin College Upheld by Appeals Court," WKYC.com, April 1, 2022, https://www.wkyc.com/article/news/local/lorain-county/oberlin-college-gibsons-bakery-judgment-upheld/95-5ba6cd73-9f1a-490e-8064-d21a46bb84c0.

88 "the Mob at Middlebury": Opinion, "The Mob at Middlebury," *Wall Street Journal*, March 5, 2017, https://www.wsj.com/articles/the-mob-at-middlebury-1488586505.

88 That same month: Abby Spegman, "Evergreen Professor at Center of Protests Resigns; College Will Pay $500,000," *Seattle Times*, September 16, 2017, https://www.seattletimes.com/seattle-news/evergreen-professor-at-center-of-protests-resigns-college-will-pay-500000/.

88 Documents unsealed in September 2021: "TV Station: Allyn D. Gibson Made Racist Facebook Posts in 2016," *Chronicle Telegram*, accessed February 15, 2022, https://chroniclet.com/news/276664/tv-station-allyn-d-gibson-made-racist-facebook-posts-in-2016/.

88 And at Evergreen: Scott Jaschik, "In Escalating Debate on Race at Evergreen State, Students Demand Firing of Professor," *Inside Higher Ed*, May 30, 2017, https://www.insidehighered.com/news/2017/05/30/escalating-debate-race-evergreen-state-students-demand-firing-professor.

91 These groups, thanks to: Generation Progress, "Building Tomorrow: The Need for Sustained Investment in America's Progressive Youth," April 5, 2017, http://youngpeoplefor.org/building-tomorrow-the-need-for-sustained-investment-in-americas-progressive-youth/.

92 The sixty-four-year-old Intercollegiate Studies Institute: "Financials—Intercollegiate Studies Institute," ISI, accessed February 13, 2022, https://isi.org/financials/.

92 "Woke World": "Lecture—Intercollegiate Studies Institute," ISI, March 13, 2019, https://isi.org/lectures/.

92 The seventy-one-year-old Foundation for Economic Education: "Financial Data—Foundation for Economic Education," FEE, June 12, 2015, https://fee.org/about/financial-data.

92 The Fund for American Studies: Fund for American Studies, Form 990–0 period ending December 2017, *ProPublica*, Nonprofit Explorer, https://projects.propublica.org/nonprofits/organizations/136223604.

92 whose central goal is: "The Fund for American Studies," Fund for American Studies, August 3, 2016, https://tfas.org.

93 "the global warming narrative": CFACT Eco-Summit 2017: The Future Belongs to the Skeptics, CFACT, August 7, 2017, https://www.cfact .org/2017/08/07/cfact-eco-summit-2017-the-future-belongs-to-the -skeptics/.

93 "the science behind climate": Campaigns, CFACT, accessed February 16, 2022, https://www.cfactcampus.org.

93 Activists clutched microphones: "Jumbotron TV–Created Equal," Created Equal, accessed February 13, 2022, https://www.createdequal.org /jumbotron-tv/.

94 In addition to its pro-gun: NRA Explore, "Refuse to Be a Victim Collegiate Edition," April 15, 2022, accessed April 15, 2022, https://rtbav -college.nra.org.

94 In addition, gun rights: NRA Blog, "NRA Releases Powerful New Ads Featuring Millennial Women," accessed April 20, 2022, https://www .nrablog.com/articles/2016/7/nra-releases-powerful-new-ads-featuring -millennial-women/.

94 In 2017, a senior: Hannah Knowles, "A conservative gun rights activist was tailed off campus by a swarm of mocking protesters," *Washington Post*, February 18, 2020, https://www.washingtonpost.com/education /2020/02/18/gun-girl-kaitlin-ohio-university/.

94 By fall 2017: "Guns on Campus: Overview—National Conference of State Legislatures," NCSL, November, 11, 2019, https://www.ncsl.org /research/education/guns-on-campus-overview.aspx; https://www.thet race.org/2015/07/the-making-of-the-campus-carry-movement/.

95 Young America's Foundation spent: Stephanie Saul, "The Conservative Force Behind Speeches Roiling College Campuses," *New York Times*, May 20, 2017, https://www.nytimes.com/2017/05/20/us/college -conservative-speeches.html.

95 Circulating online: "Video: Instructor Arrested for Attacking A Conservative Student," Campus Reform, September 18, 2017, https://www .campusreform.org/?ID=10171.

95 Another video that went viral: Jordan Hall, "Former Graduate Instructor,

Blacklisted Over Testy Exchange with TPUSA Students, Sues University of Neraska–Lincoln," FIRE , August 31, 2021, https://www.thefire.org /former-graduate-instructor-blacklisted-over-testy-exchange-with -tpusa-student-sues-university-of-nebraska-lincoln/.

96 There were plenty: "Student Freaks Out at Donald Trump Sign on Campus," Campus Reform, May 12, 2017, https://www.campusreform .org/?ID=9171.

96 Just eight months earlier: Chris Quintana and Nicole Perez, "UNM Speech Draws Hecklers, Protesters," *Albuquerque Journal*, January 27, 2017, https://www.abqjournal.com/937724/hundreds-of-protesters-gather -outside-unm-for-controversial-speaker-milo-yiannopoulos.html.

97 Also making their: "CFACT expands into New Mexico with the launch of UNM Chapter," CFACT, accessed February 15, 2022, https://www .cfactcampus.org/cfact-expands-into-new-mexico-with-the-launch-of -unm-chapter/.

97 "Keep Calm, Climate Changes": "CFACT—Collegians For A Constructive Tomorrow," accessed February 15, 2022, https://www.cfactcampus .org/#campaigns.

97 PragerU was founded: Mark Oppenheimer, "Inside the Right-Wing YouTube Empire That's Quietly Turning Millenials Into Conservatives," *MotherJones*, April/May 2018, https://www.motherjones.com /politics/2018/03/inside-right-wing-youtube-turning-millennials -conservative-prageru-video-dennis-prager/.

97 By 2021, that number: PragerU, "10 Years and 5 Billion Views: PragerU is the Undeniable Conservative Media Leader of the Next Generation," accessed April 20, 2022, https://www.prageru.com/press/10-years-and-5 -billion-views-prageru-is-the-undeniable-conservative-media.

97 Witt was hired: "Understanding The Women's March," PragerU, January 22, 2018, https://www.prageru.com/video/understanding-the -womens-march.

CHAPTER SEVEN: "TIRED OF LOSING"

99 The thundering sound: "Barry Goldwater at 1964 Republican National Convention," CSPAN, July 16, 1964, https://www.c-span.org /video/?320250-1/reel-america-barry-goldwaters-1964-acceptance -speech.

101 That same year: Mapping American Social Movements Projects, "SDS Chapters," accessed April 20, 2022, https://depts.washington.edu/moves /sds_map.shtml.

102 One Goldwater-ite: Lloyd Grove, "The Graying of Richard Viguireie,"

Washington Post, June 29, 1989, https://www.washingtonpost.com
/archive/lifestyle/1989/06/29/the-graying-of-richard-viguerie/17567
53f-5b37–4600–8da3–000f206fb1fa/.

102 Paul Weyrich, the devout: Bruce Weber, "Paul Weyrich, 66, a Conservatist Strategist Dies," *New York Times*, December 18, 2008, https://www
.nytimes.com/2008/12/19/us/politics/19weyrich.html; Robert O'Harrow
Jr., "God, Trump and the Closed-Door World of a Major Conservative
Group," *Washington Post*, October 25, 2021, https://www.washington
post.com/magazine/2021/10/25/god-trump-closed-door-world-council
-national-policy/.

103 With a $24 million coffer: "The Leadership Institute's Finance Page,"
LI, accessed February 15, 2022, https://www.leadershipinstitute.org
/aboutus/finance.cfm.

103 up from $19.4 million: Leadership Institute, Form 990–0 Period Ending
December 2015, *ProPublica*, Nonprofit Explorer, https://projects.pro
publica.org/nonprofits/organizations/510235174.

106 During an interview: Alexander Zaitchik, "The Zealot: Larry Pratty is
the Gun Lobby's Secret Weapon," *Rolling Stone*, July 14, 2014, https://
www.rollingstone.com/culture/culture-news/the-zealot-larry-pratt-is
-the-gun-lobbys-secret-weapon-87059/.

107 So Blackwell bought: Michael Dobbs, "Swift Boats Accounts Incomplete," *Washington Post*, August 22, 2004, https://www.washingtonpost
.com/wp-dyn/articles/A21239–2004Aug21.html; Jim Rutenberg, "Delegates Mock Kerry's Wounds, Angering Veterans," *New York Times*, September 1, 2004, https://www.nytimes.com/2004/09/01/politics/cam
paign/delegates-mock-kerrys-wounds-angering-veterans.html.

111 There is the Abe Lincoln Four-Step: Morton Blackwell, "The Abe Lincoln Four-Step," *National Review*, November 19, 2012, https://www
.nationalreview.com/2012/11/abe-lincoln-four-step-morton-blackwell/.

CHAPTER EIGHT: "I HATE BLACK PEOPLE"

117 In October 2017: David Britton, "Conservative Group Dons Diapers to
Protest Safe Spaces at Kent State," The Daily Dot, October 19, 2017,
https://www.dailydot.com/unclick/tpusa-diaper-protest-kent-state
/#diapergate.

117 A very public: Michael Vasquez, "Turning Point USA is Accused of
Abandoning Kent State Chapter Following Diaper Fiasco," *The Chronicle of Higher Education*, February 16, 2018, https://www.chronicle.com
/article/turning-point-usa-is-accused-of-abandoning-kent-state
-chapter-following-diaper-fiasco/?cid2=gen_login_refresh&cid=gen

_sign_in; Kaitlin Bennett, "I'm Turning Point USA's Top Activist in the Country, & I Quit This Shitty Organization," Liberty Hangout, February 12, 2018, http://libertyhangout.org/2018/02/im-turning-point-usas-top -activist-in-the-country-im-quitting-this-shitty-organization/.

118 It was hardly: Jodi Kantor and Megan Towey, "Harvey Weinstein Paid Off Sexual Harassment Accusers for Decades," *New York Times*, October 5, 2017, https://www.nytimes.com/2017/10/05/us/harvey-weinstein -harassment-allegations.html.

118 "The so-called diaper": Deidre Olsen, "How a 'Diaper Protest' Imploded a Conservative Student Group," *Salon*, March 25, 2018; https://www .salon.com/2018/03/25/how-a-diaper-protest-led-to-the-implosion-of -a-conservative-student-group/; Emily Shugerman, "Turning Point USA: How One Student in a Diaper Caused an Eruption in a Conservative Youth Organization," *Independent*, February 26, 2018, https://www.inde pendent.co.uk/news/world/americas/diaper-turning-point-usa-kent-state -student-conservative-youth-repulican-kaitlin-bennett-a8230021.html.

118 to amass close to: Turning Point USA Inc., Form 990–0 Period Ending June 2016, *ProPublica*, Nonprofit Explorer, https://projects.propublica .org/nonprofits/organizations/800835023.

119 a McCarthyesque Professor Watchlist: "Professor Watchlist," Professor Watchlist, accessed February 15, 2022, https://professorwatchlist.org.

119 After a Black sociology professor: Dan Lieberman, Davide Cannaviccio, Jeff Simon, and Zach Wasser, "Death Threats Are Forcing Professors off Campus," *CNN*, December 21, 2017, https://www.cnn.com/2017/12/21 /us/university-professors-free-speech-online-hate-threats/index.html.

120 That December, the American: American Association of University Professors, "Open Letter Regarding the Professor Watchlist," accessed April 20, 2022, https://www.aaup.org/open-letter-regarding-professor -watchlist.

121 And eventually, even a spokesperson: James Hohmann, "The Daily 202: Koch Network Warns of 'McCarthyism 2.0' in Conservative Efforts to Harass Professors," *Washington Post*, August 1, 2018, https://www .washingtonpost.com/news/powerpost/paloma/daily-202/2018/08/01 /daily-202-koch-network-warns-of-mccarthyism-2-0-in-conservative -efforts-to-harass-professors/5b611a871b326b0207955e90/.

121 Michael Vasquez: Michael Vasquez, "Inside a Stealth Plan for Political Influence," *The Chronicle of Higher Education*, May 7, 2017, https:// www.chronicle.com/article/inside-a-stealth-plan-for-political-influ ence/.

121 In a series of January 2017 texts leaked: Nick Roll, "Conservative Turn-

ing Point USA Quietly Funding Student Government Campaigns Across U.S.," *The Lantern*, February 28, 2017, https://www.thelantern .com/2017/02/leaked-documents-audio-conservative-turning-point-usa -quietly-funding-student-government-campaigns-across-us/; "New Revelations in the Curious Case of Turning Point USA and Ohio State's USG Elections," *The Tab*, March 2, 2017, https://thetab.com/us/ohio -state/2017/03/02/turning-point-usa-ohio-state-8388.

121 In a recorded phone: Roll, "Conservative Turning Point USA Quietly Funding Student Government Campaigns Across U.S."

122 In multiple cases: Vasquez, "Inside a Stealth Plan for Political Influence."

122 "the best hire we ever could have": Kirk and Hamachek, *Time for a Turning Point*, 13.

122 had sent a nauseating text: Mayer, "A Conservative Nonprofit that Seeks to Transform College Campuses."

123 When asked by Mayer: Ibid.

123 Clanton did not respond: Ruth Marcus, "Opinion: The Curious Case of the Clerk and the Racist Texts, *Washington Post*, January 18, 2022, https://www.washingtonpost.com/opinions/2022/01/18/clerk-texts -appeals-court-clanton/; Bill Rankin: "Judge Pryor Cleared of Allegations Involving Hiring of Controversial Clerk," *The Atlanta Journal-Constitution*, January 14, 2022, https://www.ajc.com/news/georgia-news /judge-pryor-cleared-of-allegations-involving-hiring-of-controversial -clerk/X3JAHI2TQBCUBMTQ5MDHO56FU4/.

123 The racism allegations: Ashley Feinberg, "Turning Point USA Keeps Accidentally Hiring Racists," *HuffPost*, April 25, 2018, https://www .huffpost.com/entry/turning-point-usa-racist-tweets_n_5ad65b06e4b02 9ebe0led1ac.

124 Clanton was hired: Caleb Ecarma, "EXCLUSIVE: Clarence Thomas's Wife Hired Ex-TPUSA Staffer Known for Saying 'I Hate Blacks,'" *MEDIAite*, September 6, 2018, https://www.mediaite.com/online/ex clusive-clarence-thomas-wife-hired-ex-tpusa-staffer-known-for-saying -i-hate-blacks/.

125 Gary Rabine, the Illinois: Feinberg, "Turning Point USA Keeps Accidentally Hiring Racists."

125 And Grooman went to: Yvonne Wingate Sanchez, "Kelli Ward Arizona GOP Chairwoman Gets Help From Volunteer Who Once Posted Racist and Homophobic Tweets," *azcentral*, February 21, 2019, https:// www.azcentral.com/story/news/politics/arizona/2019/02/21/kelli-ward -volunteer-once-posted-racist-and-homophobic-tweets-arizona-republic an-party/2915262002/.

CHAPTER NINE: CONFERENCE CRUSADERS

In this chapter, the reporting on YALCON 2018, was all first-hand, save for the Rand Paul speech. For that, I relied on a video of the event.

The sexual harassment allegations were based on interviews with former YAL members, employees, and contractors, and other young libertarians who circulate frequently within the YAL community. I also used written responses from YAL founder and board chair Jeff Frazee.

Later reporting in this book came from a series of letters and videos the young women who made the allegations posted in January 2021, on Facebook and Twitter—resulting in a lengthy, public online dialogue about their personal experiences at YAL. The women said they had turned to the web because their complaints had gone unheard when they kept them within the YAL community.

128 Cliff's Young Americans for Liberty Foundation: "Young Americans for Liberty Foundation, Form 990 for Period Ending Dec 2018," *ProPublica*, Nonprofit Explorer, accessed February 14, 2022, https://projects.pro publica.org/nonprofits/display_990/453503672/06_2020_prefixes_42 –46%2F453503672_201812_990_2020060917182815.

131 that would clock: Influence Watch, "Free the People," accessed February 13, 2022, https://www.influencewatch.org/non-profit/free-the-people/.

134 In 2018, Young Americans for Liberty Inc.: "Young Americans for Liberty Inc., Form 990 for Period Ending Dec 2018, *ProPubica*, Non-Profit Explorer, https://projects.propublica.org/nonprofits/organiza tions/262417908.

135 That night, the ballroom: "Ron Paul Live at YALCON," Young Americans for Liberty, Facebook, July 28, 2018, https://www.facebook.com /watch/live/?ref=watch_permalink&v=10155766839115197.

139 "I don't throw up when I drink like ever": "Ex-TPUSA Employee Tells All," The Pirater, *YouTube*, January 4, 2021, https://www.youtube.com /watch?v=BAlcFEjvReQ.

140 In 2018, the *Washington Examiner*: Philip Wegmann, "Turning Point USA struggles with allegations of allegations of student sexual assault, harassment," *Washington Examiner*, June 2018, https://www.washing tonexaminer.com/opinion/turning-point-usa-struggles-with-allegations -of-student-sexual-assault-harassment.

140 In 2021, a young woman: Olivia Rondeau @rondeaulivia, "Here are the details of the circumstances that lead to me being assaulted . . . ," Twitter, January 31, 2021, https://twitter.com/rondeaulivia/status/13 55965149358809090.

140 The woman said: Olivia Rondeau @rondeaulivia, "I will note that the

director who banned me . . . ," Twitter, January 31, 2021, https://twitter
.com/rondeaulivia/status/1355965167520141319; Owens exchange with
author.

140 Two years later: Olivia Rondeau @rondeaulivia, "Candace listened to
me and believed me," Twitter January 30, 2021, https://mobile.twitter
.com/rondeaulivia/status/1355735611265708037; Owens exchange with
author.

140 At another TPUSA conference: Caleb Hull, "Exclusive: 30 Sources
Expose Sexually Explicit Evidence of Harassment by Ohio GOP Rep.
Wes Goodman," *Independent Journalism Review*, November 20, 2017,
https://ijr.com; Hannah Parry, "Married Republican Lawmaker Sent
Naked Photos and Lewd Messages to Male College Students and Trawled
Craigslist for Gay Hookups Before Being Forced to Step Down Amid
Sex Scandal," *Daily Mail*, November 21, 2017, https://www.dailymail
.co.uk/news/article-5104591/Wes-Goodman-sent-naked-photos-male
-college-students.html.

141 According to documents uncovered by the *Washington Post*: Kimberly
Kind and Elise Viebeck, "How a Conservative Group Dealt with a Fondling Charge Against a Rising GOP Star," *Washington Post*, November 17, 2017, https://www.washingtonpost.com/politics/how-a-conser
vative-group-dealt-with-a-fondling-c.

141 In fact, by summer 2018: Addyson Rae Garner @realPOTUS2040, "I'm
speaking up about my experience with sexual misconduct at Young
Americans for Liberty," Twitter, January 8, 2021, https://twitter.com
/realpotus2040/status/1347702060007960582.

142 One woman told me: Mantis Girl @SonjaMantis, "When I interned at
YAL, I couldn't even come forward . . . ," Twitter, January 9, 2021,
https://twitter.com/SonjaMantis/status/1347805201286230017.

142 Another woman told me: jessi @jessinicoleb, "Aight, let's do this. #YALtoo
#FireCliff," Twitter, January 9, 2021, https://twitter.com/jessinicoleb
/status/1348042683391029256; Interview with the author.

CHAPTER TEN: CANDACE'S CONVERSION

The reporting on Candace's Social Autopsy Project came from a variety of
sources, including *New York* magazine, Breitbart News, and Candace's own
telling of the incidents. Other details from this chapter come from Candace's
book and an interview with one of her sisters.

145 At Stanford, Charlie told the crowd: "WATCH LIVE! Charlie Kirk and
Candace Owens are live at Stanford College Republicans," Turning Point
USA, Facebook, May 29, 2018, https://www.facebook.com/Stanford

GOP/videos/watch-live-charlie-kirk-and-candace-owens-are-live-at -stanford-college-republica/1686666311382078/.

145 Today, at UCLA: "Hard Truths Tour w/ Charlie Kirk & Candace Owens—UCLA," Video, Turning Point USA, April 18, 2018, https://www .facebook.com/watch/live/?ref=watch_permalink&v=1643504072364969.

152 In February 2007: Candace Owens, *Blackout: How Black America Can Make Its Second Escape from the Democrat Plantation* (Simon & Schuster, 2020), 27.

152 It turned out: Ibid., 28.

152 The story made: "Racists Threats Case Filed by Stamford High School Students Settled for $37,000," *Danbury News-Times*, January 23, 2020, https://www.newstimes.com/news/article/Racist-threats-case-filed-by -Stamford-High-107476.php.

152 Her classmate: Ibid.

153 First, she launched: Sam Mire, "Does Donald Trump Have a Small Penis?," Degree 180, Wayback Machine, March 18, 2016, https://web .archive.org/web/20160426214430/http://degree180.com/does-donald -trump-have-a-small-penis-a-washington-outsider-investigation/.

153 she herself wrote: Candace Owens, "F*** 'Girl Code': I Can Hook Up With Your Ex-Boyfriend If I Want To, Degree 180," Wayback Machine, December 27, 2015, https://web.archive.org/web/20160503031132/http:// degree180.com/f-girl-code-i-can-hook-up-with-your-ex-boyfriend-if-i -want-to/.

154 When Zoe Quinn: Jesse Singal, "The Strange Tale of Social Autopsy, the Anti-Harassment Start-up That Descended into Gamergate Truther- ism," *New York Magazine*, April 18, 20016, https://nymag.com/intelli gencer/2016/04/how-social-autopsy-fell-for-gamergate-trutherism .html; Allum Bokhari, "Why Are 'Anti-Abuse' Activists Zoe Quinn and Randi Harper Trying to Protect Anonymous Trolls?" Breitbart, April 27, 2016, https://www.breitbart.com/tech/2016/04/27/why-are-anti-abuse -activists-zoe-quinn-and-randi-harper-trying-to-protect-anonymous -trolls/; "On Her Journey from Left to Right|Candace Owens," The Rubin Report, *YouTube*, accessed February 14, 2022, https://www.you tube.com/watch?v=BSAoitd1BTQ.

155 Candace sometimes tells audiences: "An Evening with Charlie Kirk & Candace Owens. The Founding of Turning Point UK," Bright- spark Media, *YouTube*, December 22, 2022, https://www.youtube.com /watch?v=zTsT3FiiXX8&t=617s; Randy Lee Harper, "An Open Letter to Social Autopsy," *Medium*, April 15, 2016, https://medium.com /@randileeharper/an-open-letter-to-social-autopsy-ae64fccdcfe.

156 And in her 2020: Owens, *Blackout*, 15,16.

156 The video that catapulted: Candace Owens, "Mom, Dad . . . I'm Conservative," *YouTube*, July 19, 2017, https://www.youtube.com/watch?v=d gKc-2rFcRw.

157 Charlie first laid eyes on: Centennial Institute, "Charlie Kirk and Candace Owens—Western Conservative Summit 2018," *YouTube*, July 13, 2018, https://www.youtube.com/watch?v=2m4NboECfGI.

159 By the time the panel: Ibid.

CHAPTER ELEVEN: BOOTS ON THE GROUND

166 The Charles Koch Institute: Alex Kotch and Jared Holt, "Koch Network Alums Are Going Full-On White Nationalists," *Sludge*, May 30, 2019, https://readsludge.com/2019/05/30/koch-network-alums-are-going -full-on-white-nationalist/.

167 The network and its: Chris Cillizza, "Republicans Have Gained More Than 900 State Legislative Seats Since 2010," *Washington Post*, January 14, 2015, https://www.washingtonpost.com/news/the-fix/wp/2015 /01/14/republicans-have-gained-more-than-900-state-legislative-seats -since-2010/.

167 And by 2016: Quorum, "Republicans Now Control More State Legislatures Than Any Point in U.S. History," accessed April 19, 2022, https:// www.quorum.us/data-driven-insights/republicans-now-control-more -state-legislatures-than-any-point-in-u-s-history/.

167 *Good Profit*: Charles de Ganahl Koch, *Good Profit: How Creating Value for Others Built One of the World's Most Successful Companies* (Crown Business, 2015), Chapter 9.

168 taking home $170,000: "Young Americans for Liberty, Inc., Form 990-O for Period Ending Dec 2018," *ProPublica*, Nonprofit Explorer, https:// projects.propublica.org/nonprofits/organizations/262417908.

168 nearly doubling the $86,000: "Young Americans for Liberty, Inc., Form 990-O for Period Ending Dec 2017," *ProPublica*, Nonprofit Explorer, https://projects.propublica.org/nonprofits/organizations/262417908.

174 drug-legalization rhetoric: Ben Terris, "The Transcendental Meditationists Who Turned an Iowa Farm Town into a Bernie Base," *Washington Post*, January 29, 2016, https://www.washingtonpost.com/life style/style/the-transcendental-meditationists-who-turned-an-iowa -farm-town-into-a-bernie-base/2016/01/29/b4de383c-c5e1–11e5–8965 –0607e0e265ce_story.html.

175 The next morning: Kevin Landrigan, "Turnout Headed for a Record," *New Hampshire Union Leader*, November 7, 2018, https://www.tf

moran.com/wp-content/uploads/2018/11/NH-Union-Leader-Front
-Page-Nov-7–2018.pdf.

CHAPTER TWELVE: CANDACE BUILDS HER FOLLOWING

178 No matter, Kushner told people: Annie Karni and Maggie Haberman, "Trump and Kushner Saw Super Bowl Ad as Way of Making Inroads with Black Voters," *New York Times*, February 4, 2020, https://www.nytimes.com/2020/02/04/us/politics/trump-super-bowl-ad.html.

179 It would later be discovered: Eric Lipton, "Jared Kushner Selling Stake in Firm That Pursued Federal Tax Break," *New York Times*, March 5, 2020, https://www.nytimes.com/2020/03/05/us/politics/jared-kushner-cadre.html.

180 A few days after: Nadra Nittle, "Kanye West Says He Wants Nothing to Do With Blexit Apparel," *Vox*, October 31, 2018, https://www.vox.com/the-goods/2018/10/30/18045104/kanye-west-blexit-t-shirts-design-candace-owens.

181 Not surprisingly for a young woman: Tim Willis, "Courting Controversy: Tatler meets George Farmer and Candace Owens," *Tatler*, June 3, 2019, WayBack Machine, https://web.archive.org/web/20200507173045/https://www.tatler.com/article/george-farmer-candace-owens-interview.

181 Candace, looking American casual: "An Evening with Charlie Kirk & Candace Owens. The Founding of Turning Point UK," Brightspark Media, *YouTube*, December 22, 2018, https://youtu.be/zTsT3FiiXX8.

182 One audience member, a millionaire: "The Candace Owens Show: George Farmer," The Candace Owns Show, PragerU, *YouTube*, September 1, 2019, https://www.prageru.com/video/the-candace-owens-show-george-farmer.

183 And things hummed along: Mark DiStefano and Alex Spence, "Candace Owens: 'If Hitler Just Wanted to Make Germany Great and Have Things Run Well, OK, Fine,'" *BuzzFeed*, February 8, 2019, https://www.buzzfeed.com/markdistefano/candace-owens-hitler-germany-nazi.

183 Soon, Candace was in: Will Sommer, "Turning Point USA Students Call on Candace Owens to Step Down," Daily Beast, February 21, 2019, https://www.thedailybeast.com/turning-point-usa-students-call-on-candace-owens-to-step-down.

184 Candace's first episode: "The Candace Owens Show: Roseanne Barr," PragerU, March 3, 2019, https://www.prageru.com/video/the-candace-owens-show-roseanne-barr.

184 who herself had gotten: Nicholas Hautman, "Roseanne Barr's Most

Controversial Moments," *Us Weekly*, May 29, 2018, https://www.us magazine.com/celebrity-news/pictures/roseanne-barrs-most-con troversial-moments/.

CHAPTER THIRTEEN: PROM NIGHT FOR THE COLLEGE CONSERVATIVE

185 Dan Crenshaw, a former Navy SEAL: Brittany Shephard, "The Mission: Make Conservatism Cool. The Strategy: A Mechanical Bull and a Cardboard Cutout of AOC," *Washingtonian*, March 1, 2019, https://www.washingtonian.com/2019/03/01/the-mission-make-conservatism-cool-the-strategy-a-mechanical-bull-and-a-cardboard-cutout-of-aoc/.

186 She had left: Jane Mayer, "The Secret History of Kimberly Guilfoyle's Departure From Fox," *New Yorker*, October 1, 2020, https://www.new yorker.com/news/news-desk/the-secret-history-of-kimberly-guilfoyles-departure-from-fox.

186 "Thank you for making me party": Alana Mastrangelo, "Turning Point USA Celebrates Its First Night at CPAC," *Breitbart*, March 1, 2019, https://www.breitbart.com/tech/2019/03/01/turning-point-usa-cele brates-first-night-of-cpac-with-americafest-after-party/.

187 "Honestly, the fact that": Alex Dent, "I Went to a Turning Point USA Party So You Don't Have To," *Daily Tar Heel*, March 3,2019, https://www.dailytarheel.com/article/2019/03/cpac-column-0303.

187 Breitbart—once aptly dubbed: Rebecca Mead, "Rage Machine," *New Yorker*, May 17, 2010, https://www.newyorker.com/magazine/2010/05/24/rage-machine.

187 Wading into the group: Emily Crockett, "Andrew Breitbart Loses It at Occupy Protesters," *YouTube*, February 10, 2012, https://www.youtube.com/watch?v=R4od4QQVK1o&t=16s.

188 According to the *New York Times*: R.W. Apple Jr. , "Dismay and Outrage Over Nixon Erupt at Conservatives' Parley," *New York Times*, January 27, 1974, https://www.nytimes.com/1974/01/27/archives/dismay-and-outrage-over-nixon-erupt-at-conservatives-parley.html.

191 the PAC funding his very own: Mobilize the Message, Vendor/Recipient Profile, 2018, OpenSecrets, https://www.opensecrets.org/campaign-expenditures/vendor?cycle=2018&vendor=Mobilize+the+Message.

191 which paid Mobilize: Mobilize the Message, Vendor/Recipient Profile, 2020, OpenSecrets, https://www.opensecrets.org/campaign-expend itures/vendor?cycle=2020&vendor=Mobilize+the+Message.

191 One project: distribute flyers: Julia Marsh, "Conservative Group Spent $32K in One Day Against Ocasio-Cortez," *New York Post*, April 23, 2019,

https://nypost.com/2019/04/23/conservative-group-spent-32k-in-one
-day-against-ocasio-cortez/.

192 That's what he'd been doing: Thomas Fuller, "A Right Hook in Berkeley
Revives Debate Over Campus Speech," *New York Times*, March 1, 2019,
https://www.nytimes.com/2019/03/01/us/berkeley-assault-campus
-free-speech.html.

193 UC Berkeley had not, in fact: Katie Mettler, "Police Have Arrested the
Man They Say Punched a Conservative Activist at UC Berkeley,"
Washington Post, February 27, 2019, https://www.washingtonpost.com
/education/2019/02/27/conservative-activist-was-punched-face-uc
-berkeley-response-enraged-right/.

194 The next day, the Daily Beast: Maxwell Tani and Will Sommer, "CPAC
2019: Turning Point USA's Charlie Kirk and Candace Owens Are the
New King and Queen of the GOP Ball," Daily Beast, March 1, 2019,
https://www.thedailybeast.com/cpac-2019-turning-point-usas-charlie
-kirk-and-candace-owens-are-the-new-king-and-queen-of-the-gop
-ball.

CHAPTER FOURTEEN: FIREBOMBING THE INTERNET

197 On a sun-drenched day: Charlie Kirk @Charliekirk1776, "Today was a
momentous Day," Instagram, March 6, 2019, Instagram, https://www
.instagram.com/p/BusCIbkFVwG/?hl=en.

197 avid supporters of the kind: CEI Annual Dinner, Competitive Enterprise Institute, July 19, 2019, https://cei.org/blog/cei-annual-dinner
-2019-rebecca-dunn/.

197 Rebecca showed up at: @Charliekirk1776, "Today was a momentous
Day."

197 It now had 150 employees: Turning Point USA Inc., Form 990–0 Period
Ending June 2019, *ProPublica*, Nonprofit Explorer, https://projects.pro
publica.org/nonprofits/organizations/800835023.

198 a Christian influencer and a former Miss Arizona: Mid-Week Rise-up,
Erika Kirk, accessed February 16, 2022, https://www.erikafrantzve.com.

198 Charlie first met Frantzve: "I'm Engaged," *Charlie Kirk Show*, accessed
February 14, 2022, https://www.youtube.com/watch?v=7lDyJIIXb_M.

198 a woman who professed: "Shop All Proclaim," Proclaim Streetwear, accessed February 16, 2022, https://www.proclaimstreetwear.com/shop.

198 He spent time with: "Happening Now, featuring Charlie Kirk, Real Life
with Jack Hibbs," *YouTube*, December 2019, https://www.youtube.com
/watch?v=yT6ju5ViWa4.

198 and a promoter of "biblical citizenship": Maya Jaradat, "What Is Biblical

Citizenship?," *Deseret News*, October 31, 2021, https://www.deseret.com /faith/2021/10/31/22740655/what-is-biblical-citizenship-rick-green -religion-politics-churches-christian-nationalism.

198 Another new friend was: Eric Metaxas, @ericmetaxas, "It was soooo much fun talking to @CharlieKirk today on the @EricMetaxasShow!," Twitter, September 4, 2019, https://twitter.com/ericmetaxas/status/116 9367772998131712.

198 But the most important new presence: Matthew Boedy, "Ten Years of Turning Point USA," Political Research Associates, January 28, 2022, https://politicalresearch.org/2022/01/28/ten-years-turning-point-usa# _ftn5.

199 McCoy had a laid-back: Rob McCoy, "God & Government," Trinity Dallas, Video, *YouTube*, January 27, 2020, "https://www.youtube.com /watch?v=nKgwDajgaOc.

199 McCoy would help Charlie: Apologia: Forum with Charlie Kirk, Westgate Chapel, *YouTube*, May 2, 2021, https://www.youtube.com/watch ?v=7_2gOjyBEE8.

199 The move had earned Bowyer: Angela Gonzales, "Board of Regents Nixes Students' Association Fee," *Phoenix Business Journal*, February 7, 2013, https://www.bizjournals.com/phoenix/blog/business/2013/02 /board-of-regents-nixes-students.html.

199 Later, defying pushback: "Donald Trump Visits Phoenix, Talks Immigration," *The Republic/azcentral*, July 11, 2015, https://www.az central.com/story/news/local/phoenix/2015/07/11/live-donald-trump -phoenix-coverage/30018843/.

202 To mock Obama's much-criticized response: Benny Johnson, "Obama Asks the Hill to Bomb Syria, As Explained by 'The Hills,'" *BuzzFeed*, September 10, 2013, https://www.buzzfeednews.com/article/bennyjohn son/obama-asks-the-hill-to-bomb-syria-as-explained-by-the-hills.

202 Now, Johnson, ever expanding: Benny Johnson, "Everything You Think You Know About Cuba Is a Lie," Turning Point, USA, *YouTube*, February 7, 2020, https://www.youtube.com/watch?v=BS2IvQWjzRY.

202 During the trip: Ibid.

203 like one Vox headlined: Matthew Yglesias, "Trump's Performance with Hispanic Voters in 2020 Should Prompt Some Progressive Rethinking," *Vox*, November 5, 2020, https://www.vox.com/2020/11/5/21548677 /trump-hispanic-vote-latinx.

204 Johnson's fondness for mixing: Benny Johnson, "Do People Who Live In AOC's District Think She Deserves A Raise?," Turning Point USA, July 7, 2019, https://www.youtube.com/watch?v=hkdK0vuz7WE.

204 Never mind that prominent: "Designating Antifa as a Domestic Terrorist Organization Is Dangerous, Threatens Civil Liberties," Southern Poverty Law Center, June 2, 2020, https://www.splcenter.org/hate watch/2020/06/02/designating-antifa-domestic-terrorist-organization -dangerous-threatens-civil-liberties; "Who Are Antifa?," Anti-Defamation League, accessed February 14, 2020, https://www.adl.org/antifa.

204 Meanwhile, in September 2020: Isaac Stanley-Becker, "Pro-Trump Youth Group Enlists Teens in Secretive Campaign Likened to a 'Troll Farm,' Prompting Rebuke by Facebook and Twitter," *Washington Post*, September 15, 2020, https://www.washingtonpost.com/politics/turning -point-teens-disinformation-trump/2020/09/15/c84091ae-f20a-11ea -b796-2dd09962649c_story.html.

204 The truthfulness of a statement: Chris Meserole, "How Misinformation Spreads on Social Media and What to Do About It," Brookings, May 9, 2018, "https://www.brookings.edu/blog/order-from-chaos/2018/05/09 /how-misinformation-spreads-on-social-media-and-what-to-do-about-it/.

205 One tweet he posted in 2019: Charlie Kirk @charliekirk11, "Remember when our @TPUSA chapter was attacked & Hayden Williams got punched . . . ," Twitter, December 31, 2019, https://web.archive.org /web/20191231195629/https://twitter.com/charliekirk11.

205 According to a piece in the *New York Times*: Keith Collins and Kevin Roose, "Tracing a Meme From the Internet's Fringe to a Republican Slogan," *New York Times*, November 4, 2018, https://www.nytimes .com/interactive/2018/11/04/technology/jobs-not-mobs.html? searchResultPosition=15.

207 On this phenomenon: Molly Ball, "The Secret History of the Shadow Campaign That Saved the 2020 Election," *Time*, February 4, 2021, https://time.com/5936036/secret-2020-election-campaign/?amp=true.

209 By mid-February: Daniel Funke, "Trump Tweeted a Video of Pelosi Ripping His State of the Union Speech. Here's What You Need to Know," *Politifact*, Poynter Institute, February 11, 2020, https://www .politifact.com/article/2020/feb/11/trump-tweeted-video-pelosi-ripping -his-state-union/.

CHAPTER FIFTEEN: THE COMEBACK KID

211 Shortly after the horrific: Nick Freitas, "Watch the Viral Video that Has Gun Owners Cheering," Facebook, March 7, 2018, https://www.facebook.com/NickFreitasVA/videos/1581169621951547/.

213 As the talk: James Broughel, "Mercatus on Policy: A Step-by-Step Guide

to Using Mercatus Tools to Reduce State Regulation Levels," Mercatus Center, George Mason University, April 2017, https://www.mercatus .org/system/files/broughel-regdata-state-guide-mop-v1.pdf.

215 But he and his local: Graham Moomaw, "Citing Missed Deadlines, Elections Board Denies Nick Freitas, Republicans, Place on Nov. Ballot in 30th District," *Daily Progress*, August 7, 2019, https://dailyprogress .com/community/orangenews/news/citing-missed-deadlines-elections -board-denies-nick-freitas-republicans-place-on-nov-ballot-in-30th /article_396f50d0-b932-11e9-96a9-d30e1c34f0d0.html.

215 His Democratic opponent: Laura Vozzella, "From Shoo In to Write In: Paperwork Stumble Forces a VA Republican to Run the Hard Way," *Washington Post*, October 23, 2019, https://www.washingtonpost.com /local/virginia-politics/from-shoo-in-to-write-in-paperwork-stumble -forces-a-va-republican-to-run-the-hard-way/2019/10/22/e1831770 -ef74-11e9-b648-76bcf86eb67e_story.html.

215 who had just been dubbed: Stephanie Saul and Danny Hakim, "The Most Powerful Conservative Couple You've Never Heard Of," *New York Times*, June 7, 2018, https://www.nytimes.com/2018/06/07/us/politics /liz-dick-uihlein-republican-donors.html.

215 swooped in with half a million dollars: Vozzella, "From shoo-in to write-in: Paperwork stumble forces a Va. Republican to run the hard way."

215 Freitas won 14,694 votes: Allison Brophy Champion, "Abundant Spelling Variations as Culpeper Certifies 5,205 Write-in Votes for Nick Freitas," *Culpeper Star-Exponent*, November 9, 2019, https://starexponent.com/news /abundant-spelling-variations-as-culpeper-certifies-5-205-write-in -votes-for-nick-freitas/article_973fa6db-37d0-567a-9f04-ea6aa56dee9f .html.

217 "It was a hard": Taylor Hall @Libertay1776, "Well, here it goes. @ YALtoo," Twitter, January 9, 2021, https://twitter.com/Libertay1776 /status/1347951951225344001.

217 Another woman: Caitlin Grimes, "Tonight, I feel compelled to add my personal story to the #YALToo conversation . . ." January 11, 2021, Video, Facebook, https://www.facebook.com/692407893/posts/101579 80699067894/?d=n.

219 According to a December 2017 Pew survey: J. Baxter Oliphant, "Women and Men in Both Parties Say Sexual Harassment Allegations Reflect 'Widespread Problems in Society,'" *Pew Research Center*, December 7, 2017, https://www.pewresearch.org/fact-tank/2017/12/07/americans -views-of-sexual-harassment-allegations/.

CHAPTER SIXTEEN: THE VIEW FROM CANDACELAND

222 At Liberty University: "Candace Owens–Liberty University Convocation," Liberty University, *YouTube*, September 26, 2018, https://www.youtube.com/watch?v=rrKOnp1dcoo&t=1048s.

223 Marriage was, apparently: Lauren Fruen, "A Meeting of Right Minds," *The Daily Mail*, October 22, 2019, https://www.dailymail.co.uk/news/article-7601719/PICTURED-Inside-Trump-Winery-wedding-conservative-activist-Candace-Owens.html.

224 As for Candace: Tim Willis, "Courting Controversy: Tatler Meets George Farmer and Candace Owens," *Tatler*, June 3, 2019, https://web.archive.org/web/20190607003733/https://www.tatler.com/article/george-farmer-candace-owens-interview.

228 Facebook posts planted: Jon Swaine, "Russian Propagandist Targeted African Americans to Influence 2016 US Election," *The Guardian*, December 17, 2018, https://www.theguardian.com/us-news/2018/dec/17/russian-propagandists-targeted-african-americans-2016-election.

229 "Go with me": "President Trump Delivers Remarks at the Young Black Leadership Summit 2019," White House, *YouTube*, October 4, 2019, https://www.youtube.com/watch?v=QaZZbg-BInc.

229 On social media: Candace Owens @RealCandaceO, "WOW. Just had a police officer called over to me and my husband at Whole Foods . . . ," Twitter, April 14, 2020, https://twitter.com/RealCandaceO/status/1250130325356888064; Candace Owens @RealCandaceO, "Can somebody PLEASE pay Prince Harry's ransom . . . ," Twitter, October 26, 2020, https://twitter.com/realcandaceo/status/1320713743190401024.

230 Candace's husband: Kara Swisher, "One Year After Jan 6 Attack, Parler's C.E.O. Grapples with Big Tech and Trump," Sway Podcast/*The New York Times*, January 6, 2022, https://www.nytimes.com/2022/01/06/opinion/sway-kara-swisher-george-farmer.html.

CHAPTER SEVENTEEN: SOWING SEEDS

231 "BREAKING": Candace Owens @RealCandaceOwens, "Removing One Page of Report That Had @AndrewGillum's Personal Address Listed Which Wasn't My Intent—but YES—BREAKING: Democrat Andrew Gillum Was Involved in a Crystal Meth Overdose Incident Last Night in a Miami Hotel. Orgy Suspected, but Unconfirmed.," Twitter, March 13, 2020, https://twitter.com/newsmax/status/1330332248906866693?s=20&t=gyg9aFidOpCR965wGvh8s.

232 But it was Candace's eighteen-minute video: Candace Owens, "Candace

Owens: 'I DO NOT Support George Floyd!' & Here's Why!," Durtty Daily, *YouTube*, June 4, 2020, https://www.facebook.com/watch/live /?ref=watch_permalink&v=273957870461345.

232 A few days after it was released: Kevin Roose, "Social Media Giants Support Racial Justice, Their Products Undermine it," *New York Times*, June 19, 2020, "https://www.nytimes.com/2020/06/19/technology/face book-youtube-twitter-black-lives-matter.html.

232 Ivanka Trump, hardly: Ivanka Trump @IvankaTrump, "People in Minneapolis are hurting for a reason . . ." Twitter, May 29, 2020, https:// twitter.com/ivankatrump/status/1266377235985862656.

232 Her book *Blackout*: Candace Owens, *Blackout: How Black America Can Make Its Second Escape from the Democrat Plantation* (Simon & Schuster, 2020).

233 "Remember the 40": Candace Owens @RealCandaceOwens, "Remember the 40 year Tuskegee Experiment . . . ," Twitter, June 17, 2020, https://twitter.com/realcandaceo/status/1273401168845320193.

235 By September 2020: "Most Americans Who Have Heard of QAnon Conspiracy Theories Say They Are Bad for the Country and That Trump Seems to Support People Who Promote Them," *Pew Research Center Journalism Project*, September 16, 2020, https://www.pewresearch.org /journalism/2020/09/16/most-americans-who-have-heard-of-qanon -conspiracy-theories-say-they-are-bad-for-the-country-and-that-trump -seems-to-support-people-who-promote-them/.

235 A few months later: Mallory Newall, "More than 1 in 3 Americans Believe a 'Deep State' Is Working to Undermine Trump," *Ipsos*, December 30, 2020, https://www.ipsos.com/en-us/news-polls/npr-misinforma tion-123020.

235 They migrated to: Rebecca Speare-Cole, "Alex Jones' QANON Rant Watched Over 2 Million Times: 'I'm Sick of It!,'" Newsweek, January 11, 2021, https://www.newsweek.com/alex-jones-qanon-rant-viral-infowars -1560394?utm_term=Autofeed&utm_medium=Social&utm_source= Twitter#Echobox=1610356258; Kelly Weill, "Roseanne Keeps Promoting QANON," the Daily Beast, March 30, 2018, https://www.thedailybeast .com/roseanne-keeps-promoting-qanon-the-pro-trump-conspiracy -theory-that-makes-pizzagate-look-tame.

236 Even relative moderates: Todd Spangler, "Why Joe Rogan's Latest Podcast With Conspiracy-Monger Alex Jones Is OK With Spotify," Variety, October 28, 2020, https://variety.com/2020/digital/news/spotify-joe -rogan-alex-jones-podcast-1234817836/; Harper Lambert, "Joe Rogan

Endorses the Deep State: 'We would be Beyond F-ed' Without It," March 21, 2022, https://www.thewrap.com/joe-rogan-endorses-deep -state-conspiracy-trump/.

237 In June of 2020, inside a North Phoenix mega church: TMZ Staff, "Arizona Church Hosting Trump's Rally Claims New Tech Kills COVID-19," TMZ, June 22, 2020, https://www.tmz.com/2020/06/22 /trump-rally-site-arizona-dream-city-church-technology-covid-clean -air/.

CHAPTER EIGHTEEN: SPREADING THE STEAL STORY

Scenes from the insurrection were taken from multiple sources that covered the same material. I credited the *New York Times* whose comprehensive investigations proved most helpful to me.

239 Standing behind a podium: *PBS NewsHour*, "WATCH: Charlie Kirk's Full Speech at the Republican National Convention," *YouTube*, August 24, 2020, https://www.youtube.com/watch?v=hV8_Bunawqg.

240 A few days later: Charles P. Pierce, "The Theme of the RNC Is Already Clear: Any Election Where Trump Doesn't Win Is Illegitimate," *Esquire*, August 24, 2020, https://www.esquire.com/news-politics/politics /a33770274/trump-republican-national-convention-speech-voter-fraud/.

240 Plans for a Toby Keith: "Charlotte RNC Loses Parties, Luster," August 21, 2020, *Charlotte Observer*, https://www.charlotteobserver.com › article 245108330.

241 A Miami pool attendant: Adam Gabbatt, "Jerry Falwell Jr 'enjoyed Watching' His Wife Have Sex, Alleged Lover Says," *The Guardian*, August 28, 2020, https://www.theguardian.com/us-news/2020/aug/28 /jerry-falwell-jr-giancarlo-granda-becki-enjoyed-watching.

241 And in March: Ruth Graham, "Conservative Activist Charlie Kirk Leaves Liberty University Think Tank," *New York Times*, March 16, 2021, https://www.nytimes.com/2021/03/16/us/charlie-kirk-liberty-falwell -falkirk.html.

242 In October, Charlie, misquoting: "Right-Wing Media Question Integrity of Pennsylvania's Election by Conflating Mail-in Ballot Applications with Mail-in Ballots," *Media Matters for America*, accessed February 17, 2022, https://www.mediamatters.org/voter-fraud-and-suppression /right-wing-media-question-integrity-pennsylvanias-election-conflating.

242 What the article: Ibid

242 responding to widespread voter suppression: Michael Scherer, "Mike Bloomberg raises $16 million to allow former felons to vote in Florida," *Washington Post*, September 22, 2020, https://www.washingtonpost.com

/politics/mike-bloomberg-raises-16-million-to-allow-former-felons-to
-vote-in-florida/2020/09/21/6dda787e-fc5a-11ea-8d05-9beaaa91c71f
_story.html.

242 told a Dallas gathering: "Paul Weyrich—'I Don't Want Everybody to
Vote' (Goo Goo)," *YouTube*, June 8, 2007, https://www.youtube.com
/watch?v=8GBAsFwPglw.

243 Twenty years later, in 2000: Joshua Green, "Karl Rove's Voter Fraud
Fetish," *The Atlantic*, April 12, 2007, https://www.theatlantic.com
/magazine/archive/2007/04/karl-roves-voter-fraud-fetish/305861/.

243 In 2011 alone: "Wrap Up of 2011 Legislative Enactments," NCLS, accessed February 17, 2022, https://www.ncsl.org/research/elections-and
-campaigns/wrap-up-of-2011-legislative-enactments.aspx.

243 slashed a whole early-voting week: Adam Liptak, "Supreme Court Won't
Restore 'Golden Week' Voting in Ohio," *New York Times*, September 13,
2016, https://www.nytimes.com/2016/09/14/us/politics/supreme-court
-wont-restore-golden-week-voting-in-ohio.html.

243 And Nebraska cut: German Lopez, "7 Specific Ways States Made
It Harder for Americans to Vote in 2016," *Vox*, November 11, 2016,
https://www.vox.com/policy-and-politics/2016/11/7/13545718/voter
-suppression-early-voting-2016.

243 In a video: Robert O'Harrow Jr., "Videos Show Closed-Door Sessions
of Leading Conservative Activists: 'Be Not Afraid of the Accusations
that You're a Voter Suppressor,'" *Washington Post*, October 14, 2020,
https://www.washingtonpost.com/investigations/council-national
-policy-video/2020/10/14/367f24c2-f793-11ea-a510-f57d8ce76e11_story
.html.

245 "cataclysmic collision": Newss19WLTX, "Charlie Kirk speaks at 2020
CPAC," *YouTube*, February 27, 2020, WLTXhttps://www.youtube.com
/watch?app=desktop&v=c-WiaPPxIHc.

247 Whether he was denying: Daniel Lippman and Tina Nguyen, "Turning
Point Co-founder Dies of Coronavirus-Related Complications," *Politico*, July 29, 2020, https://www.politico.com/news/2020/07/29/turning
-point-usa-founder-dies-coronavirus-complications-387077.

248 Just before midnight: MLive, "Donald Trump's Last Rally before Election Day," *YouTube*, November 3, 2020, https://www.youtube.com
/watch?v=ZJ15XMQ4ns0.

248 And Charlie was headed there: Charlie Kirk @CharliKirk11, "The line to
get in to President @realDonaldTrumpsss's rally . . . ," Twitter, November 2, 2020 https://twitter.com/charliekirk11/status/132344679707996
5697.

249 On the evening on November 3: "How the #sharpiegate Election Fraud Narrative Went Viral," *Yonder*, November 5, 2020, https://www.yonder -ai.com/resources/blog/how-the-sharpiegate-election-fraud-narrative -went-viral/.

250 That night, as Charlie: Charlie Kirk, "Charlie Kirk—The Charlie Kirk Show LIVE On Air—November . . . ," Facebook Watch, November 3, 2020, https://www.facebook.com/watch/live/?ref=watch _permalink&v=917611485712934; Charlie Kirk, "The Charlie Kirk Show LIVE On Air—November, 4 2020," Video, YouTube, November 4, 2020, https://www.youtube.com/watch?v=5RlHM48k8mg.

250 Charlie was also sure: Ibid

251 During the 2018 midterms: Roger Sollenberger, "How Two Friends' Farcical, Failed Schemes Ended with the Biggest Fail of All: Stop the Steal," *Salon*, January 19, 2021, https://www.salon.com/2021/01/19 /how-two-friends-farcical-failed-schemes-ended-with-the-biggest-fail -of-all-stop-the-steal/.

251 On the night of November 4: Mike Cernovich @Cernovich, "On a 7 hour road trip to Arizona, ask me anything!," Twitter, November 4, 2020, https://twitter.com/Cernovich/status/1324162931966140417; *Arizona Republic*: "Arizona Election Updates, Joe Biden's Lead Tightens in Updated Results," *azcentral*, November 4, 20202, https://www.azcentral.com /story/news/politics/elections/2020/11/04/arizona-election-live -updates-2020-presidential-election/6093637002/.

252 There were grizzled Trump supporters: Brianna Sacks @bri_sacks, "Back at the Maricopa counting center . . . ," Twitter, November 6, 2020, https://twitter.com/bri_sacks/status/1324831801278259200?s=20&t=2 wkQaR096KF2BWNDdoQrXw: Thomas Hawthorne, "Alex Jones Returns to Speak to Trump Supporters Outside the Maricopa County Election Center in Phoenix," *azcentral*, November, 6, 2020, https://www .azcentral.com/videos/news/politics/elections/2020/11/06/alex-jones -returns-speak-trump-supporters-outside-maricopa-county-election -center-phoenix/6190304002/.

CHAPTER NINETEEN: THE INSURRECTIONISTS

253 "You have every right to be suspicious": Benny Johnson, "You Have Every Right to Be Suspicious," Benny Report, Newsmax, Twitter, November 21, 2020, https://twitter.com/newsmax/status/133033224890686 6693?s=20&t=gyg9aFidOpCR965wGvh8s.

253 Johnson went on: David Charns, "Judge: 'No Evidence to Support Voter

Fraud Across Nevada,' I-Team Digs into Allegations, Evidence," 8news now.com, December 4, 2020, https://www.8newsnow.com/i-team/judge -no-evidence-to-support-voter-fraud-across-nevada-i-team-digs-into -allegations-evidence-trump-republicans-lawsuit-las-vegas-clark-county/.

254 and the company would file: Alison Durkee, "Dominion Sues Newsmax, OANN And Ex-Overstock CEO Byrne In New Defamation Suits Over Election Conspiracy Theory," *Forbes*, August 10, 2021, https://www .forbes.com/sites/alisondurkee/2021/08/10/dominion-sues-newsmax -oann-and-ex-overstock-ceo-byrne-in-new-defamation-suits-over -election-conspiracy-theory/?sh=60bcb0a65440.

255 Numerous news organizations: Ben Collins and Brandy Zadrozny, "Extremists Made Little Secret of Ambitions to 'Occupy' Capitol in Weeks Before Attack," *NBC News*, January 8, 2021, https://www.nbcnews.com /tech/internet/extremists-made-little-secret-ambitions-occupy-capitol -weeks-attack-n1253499.

256 Charlie had originally: Mikael Thalen, "Charlie Kirk Deletes Tweet Saying He Sent '80+ buses full of patriots' to D.C.," *Daily Dot*, January 9, 2021, https://www.dailydot.com/debug/charlie-kirk-delete-tweet -buses-capitol/.

256 Turning Point Action appears to have transported: Sarah Al-Arshani, "A Former Firefighter Charged in the Capitol Riot Took a Bus Organized by Turning Point USA to DC, Filing Says," *Business Insider*, March 3, 2012, https://www.businessinsider.com/man-charged-capitol-riot-went-dc -bus-turning-point-usa-2021-3. (https://storage.courtlistener.com/recap /gov.uscourts.dcd.227169/gov.uscourts.dcd.227169.8.0.pdf), criminal complaint (https://www.justice.gov/usao-dc/press-release/file/1354756/down load)

258 Others pushed their way: "Capitol Riot Investigations," *New York Times*, accessed February 17, 2022, https://www.nytimes.com/spotlight/us -capitol-riots-investigations.

258 But Charlie, recording his live podcast: Charlie Kirk, "CHAOS AT THE CAPITOL—Joint Session of Congress Interrupted in Washington DC," *YouTube*, January 6, 2021, https://www.youtube.com/watch?v=X8a 9rvwJUCw&bpctr=1644531195.

262 One woman reported: Addyson Rae Garner @realPOTUS2040, "dm shared with permission The utter disrespect and misogyny on display by Cliff Maloney makes my skin crawl," Twitter, January 9, 2021, https:// twitter.com/realpotus2040/status/1347702060007960582.

262 Another young woman claimed: Syd @sSyd_Travis, "I was harassed by

a member of the YAL staff at a conference in 2018," Twitter, January 9, 2021, https://twitter.com/syd_travis/status/1348059408736133123?s=19? ref_src=twsrc%5Etfw.

262 And a former intern: Deleted tweet. Can be found here: TWunroll, https://twunroll.com/article/1347702060007960582.

262 Yet another alleged victim: Maggie @LibertyAnders, "My #YALtoo story," Twitter, January 10, 2021, https://twitter.com/libertyanders /status/1348423269431578628.

263 In the words of: Grace Fendrick @Grace4Liberty, "It's really unfortunate that YAL gave many of us a start in this movement," Twitter, January 8, 2021, https://twitter.com/Grace4Liberty/status/134791904110988 9024.

263 Thanks to that work: Young Americans for Liberty, "'Liberty Wave' Sweeps America's State Legislatures as YAL Secures 123 Wins!," *Young Americans for Liberty*, accessed November 20, 2020, https://www.globe newswire.com/news-release/2020/11/20/2131138/0/en/Liberty-Wave -Sweeps-America-s-State-Legislatures-as-YAL-Secures-123-Wins .html.

263 Cliff's own private company: "Vendor/Recipient Profile: Mobilize the Message," OpenSecrets, 2020, https://www.opensecrets.org/campaign -expenditures/vendor?cycle=2020&vendor=Mobilize+the+Message.

264 Justin Amash, began to demand: Justin Amash @justinamash, "at a minimum, any investigation should be conducted by persons independent of YAL," Twitter, January 10, 2021, https://twitter.com/justinamash /status/1348453494479589380?ref_src=twsrc%5Etfw.

264 On January 11, 2021: Young American for Liberty @YALiberty, "Official Statement: YAL will address these issues head-on and begin the process of healing," Twitter, January 11, 2021, https://twitter.com/YALiberty /status/1348823314391855105.

264 Two days later: Young American for Liberty @YALiberty, "Today, the Young Americans for Liberty (YAL) Board of Directors terminate Cliff Maloney . . . ," Twitter, January 13, 2021, https://twitter.com/yaliberty /status/1349429887187247104.

266 This year, attention: Addy Baird and Brianna Sacks, "Danger Warning": Women Say Madison Cawthon Harassed Them In College," *Buzzfeed*, February 26, 2021, https://www.buzzfeednews.com/article/addybaird /madison-cawthorn-sexual-misconduct-allegations-patrick.

266 Matt Gaetz: Amber Phillips, "The Sex-Trafficking Investigation That's Zeroing in on Matt Gaetz, Explained," *The Washington Post*, January 27,

2022, https://www.washingtonpost.com/politics/2022/01/27/sex-traff
icking-allegations-matt-gaetz/.

CHAPTER TWENTY: ARMED FOR THE FUTURE

270 Candace devoted much of: Candace Owens @RealCandaceo: "Twitter
has unnecessarily slapped a label on my entirely truthful tweet," Twitter,
April 1, 2021, https://twitter.com/RealCandaceO/status/13774805162
87488001.

271 Cliff, who was: Alexis Loya, "Man Charged with Raping Unconscious
Woman at UPJ in 2013," April 27, 2022, https://www.wearecentralpa
.com/news/local-news/man-charged-with-raping-unconscious-woman
-at-upj-in-2013/.

272 That fall of 2021: Cathryn Stout and Thomas Wilburn, "CRT Map: Efforts to Restrict Teaching Racism and Bias Have Multiplied Across the
U.S.," *Chalkbeat*, February 2022, https://www.chalkbeat.org/22525983
/map-critical-race-theory-legislation-teaching-racism.

272 In rural Eatonville: Hannah Allam, "A Rural Washington School Board
Race Shows How Far-Right Extremists are Shifting to Local Power,"
Washington Post, January 8, 2022, https://www.washingtonpost.com
/national-security/2022/01/08/far-right-school-boards/.

272 Earlier that year: TPUSA Faith, "Together We Can Restore America,"
Turning Point USA, accessed April 10, 2022, https://www.tpusa.com
/FAITH.

272 School Board Watchlist: Greg Childress, "National Watchlist for 'Radical Left' Policies Includes 5 North Carolina School Boards," *North
Carolina Policy Watch*, September 7, 2021, https://pulse.ncpolicywatch
.org/2021/09/07/national-watchlist-for-radical-left-policies-includes-5
-north-carolina-school-boards/#sthash.S3rochBy.dpbs.

273 He also announced: Turning Point USA, "Turning Point Academy,"
Turning Point USA, accessed April 10, 2022, https://www.tpusa.com
/academy.

273 As of February 2022: Isaac Stanley-Becker and Beth Reinhard, "Firm Saw
$40 Million Potential in Charlie Kirk's 'America-First' Academy. Then
It's Plans Fell Apart," *The Washington Post*, February 8, 2022, https://
www.washingtonpost.com/politics/2022/02/08/charlie-kirk-turning
-point-academy-strongmind/.

274 So it could: Laurie Roberts, "How Many Elections Are They Going to
Steal Before We Kill These People?" October 27, 2021, *azcentral*, https://
www.azcentral.com/story/opinion/op-ed/laurieroberts/2021/10/27

/when-do-we-get-use-guns-tpusa-owns-and-others-too/857081
2002.

EPILOGUE

277 Swing Left had since: Swing Left, "Protect the New Democratic Tri-
fecta and Defend Democracy," Swing Left, accessed February 17, 2022,
https://swingleft.org.

278 To help rectify that: Swing Left, "Impactful Individual Political Contributions," Blueprint by Swing Left, accessed February 17, 2022, https://
blueprint.swingleft.org.

278 There to help bring: LUCHA Arizona, "Home," LUCHA Arizona, accessed February 17, 2022, https://www.luchaaz.org.

279 But perhaps most importantly: One Arizona, "People's Movement for a
New Arizona," One Arizona, accessed February 17, 2022, https://one
arizona.org.

279 A recount conducted: Rosalind S. Helderman, "Arizona Ballot Review
Commissioned by Republicans Reaffirms Biden's Victory," *Washington Post*, September 24, 2021, https://www.washingtonpost.com/politics
/arizona-ballot-review-draft-report/2021/09/24/7c19ac08–1562–11ec
-b976-f4a43b740aeb_story.html.

280 courtesy of FreedomWorks: "Arizona Election Updates: More Ballot
Result, Expected Friday," *azcentral*, November 6, 2020, https://www.az
central.com/story/news/politics/elections/2020/11/05/arizona-election
-live-updates-2020-presidential-election/6093756002/.

INDEX